OPERATION
NEPTUNE

A section of men that has just landed in Ruquet in St Laurent sur Mer, on the rocks along the shore of Omaha littered with abandoned equipment. To the right, a DUKW. The name was not an acronym; it came about from GMC terminology. 'D' indicated a vehicle designed in 1942, 'U' meant 'utility', 'K' indicated driven by front wheels, 'W' indicated two powered rear axles.

Omaha Beach, with reinforcements landing.

OPERATION NEPTUNE

KENNETH EDWARDS

FONTHILL

Fonthill Media Limited
Fonthill Media LLC
www.fonthillmedia.com
office@fonthillmedia.com

First published in the United Kingdom 1946
This revised edition first published 2013

British Library Cataloguing in Publication Data:
A catalogue record for this book is available from the British Library

Copyright © The Estate of Commander Kenneth Edwards 2013

ISBN 978-1-78155-127-1

The original 1946 edition was dedicated by the Author to the Memory of
Admiral Sir Bertram H. Ramsay, KCB, KBE, MVO.
Allied Naval Commander, Expeditionary Force
'Who Wrought and Wielded Neptune's Trident

The 1946 edition had a small section of illustrations, most of which have
been included in this edition. This full-illustrated 2013 edition has addition
photographs and captions.

Typeset in 10/13 pt Sabon
Printed and bound in England

Part One

PREPARATION

CHAPTER I

BY FORTITUDE, FAITH
AND FORESIGHT

The beginning of the planning—Early thoughts of invasion in the Pas de Calais area—Preliminary concentration on the Mediterranean—Choice of site for invasion of Northern France—The "X Staff"—The "COSSAC Plan"—Decisions of the Quebec Conference—Appointment of Admiral Ramsay.

When Mr Winston Churchill made his second statement to a crowded and cheering House of Commons on D-day he announced that the commanders on the spot had reported that so far everything was going according to plan. He paused significantly and added, "and what a plan!"

Those four words were a just tribute to all those who had worked unremittingly behind the scenes for so long in the preparation of a plan which provided for every possible contingency, and in which all the manifold and intricate parts fitted together with minute exactness and were carefully dovetailed with other movements far removed from the English Channel. Some idea of the magnitude of the task of planning this great expedition may be gained from the fact that the orders for "Operation Neptune" which was only the naval component of the invasion—amounted to a printed book of foolscap size three inches thick.

The planning of the invasion of North-west Europe naturally sprang from small beginnings, and it passed through many vicissitudes, even before the final detailed planning of the operation was begun.

The story begins in 1941, when two radical changes had taken place in the strategic aspect of the war. These were the entry of the United States of America into the war following Japan's treacherous attack on Pearl Harbor, and Hitler's assault on Russia. Both of these led indirectly to a review of plans for the establishment of a "second front" in Western Europe.

The vast war-potential of the United States was beginning to make itself felt. American production of war materials was keyed to a pitch which already enabled it to expedite delivery in the West as well as the East, and the enormous planned expansion of the United States Army formed a potential strategic reserve—a reserve the lack of which had hitherto circumscribed all Allied strategy.

At the other side of the world, Russia was being very hard pressed and was asking repeatedly for the establishment of a land front against Germany in the West in order to draw off some of the divisions of the German army, nearly the whole strength of which was being hurled against her.

On both counts the establishment of a "second front" in North-west Europe seemed a tempting prospect, the more so as it would force Germany to fight the "two-front war" which had always been dreaded by the German High Command.

Thus, towards the end of 1941, the Chiefs of Staff Committee charged Lord Louis Mountbatten, Air Marshal Sir Sholto Douglas and General Sir Bernard Paget to examine the possibilities and prepare a tentative outline plan for an assault on Europe across, the English Channel. Lord Louis Mountbatten was the Chief of Combined Operations; Sir Sholto Douglas was Air Officer Commanding-in-Chief Fighter Command of the Royal Air Force, and Sir Bernard Paget was Commander-in-Chief, Home Forces. These three officers did much valuable and careful, work in examining the plethora of factors which of necessity influenced the choice of areas in which a footing on the continent might possibly have been obtained, having regard to the potentialities of the sea; air and land forces at that time available.

The more these problems were studied the larger loomed the difficulties and the risks. The mere question of availability of ships and landing craft then restricted the possible area of assault to the heavily defended Pas de Calais area, and it seemed that, although beachheads might be secured, the shipping resources might prove insufficient to provide a sufficient "build-up" of the forces ashore to allow the beachheads to be exploited and consolidated to a degree which would ensure their ability to withstand the inevitable strong counter-attack of major German forces. Nevertheless, these three officers produced a tentative outline plan, making the best use of everything that was likely to be available.

In May, 1942, Admiral Sir Bertram Ramsay, who was at that time commanding at Dover, was temporarily relieved of his command and summoned to London. His absence from Dover was at that time intended to be only temporary, but he did not return to that command, for from that time on he was fully engaged in the planning and execution of amphibious operations.

Admiral Ramsay was the naval commander designate for the projected operation against the Pas de Calais area, and General Freyberg was to be military Force Commander. The air component was to be commanded by Sir Trafford Leigh-Mallory. These officers formed what was called a "Round-up Planning Staff," and their first duty was to examine the outline plan for the invasion of the Pas de Calais and build around it a detailed plan for the proposed operation. It was not long before they found that the resources available or likely to be available to them would not allow of the plan being implemented without the acceptance of risks which they considered unjustifiable, not only because of the losses which would inevitably be incurred by failure, but also because failure would obviously lengthen the war and have a very serious effect upon our Allies and upon neutral opinion.

The chief responsibility for deciding whether the proposed landing in the Pas de Calais area was, or was not, feasible rested with Admiral Ramsay and General Freyberg. When, on detailed examination of the situations which were likely to arise in the event of the attempt being made, General Freyberg found himself doubtful of the ability to take a certain vitally important objective unless he could be assured of a certain speed and volume of "build-up," and Admiral Ramsay found that he could not be sure of providing that rate of "build-up" with the forces available to him, it was obvious that the proposed operation was unsound, and a definite report in this sense was made to the Chiefs of Staff Committee.

There followed the mid-summer meeting between Mr Churchill and President Roosevelt in Washington.

At their conference at Washington Mr Churchill and President Roosevelt examined the war situation in the light of the impracticability of attempting a cross-Channel invasion of France at that stage in the war, and they decided to adopt an alternative which had originally been suggested by Lord Louis Mountbatten. This was the invasion of French North Africa which, coupled with a great reinforcement of the strength of the Eighth Army, might be relied upon to clear the enemy from the whole of North Africa. This would in turn enable Italy to be invaded, in which case the surrender of Italy could be expected. Such a train of events would, by opening the Mediterranean, effect such a saving in shipping that the eventual invasion of Northern France would be brought nearer.

This was not an easy decision for President Roosevelt to take. A large section of public opinion in the United States had been impatiently awaiting the invasion of Hitler's "European Fortress" ever since the announcement, in February, 1942, of the arrival in the British Isles of the first contingent of United States troops. There was some excuse for such an attitude among a public far removed from the theatre of active warfare and without vivid and painful experience of German strength. Americans felt that if their men were to be overseas they might as well "get on with it and get it over" in the west so that the whole energies of the Allies might be diverted to the crushing of

Japan. They blamed British dilatoriness when they received letters from the troops expressing boredom and homesickness, but containing no news of impending invasion. Even in some high places in the United States there was impatience and a conviction that the British were being over-cautious—but the justification of that caution came in August with the experience at Dieppe.

The outcome of the talks at Washington was the victorious campaign of the Eighth Army, beginning with the battle of El Alamein in October, and the Allied invasion of French North and West Africa in the following month.

The needs of "Operation Torch"—as the French North African invasion was called—entailed the diversion overseas of practically all the equipment which had up till then been earmarked for the proposed invasion of the Pas de Calais area of France. The British First Army and the United States Second Corps had to be taken to the Mediterranean, together with vast quantities of equipment and stores both for the armies and the air forces. The shipping commitments were tremendous, the numbers of ships and craft running into thousands. Most of the planning staff which had been working on the possibility of an invasion of Northern France were also diverted to "Torch," from which they followed on almost automatically to "Operation Husky"— the invasion of Sicily.

There remained in England, however, a skeleton planning staff whose work—and it was at this time mostly research—was still attuned to the invasion of France from Great Britain.

By April, 1943, the situation in the Mediterranean had clarified. The whole of the North African coast from the frontier of Spanish Morocco opposite Gibraltar to Suez and beyond was dominated by the Allies. Convoys were already able to pass through the Mediterranean without provoking major naval and air battles. The requirements for the invasion of Sicily had been worked out. It was possible to think again about the invasion of Northern France without feeling that it was largely an academic study which might have to be postponed for so long that much of the preparatory work might prove useless.

At this time it was considered that the naval Commander-in-Chief at Portsmouth would be the Allied Naval Commander-in-Chief for any cross-Channel invasion. Geographically this was perfectly sound. As a result of the preliminary research it had been decided in June, 1943, that the invasion landings would take place on the Normandy coast between the rivers Orne and Vire.

It was a bold decision, taken by the then Combined Commanders, of which Admiral Ramsay was one, because any invasion on that coast would have the enemy-held naval bases of Le Havre on one flank and of Cherbourg on the other. Among the various points in favour of this choice, which was to be so amply justified by events, was that it would be sheltered by the Cotentin

Senior officers on board USS
Ancon, 6 January 1944. Walking
in front are (from left to right):
Rear Admiral Alan G. Kirk,
USN; Rear Admiral John L. Hall,
Jr., USN; and Rear Admiral John
Wilkes, USN.

At Admiral Ramsay's headquarters at Norfolk House there reigned a spirit of driving energy, coupled with determination that no small difficulties should become magnified and threaten the goodwill and close co-operation of the Allies. That there should have been small difficulties from time to time was inevitable, for the two navies had very different ways of doing some things.

At one time difficulties arose because the American authorities on the spot were reluctant to take decisions of far-reaching importance without referring them to Washington. Nobody had the slightest desire to keep the high authorities in Washington in the dark regarding the progress and needs of the plan, but the continual reference of comparatively unimportant matters to departments in Washington obviously jeopardised secrecy, since it meant that a great many more people were privy to them. Moreover, it greatly increased signal traffic and made for delay. On the other hand, it was all very well for the British to complain, since they were not faced with the difficulties of distance. The Admiralty was a bare five minutes' walk from Norfolk House, and the Cabinet Offices not much farther. The problem was solved by the departments in Washington giving greater authority to their representatives in London.

A greater difficulty, because it struck at the root of the planning, arose out of the differences between the British and American approaches to a naval plan. The British idea is to have a detailed plan covering every facet of a complicated operation, and Admiral Ramsay, with his experience of planning and carrying out invasions requiring the use of all three arms of an Allied force, was determined that the final plan for the invasion of Normandy would leave nothing to chance and no loophole for error. The American idea of a plan was very different. The Americans were used to being given broad directives but not detailed plans, and they felt that the latter tied them down too rigidly and left no room for the exercise of their own initiative. This point of view was well expressed to Admiral Ramsay by a senior officer of the United States

Navy who said: "When I'm wanted to do something I like to be told what to do, but not how to do it. How I do it is my business."

In principle there is a great deal to be said for the American point of view, particularly in ordinary simple naval operations. It is virile, imaginative, and leaves great scope for the individual commander. In an operation such as the invasion of Normandy, however, it would have led to chaos. In that invasion there was no room for discrepancies in timing or position such as would have been certain to arise if matters had been left to individual initiative. There were many thousands of different parts, even to the initial assault, and yards and minutes might well have meant the difference between success and failure too disastrous to contemplate. Nor could the invasion of Normandy be regarded solely as a combined operation of war—albeit the greatest combined operation ever contemplated.

England is a small and crowded country from which to launch such an operation. Port facilities, internal transport, and coastal transport had to remain available to the ordinary needs of the country if the British people were not to be left without food, light, power or fuel; and the wheels of industry going "all out" on war production were not to slow down and stop. The needs of the invasion, therefore, had to be dovetailed into all these other factors, and even into the movements of convoys to be assembled on the other side of the Atlantic. It was a vast jigsaw puzzle in which the wrong placing of a single piece might throw things out of gear over thousands of miles of distance and vital weeks of time. It was only by rigid and most detailed planning that all these factors could be co-ordinated into a scheme which was not only workable, but left no room for error.

When Admiral Ramsay explained the intricacies of the planning of the invasion to the Americans, who of course were unaccustomed to mounting enormous operations from a small country whose external and internal economy had to be considered in conjunction with the purely naval, military and air aspects, they were quick to see the necessity for detailed and rigid planning. Nevertheless, they still thought that the consequent operations orders for "Operation Neptune" were too voluminous and detailed.

On looking back after the event, Admiral Ramsay was rather inclined to agree with this criticism, and admitted that the orders, as issued to every authority taking part in the invasion, might have been less bulky. He was, however, the last man in the world to risk confusion or failure through under-organisation during the planning stage, and for this, among many other things, both Britain and the United States have great reason to be grateful to him, observing that any slip might well have led to a tremendous increase in the Allied casualties both afloat and ashore.

It seems as well to cite these inter-Allied difficulties and to examine their causes, for their very smallness in relation to the gigantic enterprise of the

Admiral Sir Bertram Ramsey, RN (centre of photograph), with Rear Admiral Alan G. Kirk, USN to his left. They are on a tour of the photographic laboratory on board USS *Ancon*, 8 March 1944. The ship's Commanding Officer, Captain P. L. Mather, USN, is conducting the tour.

invasion of Northern France is a measure of the accord which existed; while to pretend that there were no difficulties would be to argue an impossible perfection, and thus to open the door to such canards as Dr Goebbels would have greatly liked to foster. In fact, there were no canards at the time, nor have there been any since concerning the naval side of the invasion, although one such has appeared regarding the military side, alleging that Mr Winston Churchill and General Eisenhower both chose a military commander of whose ability they were doubtful.

In the month after the appointment of Sir Bertram Ramsay as Allied Naval Commander-in-Chief, Sir Trafford Leigh-Mallory and Sir Bernard Paget were appointed as the commanders of the air and military components respectively of the British invasion forces. Sir Bernard Paget was then commanding the 21st Army Group, which was designated as the British Expeditionary Force.

There was still no Supreme Allied Commander designate, and it seemed probable that Sir Bernard Paget's command of the 21st Army Group was of only a temporary nature. Nevertheless, both these air and military commanders had had experience in the planning of combined operations, and as soon as they had settled down and collected the requisite staffs, the combined planning began at the headquarters of No. 21 Army Group.

It may be as well to explain here that the planning of the naval side of the operation—which was by far the most complicated from the point of view of both planning and execution—was already fairly far advanced. It continued in the purely naval sense while the combined planning began at the headquarters of the 21st Army Group on 15 December 1943. This combined planning was a matter of fitting the naval, air and military plans together into what might be termed "the master plan" for the whole operation of invasion.

CHAPTER II

SHIPS AND YET MORE SHIPS

First naval requirements—Admiralty reactions—Possible German strength—
General Montgomery appointed—His requirement of a larger scale of
assault—Planning on the new basis—Appointment of Rear-Admiral Sir
Philip Vian—Ever-increasing naval needs.

By the middle of December, 1943, when the Combined Planning of the invasion of Northern France began at the Headquarters of No. 21 Army Group, the naval plan had crystallised to a point at which Admiral Sir Bertram Ramsay could make some preliminary estimate of the naval requirements for the invasion. The naval plan was at that time based upon the outline "COSSAC Plan" which had been approved by the Combined Chiefs of Staff at Quebec.

In December, 1943, it was still believed that no United States naval forces would take part in "Neptune." It had been agreed by Mr Churchill and President Roosevelt at their meeting in Cairo that the naval forces required for the invasion of Normandy would he provided by the British Navy, with such assistance as could be given by the Dominion navies and by the navies of our European allies. It was realised that, with the best will in the world, these Dominion and Allied contributions would be small by comparison with the total naval requirements.

Admiral Sir Bertram Ramsay—the Allied Naval Commander-in-Chief—was of the opinion that the United States Navy would, in the event, wish to be adequately represented. That, however, was then only an opinion, and an opinion is not a good substitute for warships. Admiral Ramsay could not plan on an opinion.

On the other hand, the Allied Naval Commander-in-Chief well appreciated the degree to which British naval resources had for so long been extended by the conduct of war in every sea. He was therefore determined that he would not add to the burdens of the Admiralty by making demands beyond those which he considered the absolute minimum necessary to ensure the safety of the invasion troops and of their supplies and reinforcements. He set his face resolutely against the temptation to work on the principle that "the more you ask for, the more you are likely to get"; and he drilled his staff and examined their findings accordingly.

Nevertheless, the preliminary estimate of the naval requirements for the invasion of Normandy made up a very formidable list. This list the Allied Naval Commander-in-Chief laid before the Admiralty during the second week of December, 1943.

It amounted to:

2 battleships.
3 monitors (or battleships).
15 cruisers.
107 destroyers (of which 20 might be old destroyers).
48 frigates or corvettes.
64 anti-submarine trawlers.
108 motor launches.
120 motor torpedo boats and motor gunboats.

That was a total of 467 warships! Nor was that all, for the figure made no allowance for the minesweeping force which would be necessary. It was appreciated that the invasion of Normandy would entail the greatest minesweeping operation in naval history, and Admiral Ramsay's staff found itself quite incapable of providing for the minesweeping requirements with less than twelve flotillas of minesweepers—six flotillas of big "Fleet" minesweepers and six flotillas of the smaller motor minesweepers for inshore work off the beaches. By the time allocation had been made for dan-buoy layers, and spare minesweepers to ensure against a breakdown of the minesweeping plan due to casualties, the minesweeping requirements amounted to close on 150 vessels.

Add these 150 vessels for minesweeping duties to the 467 other warships required, and one can scarcely wonder that the Admiralty were somewhat shocked at Admiral Sir Bertram Ramsay's needs.

It is only right, however, to record that the Admiralty appreciated that these requirements had been worked out as a preliminary assessment which might well have to be increased. This realisation tended to add to the horror of the Admiralty when confronted with these figures.

In dealing with the Admiralty's reception of these demands one must take into consideration the fact that, in the Admiralty's view, the invasion of Normandy was but one operation among many for which ships had to be found. Everybody in the Admiralty appreciated that "Neptune" would be the most important naval operation of the whole war, but this in no degree blinded them to the fact that they were responsible for the conduct of naval affairs in all the seven seas. There was no desire to curtail the resources for the invasion, and certainly no tendency towards obstruction on the ground that one commander might have more ships under his control than the Admiralty themselves.

On the other hand, there was a very definite doubt in the Admiralty whether the other essential naval commitments could be adequately discharged if the demands for invasion were met in full. It has been said that, from the production point of view, the United States were at that time leaving the shadow of "too little" and entering the light of "plenty"; but this increased production was not leading at that time to an increase in British naval strength sufficient, to enable the Admiralty to view with equanimity its worldwide commitments and at the same time earmark a great fleet to be immediately available for a gigantic combined operation.

In the circumstances it was not surprising that the Admiralty did not accept Admiral Ramsay's requirements without question. They examined them in the light of the world naval situation and concluded that to allocate a total of 232 ships capable of working as convoy escorts and anti-U-boat vessels to "Operation Neptune" would be likely to impose an intolerable strain upon such vessels as remained available for these duties outside the invasion area, and might therefore lead to disastrous setbacks in other theatres.

The Admiralty also appreciated that, if Admiral Ramsay's requirements in minesweepers were to be met, there would be few minesweeping flotillas left to deal with the day-to-day requirements all round our coasts—and who was to say that the enemy might not at any moment embark upon another sudden and concentrated mining offensive such as that which had cost us so dear in the autumn of 1939?

The outcome was that the Admiralty asked Admiral Ramsay to reduce his requirements in naval vessels, particularly in ships suited to act as convoy escorts and in minesweepers.

So strongly did the Admiralty feel on the subject of convoy escorts that Admiral Ramsay was invited to reduce his requirements in these types of ship by as much as 40 per cent. This was not a flat request. The Admiralty suggested that it might be possible to reduce the convoy escort requirements by this amount if Admiral Ramsay could see his way to substitute for his plan of escorting all convoys a system of patrols on each flank of the convoy route between Britain and the Normandy beaches.

This Admiral Ramsay found himself unable to do. The working out of the detailed plan had made it clear that, in addition to the vast number of ships of all types which would have to be at sea on D-day, the minimum "build-up" requirements would be for the daily passage of at least 8 ship-convoys and 10 or 12 landing craft groups—which would have to be continued day in and day out for a minimum of five or six weeks. Tactical surprise might, if it could be achieved, prove a great factor for the safety of the shipping on D-day, but it was only to be expected that the enemy would subsequently bring all possible weapons into action in an attempt to cut our vital sea lines of communication with the armies in Normandy.

Admiral Ramsay and his staff could only assess the probable strength of the enemy's counter-attacks against this sea-lane in the light of the latest intelligence of the German forces available or likely to be available. Nor could he ignore the fact that the landings and the initial "build-up" of our invasion troops in the Bay of the Seine would have to be conducted along a sea route with a major German naval base close on either flank—Le Havre to the east and Cherbourg to the west.

It was known that the Germans had in the west at that time five destroyers of the powerful "Narvik" class, and about nine of the smaller destroyers of the "Elbing" class. This force, it was estimated, might be reinforced rapidly by six more big German destroyers from the Baltic, the Heligoland Bight or Norwegian waters. Such reinforcement of the German destroyer strength in the west would, however, leave no destroyers in the north-west to act as screens for the German heavy ships and would therefore indicate that the German High Command did not propose to use the heavy ships in an attempt to interfere with our invasion of France. On the other hand, it would in no way indicate that the German heavy ships were to be kept inactive. The great British naval responsibility of preventing them from breaking out on to the Atlantic convoy routes would continue and be of added rather than diminished importance, for destroyer screens would be only an encumbrance in an attempted break out for a raiding expedition in the Atlantic.

Between fifty and sixty E-boats might be expected in the English Channel, and about the same number of R-boats, in addition to between 25 and 30 minesweepers and some 60 other small craft of various types.

The minesweepers and the other small craft might easily and quickly be fitted to adopt an offensive role; but it was the E-boats and R-boats which caused the greatest anxiety. They would almost certainly be operating from bases close to the flanks of the cross-Channel convoy routes and close to the conglomeration of shipping which would be inevitable off our Normandy beachheads.

Then there was the U-boat menace. In the light of all the information available in Allied hands it was calculated that, even if tactical surprise were effected with the initial assault, about 130 U-boats might reach the invasion area from the Biscay ports and the Eastern Atlantic within forty-eight hours of a general alarm being broadcast by the German High Command. Nor was this all. There was a possibility of this U-boat force being reinforced by a further 70 vessels within a fortnight of D-day—and Admiral Ramsay had to think in terms of several fortnights. There was also the possibility that up to 25 short-range U-boats might be available to operate off the British east coast during the invasion operations.

Although the problem of dealing with enemy air attack by day could be safely left to our undoubted air superiority, there was the possibility of night air attack. Although night air attack on the convoys at sea might not assume serious proportions, there was no denying that the mass of shipping which would necessarily be collected off our Normandy beachheads would provide the *Luftwaffe* with a tempting and perhaps a profitable target. Night fighter patrols were organised and the anti-aircraft armament of nearly every ship taking part in the invasion was increased, but still it was necessary to allow a margin for ships which might be sunk or damaged.

A margin to cover ships lost or damaged had also to be allowed in respect of other means whereby the enemy might seek to attack our convoys or our shipping off the beachheads. The Naval Commander-in-Chief of the Expeditionary Force had to be prepared to meet the unknown. There had been much talk of German "secret weapons." This certainly could not be taken at its face value, but there was, nevertheless, no denying the ingenuity of the Germans in weapon production. They had produced the glider-bomb, the acoustic torpedo and the magnetic and acoustic mines, all of which had inflicted losses upon us at sea, and it would have been quite unjustifiable to plan the invasion on the assumption that Germany had nothing new for use against our invasion forces. In the event, the Germans produced no less than four so-called "secret weapons" for use against our ships during the invasion of France. All were dangerous and difficult to counter, and only one of them had previously put in an appearance.

In addition to the margins necessary to guard against and to cover losses which might be incurred by methods of direct enemy attack, allowances had to be made in respect of probable losses due to mines and to stress of weather, breakdowns, and accidents such as collisions. The invasion of Normandy and the cracking of Hitler's "West Wall" was certainly not an operation which could be contemplated without an adequate "factor of safety."

When one considers the magnitude and variety of the threats to the convoy routes and anchorages—upon the safety of which would hang the success of the entire invasion—it is not surprising that Admiral Ramsay could not see his way to adopt the Admiralty's suggestion of a reduction of 40 per cent in his requirements of escort ships.

Nor could he accept a reduction in his requirements in minesweepers. It was already known that the Germans had been laying an anti-invasion barrage of moored mines off the French coast for nearly the whole length of the English Channel, and there was every possibility that the German defensive mining would greatly increase before D-day. Moreover, there was no knowing what might be encountered on the French side of the German anti-invasion mine barrage. It was to be expected that the approaches to all possible beaches would be heavily mined. Moreover, Admiral Ramsay considered that one of the German reactions to our invasion would be a great increase in their mining activities in the invasion area, and particularly off the beachheads, where the sinking of a ship might not only lead to the loss of that ship, but cause a wreck in such a position that it might seriously interfere with other movements to and from the beaches. Events were to prove that Admiral Ramsay was right in his assessment of the probable German reactions to our invasion, and it was providential that there were available a sufficient number of minesweepers to deal with a situation which at one time became very serious, with the minesweeping resources strained to the very utmost.

There was yet another factor which made the Allied Naval Commander-in-Chief determined to accept no reduction in the naval requirements as presented to the Admiralty at this stage. This was the outcome of his experience in the planning and conduct of invasion operations. As a result of this he was convinced that as the Combined Planning progressed the naval commitments would increase, and that this would entail an expansion, rather than any contraction, in the demands for warships which he would have to make to the Admiralty. It would obviously have been unfair and would have been likely to cause confusion if he had accepted a reduction in his initial requirements and then, at a later stage, had found it essential not only to go back upon agreed reductions but also to increase the total naval requirements above those initially presented to the Admiralty.

It must be emphasised that there was no disagreement between the Admiralty and Admiral Ramsay over these naval requirements. It was a perfectly normal procedure. The Allied Naval Commander-in-Chief asked for certain ships to be made available to him. The Admiralty, finding these requirements large in relation to their other naval commitments, asked the Commander-in-Chief whether it would not be possible to reduce his requirements, possibly by some modification of his plan. The Commander-in-Chief reconsidered the matter and found himself unable to accept a reduction in the number of warships which he felt to be the minimum necessary to ensure the success of the operation. The Admiralty then accepted the position and set about the task of finding the necessary ships.

As events were to show, it was as well that Admiral Ramsay did not accept any reduction in his initial naval requirements; for he was right in expecting the naval commitments to be increased as the planning progressed. It is doubtful, however, if even he had expected as great an increase as actually took place in the naval commitments for which he was responsible.

On Christmas Day, 1943, General Sir Bernard Montgomery was appointed to take over the command of No. 21 Army Group—the Army group which was to form the British military component of the invasion. General Montgomery arrived in London on 3 January 1944, and then saw for the first time the outline plan for the invasion. This, it will be remembered, was the "COSSAC Plan" which had received the approval of the combined British and American Chiefs of Staff at the Quebec Conference. This plan provided for an assault of the Normandy beaches on a three-divisional front, with an immediate follow-up of two divisions. It had been on this basis that all the planning had so far been done, and the requirements for the invasion worked out.

General Montgomery examined the outline plan, in conjunction with all the available intelligence of German defences and military strength in the west, and in the light of his experience in the invasion of Sicily, in which he had been the British Military Force Commander. He came to the conclusion that the assault, as contemplated, would be on too narrow a front. Moreover, he felt that it would be essential to have a greater number of troops in the first wave of the assault.

General Montgomery accordingly demanded that the plan should be re-drafted to provide for an initial assault on a five-divisional front instead of a three-divisional front. He was content that the immediate follow-up should remain at two divisions.

Thus the strength of the first wave of the assault was to be nearly doubled. The extent to which this increased the commitments of the Allied Naval Commander-in-Chief was enormous. It affected not only the initial assault, but the immediate "build-up" requirements, in order that two more divisions could be supplied and sustained during the early stages. Thus the increased commitments were concerned not only with naval vessels and the ships and landing craft to take part in the assault, but with the merchant ships and craft which were to bear the brunt of the "build-up."

The assault on a three-divisional front had been worked out on the basis that this would absorb practically all the ships and craft which were likely to be available at the time when the invasion had been planned to take place. The extension of the scope of the assault to a five-divisional front could only, therefore, be accepted if certain adjustments and compromises were made.

In the first place it was found to be essential to postpone the "target date" for the invasion by one month, in order that the necessary ships and craft for the two extra divisions of the assault should become available and the necessary training of these two extra divisions be undertaken. The invasion had been planned for the first week in May, but it had to be put back to the first week in June. It could not possibly have been undertaken any earlier on the new five-divisional front basis, and even as it was the two extra divisions had not—by early June—achieved such a high degree of training in amphibious assault warfare as the three divisions originally allocated for the initial landings.

It was realised that even by June there would not be available a sufficient number of ships and craft to convey to France with the initial assault as many vehicles *per* division as had been envisaged in the three-divisional front plan.

In all great amphibious operations it is the sea transport of the army's land transport which presents the greatest difficulties to those in charge of the maritime side of the expedition. The laden vehicles form a clumsy and cumbersome cargo. They take up far more space than men or stores, and are far more difficult and slower to load or unload except from Tank Landing Craft and Tank Landing Ships, from which they can be driven ashore. In the case of ordinary ships, special slings and often special derricks have to be provided for handling them.

These factors made it necessary to ask General Montgomery to accept a reduction in the number of vehicles to be landed with the assault divisions, and he agreed to a reduction in the number of vehicles from 3,200 to 2,500 *per* division. It was also necessary for General Montgomery to accept some reduction in the number of gun-support craft allocated to each division along the front of the assault. The craft allocated to give gunfire support to the troops ashore did not mean only the naval bombardment ships and the destroyers, which would provide a good proportion of the gunfire at fairly short rage in the initial stages. They included vessels being specially designed and built for the purpose, notably types of landing craft on which were mounted batteries of guns or batteries for the launching of rocket projectiles.

The increase in the scope of the initial assault was naturally accompanied by a great increase in the responsibilities of the Allied Naval Commander-in-Chief. Up to this stage in the planning of the invasion it had been accepted that Admiral Sir Bertram Ramsay as Allied Naval Commander-in-Chief-would not only have charge of all vessels engaged, but would also assume active command at sea.

With the great increase in the scope of "Operation Neptune" it became apparent that it would not be humanly possible for the Commander-in-Chief to conduct the whole operation and also to command at sea in charge of the tactical handling of ships and squadrons, with duties as widely different as bombarding in support of the army and convoy protection and seaward offensive patrols against the German destroyers and U-boats which were likely to try to interfere.

It was therefore decided that, while the Commander-in-Chief should conduct the operation and have general control of all ships in the invasion area, it would be necessary to appoint a Flag Officer to take command at sea of the British Task Force.

Rear-Admiral Sir Philip Vian was selected for the command. Rear-Admiral Vian had proved himself time and again as a dashing but not reckless sea commander; one who was willing to take enormous risks if they were in his

Admiral of the Fleet Sir Philip
Louis Vian, RN, (1894-1968).
Admiral Halsey and Vice
Admiral Vian aboard USS
Missouri, c. May-Aug 1945; the
other officers were Commander
William Kitchell and Captain
Joel Boone.

view justified by the circumstances and the situation, and with the power to
size up a situation very rapidly and seize the initiative. It had been he who had
rescued 300 British merchant seamen who were being taken to Germany in the
tanker *Altmark* and had earned a message from Winston Churchill, then First
Lord of the Admiralty: "The force under your orders is to be congratulated
on having in a single day achieved a double rescue, Britons from captivity
and Germans from drowning." (The latter because he had rescued the crew
of the German ship *Baldur* which they had scuttled). Rear-Admiral Vian had
successfully accomplished other missions in the Arctic, notably the expedition
to Spitzbergen and the action in which the German cruiser *Bremse* and other
ships were sunk. The great battleship *Bismarck* had been held in a "box"
made by Rear-Admiral Vian's destroyers throughout the wild night before the
German battleship was sunk. Later, in the Mediterranean, he had commanded
a force of light cruisers and destroyers with which he successfully fought off
Italian battleships and heavy cruisers from a Malta convoy, in what has been
described as "one of the most brilliant actions against greatly superior forces
ever successfully brought off." Rear-Admiral Vian had, moreover, first-hand
experience of invasion, for he had commanded one of the British Assault
Forces during the invasion of Sicily, an appointment in which he had served
under Admiral Ramsay, who had been in command of the British Task Force.

The Combined Planning of the invasion on the altered basis—that is with
a five-divisional instead of a three-divisional front for the initial assault—was
begun on 4 January 1944, although the concurrence of all the authorities
concerned had not by that time been obtained to the change of plan. It was,
in fact, not until 7 February that the concurrence of the United States to the
greater assault was received, but it was essential that the Combined Planning
should be rushed ahead, even without approval, if delays were to be avoided.

Even when official sanction had been obtained for the assault on the wider

better fitted for their invasion duties. It was heard in thousands of inland workshops and garages. In these, men and machines which had been for long devoted to constructional engineering and motor repair diverted their labours to produce parts and sections for prefabricated landing craft.

Most astounding of all, it was heard in the waterside glades of the New Forest and in hundreds of little streets running down to the banks of rivers and canals all over the country. To these came the devil of urgency, which with truly devilish ingenuity converted them into shipyards. In the roadways were laid improvised slipways. Gantries were swung across between the windows of opposite houses. Lorries brought strange-shaped structures of steel plate. The sound of pneumatic riveters took the place of the shouts of children at play, and the children stood goggle-eyed at the brilliance of the welding arcs which so far outshone the neon cinema lights which many had never seen.

These street dockyards became part of the life of the streets which they occupied. There were, of course, the regular workers, doing their shifts as they would have done on any other organised industrial labour, but there was also a tremendous amount of casual labour. Men and women on their way home or on their way to work or to shop stopped and lent willing hands. A community spirit was built into the landing craft put together in these streets and launched into river or canal, and Water Street was for ever trying to outdo Canal Street. The methods were ultra-modern; the scene was ugly twentieth century; but there was something intimately Elizabethan in the spirit. Had it not been so, D-day could hardly have marked so great a turning point in the history of freedom. As it was, it may well be that centuries to come will find that the essence of the success of that great day was the product of struggle between slave labour and labour "directed" in emergency but basically free.

Yet the work being done on the production of landing craft, great and widespread as it was, amounted only to a tithe of the tasks being undertaken for the maritime side of the invasion. Only an astronomer could visualise the number of man-hours and women-hours of work which went to the building of successful invasion.

The shipyards proper were crammed with work, and even the stringent blackout regulations took second place to an urgency which made small fry of "priorities" and kept the shifts working day and night.

The breaching of Hitler's "Atlantic Wall"—Todt-armoured by four years of German ingenuity provided with almost limitless slave labour—was not a project lightly to be undertaken. It was in no sense an operation to which the war-time "standardised" shipping such as the "Liberty Ships" and the "Victory Ships" could be diverted from their ocean-going work with confidence that they would prove as useful off the beaches as in the Atlantic. Utterly different conditions would obtain during invasion, and if this were not to be built upon dangerous makeshift, the ships had to be altered to meet the requirements of their altered service. They had to be fitted to carry combinations of cargoes and of cargo and passengers such as had not been thought of in their design and construction. They had to be fitted to meet a scale of air attack undreamt of on the great trade routes of the open ocean. Arrangements and alterations had to be made to enable them to discharge their cargoes quickly and efficiently off open beaches and in improvised shelter harbours instead of in the long-established and efficient ports to which they were accustomed.

It had been recognised that in the early stages of the invasion, until something in the nature of port facilities had been either captured or devised on the French coast, the merchant ships upon which the greatest burden would fall would be the small coasting vessels. Apart from the specially designed landing ships and craft, the first stages of the invasion would be predominantly a coaster's job.

Being small, the coasters would be less vulnerable than big ocean-going ships, and they could be handled with greater freedom. The main reason for using coasters, however, lay in the fact that they were almost flat-bottomed and fairly light when unladen, although very strong for their size. The problem of the rapid landing of large quantities of stores and equipment on open beaches could only be solved by running the ships themselves ashore. Where a big ship would be likely to break her back on the falling tide and would, at the least, require tugs to haul her off the beach on the next high water, the coasters would be quite safe and independent. They could run themselves ashore on the beaches at or near high water, laying out a stern anchor as they did so. They would "dry out" completely at low water and be able to land their cargoes directly on to the beaches without the use of lighters or other craft. When high and dry they would remain upright and be immune to the strains which would probably damage a bigger ship in similar circumstances. And when the tide rose sufficiently for them to be once more water-borne they could "kedge" themselves off the beach without assistance, by the simple process of heaving in on the hawser attached to the anchor laid out astern.

Most of the coasters chosen, however, had to undergo a certain amount of structural alteration to fit them for their duties. Here was yet more work for the shipyards, and it was work which was complicated by the fact that it could not in any way be standardised. There is no less standardised fleet of vessels in the world than the coasters which ply round the British coasts, and every coaster had to be treated in a way peculiar to itself.

The most frequent alteration required to be made to the coasters was the fitting of stouter derricks to enable them to unload their heavy cargoes on to beaches where there would be no facilities whatever. The fitting of stouter derricks in many cases entailed the fitting of stronger masts or the strengthening of the mast-step and the heel fittings of the derricks. Many of the coasters had also to be fitted for the carriage of specialised and dangerous cargoes such as cased petrol and ammunition.

To these commitments of the shipyards there was added yet another. Ships and craft had to be fitted as water-boats, tenders, hospital carriers, and a great number of "dumb" and power-driven lighters and barges and tugs produced. Even floating kitchens had to be provided.

The vast amount of fitting-out work required imposed a tremendous strain on the shipyards of this country, and the work had to be finished in very quick time at the last moment, for it was essential that no ships should be withdrawn from their normal service until it was absolutely necessary. This was in order to avoid dislocation of the country's distributive organisation or any premature reduction in the imports of food and essential war materials.

Not only was it essential that the deep-sea merchant ships should continue to transport to this country large numbers of American troops and the vast amount of war material to be accumulated for the invasion, but it was essential that the coaster fleet should continue until the last possible moment to play its part in the transport system of the country and build up stocks of various commodities in various places. In no case was this more important than in building up stocks of coal at the riverside power stations and other plants upon which so much of the war potential depended.

It was inevitable that much of the shipbuilding and nearly all the alteration work should be done in the crowded shipyards of the United Kingdom. Although shipyards in the United States and Canada were also working "all out" for D-day, their work was predominantly one of production. In 1943 the United States shipyards turned out no less than 21,525 landing craft, and did this on a rapidly rising production schedule which was still soaring after D-day in Normandy. By no means all the American-produced landing craft were, however, allocated to the European theatre of operations, for the swing to the offensive in the Pacific was calling more and more urgently for landing craft. The contribution from across the Atlantic in landing craft for the invasion of Normandy was, however, great and vital. In most cases these landing craft made the voyage across the Atlantic under their own power, and a number of very daring and gallant voyages were made in these little craft. Before the war such voyages would have been "front page news" throughout the world, but they were shrouded in the essential secrecy which cloaked all the invasion preparations.

For all the effort expended on the western side of the Atlantic the British production in landing craft was prodigious. Its rapid growth from very small beginnings was illustrated by the following sentence—carefully phrased to avoid giving total figures—used by the First Lord of the Admiralty when presenting Navy Estimates to Parliament on 7 March 1945:

"In the first quarter of 1942 four times as many major landing craft were built as in the first quarter of 1941; in the first quarter of 1943 ten times as many; and in the first quarter of 1944 sixteen times as many."

As the plans advanced it was appreciated that even the combined facilities of the southern ports of England would not be sufficient to handle the vast cross-Channel traffic which was contemplated. Fortunately the design of tank landing craft and tank landing ships, with ramps in the bows which had been dictated by the need for disembarking their loads on open beaches, simplified the loading problem. Instead of having to build jetties and supply them with cranes, loading facilities for those craft could be produced in Britain by the building of "hards." These are, in effect, hard roadways sloping down into the sea. The LCT's and LST's could nose in against them, let down their ramps, and the tanks and vehicles could be driven straight into the ships. A very large number of these "hards" had to be built along the south coast of England to ease the pressure on the established port facilities and, incidentally, they greatly reduced the time of loading these craft.

Meanwhile there were under construction in the United Kingdom the components of a project which has been described as the greatest constructional engineering feat in history.

So long as an invading army has no efficient port at its back and is dependent upon reinforcements and supplies landed over open beaches, its reinforcements and supplies must be to a great extent at the mercy of the vicissitudes of the weather. It is quite true to say, therefore, that even the first phase of invasion and the firm establishment of the invading army cannot be called successful until the invaders are in possession of a port.

This fact had greatly exercised the planners from the very outset of their task. The ideal would, of course, be to capture a major port in the initial assault, but the enemy well appreciated the importance of the ports and had specially strengthened their defences. The experience of the Dieppe raid and all subsequent intelligence went to prove that the ideal would not be attainable against an enemy of Germany's calibre. The alternative was to land on beaches where the configuration of the coast would give good shelter against the prevailing winds, and with ports in the vicinity which might be captured within a reasonable time after the initial landings. It had been these factors which had been chiefly responsible for the selection of the Bay of the Seine area for the invasion of Northern France. It was hoped to be able to capture the port of Caen and the canal leading to it very early in the operation, and within a reasonable period to cut off and capture the great port of Cherbourg. These, however, could not be guaranteed—and invasion cannot be undertaken on a gambler's charter.

It was at this early stage that Commodore Hughes-Hallett, then head of the "X Staff" planning the invasion, had his great idea. It was not a new conception, but a development of a technique. He argued that since urgency had shown it to be possible to prefabricate most big structures it should be possible to prefabricate a port, take it in sections across the Channel, and set it

A Mulberry caisson under construction in a temporary scooped out 'dry dock' off the Beaulieu River.

At twelve places close to the Thames mechanical excavators got to work and scooped out twelve great holes in the ground. Their depth was far below the river level at high tide, and, the ground being very porous, pumps had to be installed to keep these great pits dry—or nearly dry. In those pits began the construction of the lower portions of the concrete caissons required for the "Mulberries." When these had reached a stage at which they would float and only the upper sections and fittings needed to be added, the pumps were stopped and excavators removed the strip of land between the pit and the river. Thus the pit was flooded and the under-water sections of the caissons could be floated out into the river. They called these pits basins, but they did not become basins until they had served their primary purpose. In effect they were improvised graving dry docks, with the strip of soil remaining between them and the river until the work on the under-water sections of the "Mulberry" sections had been completed serving as a natural caisson closing the entrance to the dock.

Here was improvisation on a truly grand scale. The men concerned—20,000 workers and hundreds of designers, planners and organisers—were too busy

One of the Beaulieu caissons afloat.

and too intent upon the great job in hand to have time to think. If they had been able to think beyond their minute to minute service they could hardly have failed to recognise the significance of these great aids to the liberation of Europe and defeat of Germany being built in craters bigger than any ever produced by German bombs in the tortured soil of the banks of the lower Thames.

The importance of this system of improvised dry docks for the building of caissons cannot be over-estimated. Without them there could have been no "Mulberries," and it is safe to say that without the great artificial harbour erected off Arromanches on the Normandy coast our armies would have had to wait upon their supplies instead of being able to exploit to the utmost every sign of weakness or indecision shown by the enemy.

The importance of these so-called "basins" in the general scheme of production of the great concrete caissons for the artificial harbours is also obvious from the statistics. A total of 146 of these reinforced concrete caissons were built for the two artificial harbours. As has been said, these were in five sizes. Sixty of the largest size displacing over 6,000 tons each were built, and the numbers of the smaller sizes diminished to only 10 of the smallest size, displacing over 1,600 tons. Thus the biggest demand was for the largest caissons.

Of the 146 caissons built, 57 were built in the eight existing dry docks which could be set aside for the purpose, while 23 were built on the four available existing slipways and 18 in the two wet docks which were suitable and could be spared for this work. The whole of the remainder—48 caissons, among them many of the largest size—were built in the pits excavated along the banks of the Thames, officially called "basins."

Each of the caissons was in some sense a ship, for it was provided with quarters for the crew which was to man it during its cross-Channel voyage. Most of the caissons, too, were armed. They had mounted on them a Bofors gun and a shelter for the gun's crew, while stowage for 20 tons of ammunition was built within the upper part of the concrete structure. These guns would form a valuable addition to the anti-aircraft defences of the harbour, for it was to be expected that the *Luftwaffe* would make determined attacks on them and on the shipping which they sheltered.

While the concrete caissons were under construction the prefabrication of sections of the road piers and the building of the "spud pierheads" went forward.

Despite the progress made as a result of the Prime Minister's energising minute, many problems had to be solved. It is no easy matter to produce a pier hundreds of feet long that can be assembled with its inshore end on a very gradually shelving beach where the rise and fall of the tide is over 20 feet, so that at low water a great length of the pier will be resting on sand, or possibly even rock. Floating pontoons of steel and concrete were, however, evolved to meet these requirements and the great flexible roadway was laid upon these pontoons, which were of two types and known as "Whales" and "Beetles."

The requirements for the two "Mulberry" artificial harbours were no less than seven miles of this flexible pier roadway, and they had to be provided with adequate anchoring arrangements to prevent them swinging—and probably breaking—with the tidal streams. The inshore ends of the piers were anchored to specially heavy steel and concrete "floats," which could be hauled up on the beach at high water. The road piers were, in fact, floating bridges of special type, and their construction was necessarily far too light to allow of any vessel discharging direct to them. Hence there was evolved for the seaward end of these piers special "spud pierheads" which could be firmly fixed to the sea bed and against which ships of small and even moderate tonnage could secure while discharging their cargoes, once unloaded, being driven ashore in trucks along the roadway pier linking the "spud pierhead" to the beach. The system was, in fact, somewhat similar to, but much more complicated than, that adopted for many decades on the Yangtze river in China. The rise and fall of that river is so great and apt to be so sudden that enormous floating pontoons capable of having a ship moored alongside are securely anchored off the river bank and connected to the land by a sliding or flexible bridge. But the dis-

Mulberry beetles constructed just off the Beaulieu River and being towed downstream for eventual cross-channel transportation.

These following five photographs show the construction of 'Whales' the road elements of Mulberry Harbour at Marchwood Military Port. Marchwood, the Beaulieu River and nearby Lepe played very important roles in the construction of temporary Mulberry Harbours, which consisted of 'Spuds' (pier heads), 'Whales' (roads) and 'Beetles' (pontoons). In November 1943 a new military port was built at Marchwood to specifically assist with Mulberry Harbour construction in the build- up to D Day and to give extra

docking space for the ever increasing number of vessels waiting in Southampton Water for the Normandy landings. It became the base for the newly formed No. 1 Port and Inland Water Transport Repair Depot, Royal Engineers. Wates Group Ltd. construction firm, who had been employed to build elements of Mulberry, also built a slipway and other facilities. Part of the waterfront was also roofed over so that Mulberry construction could continue in bad weather.

tance between the pontoon, which amounts to a floating wharf provided with "godowns" and the rest, is in the Yangtze a matter of a few yards, and the current does not change its direction every few hours.

A "spud pierhead" is a steel pontoon structure which is anchored to the sea bed by piles. As the tide rises and falls the pierhead floats up and down, sliding up and down these piles. Thus, while there is vertical movement dictated by the rise and fall, there is no lateral movement in obedience to tidal stream, current or wind.

The "spud pierheads" used in the "Mulberries" were great steel structures displacing about 1,000 tons each. They consisted of a main steel pontoon 200 feet long and with a beam of 60 feet. These had four "spuds," or pillars with which they were securely held to the sea bed and on which they could rise and fall with the tide. Provision was also made for the lengthening of a pierhead from 200 feet to 280 feet by the attachment of specially designed concrete intermediate pontoons.

The "spud pierheads" were built almost as ships are built, and contained generating sets, storage space, and accommodation for their crews, which would not only tend them during their cross-Channel voyage in tow, but also serve in them when they were in operation, securing and casting off ships, arranging traffic both at sea and on the pier roadways and so on. They were unhandy things to tow, and they had farthest to go before they reached the Normandy coast, for they were built in Scottish ports. These "spud pierheads" were provided with yet another refinement. This amounted to a sort of false beach made of steel which sloped down into the water. LST's could nose in against this, lower their ramps, and discharge their vehicles, which could be driven straight ashore along the pier roadway. And while this was going on coasters could lie alongside the other parts of the pierhead and discharge their cargoes straight into waiting lorries.

The whole design of the "Mulberries" was keyed to rapid unloading of ships as well as to providing shelter for them from the weather during this operation. It was clear, however, that the "spud pierheads" could hope to deal only with coasters and LST's, and that the "Liberty" ships lying within the concrete caisson breakwaters—the concrete caissons were called "Phoenixes"—would have to unload into barges, lighters, DUKW's (amphibious lorries), and all sorts of small craft. These formed a ferry service of such dimensions that it consisted of between 2,0000 and 3,000 craft, exclusive of DUKW's, and employed some 15,000 men.

The need to provide shelter from the weather for these small craft would obviously be an earlier commitment than the completion of the "Mulberries," for the ferry service would have to begin to operate immediately after the "touch down" of the initial assault, and much of the early stages of the "build up" would be dependent upon its work. The country had been combed to provide the craft for this ferry service, so that practically no replacements were available. It therefore became imperative that arrangements should be made to give them shelter from the weather.

From the realisation of this need there arose the "Gooseberries." These were to be shelter harbours formed by the sinking of blockships. These could only enclose a shallow water area, since, in order to be efficient units of the breakwater, the blockships, when resting on the bottom, would have to have the top strakes of their hulls above high-water mark, otherwise the sea would break over them at high tide, making the shelter within the blockship breakwaters inefficient, and threatening to break up the blockships themselves. While the "Gooseberries" could not, therefore, provide shelter for ships, they would do so for the more vulnerable small craft of the ferry service, the preservation of which from loss or damage due to weather was a matter of the utmost importance.

It was decided that there were to be five of these "Gooseberry" shallow water harbours, that off Arromanches and that off St Laurent to form extensions of

have absolutely no mercy upon any grain of sand in the working parts—and he saw to it personally that they really were working parts.

General Eisenhower brought this creed of co-operation to the staffs which had been working on the combined planning of the invasion of Northern France. That is not to say that there had been discord before his advent. There certainly had not been; but it was inevitable that there should, in the absence of a supreme commander, have been certain watertight compartments and minor misunderstandings for lack of overriding authority.

One of the first things that General Eisenhower did on taking up his new appointment was to assemble the combined British and American staffs in the big conference room at Norfolk House. To them he said: "WE are not Allies. We have plenty of Allies among the United Nations, but we who are to undertake this great operation are one indivisible force with all its parts more closely integrated than has ever been the case in any force before." General Eisenhower was certainly not decrying the value of the other United Nations, the armed forces of many of whom had served him so well in the Mediterranean theatre of war and were to serve him so well farther north; but he instilled into the staff and into the troops, ships' crews and air crews allocated for the invasion of North-west Europe a spirit of mutual confidence that transcended mere co-operation.

By the time General Eisenhower was appointed as Supreme Allied Commander in January, 1944, an immense amount of work had already been done by the planning staffs and by the various departments and organisations working to the instructions of the naval, military and air commanders. Such instructions had, of course, to be issued as the various details of the plan materialised. Had they not been, a long period of preparation would have been necessary after the final plans had been completed—a delay which would have postponed the invasion until the following year.

The ramifications of the planning and preparation of the invasion of Normandy were so vast that it is even now difficult to grasp them in their entirety.

For a long time even before the area of the invasion or its probable date had been decided upon, the intelligence staffs had been busily engaged in the collection and collation of all manner of details about the enemy coasts and their immediate hinterland. Advertisements had appeared in the Press from time to time for photographs and information dealing with certain areas. As a result, hundreds of thousands of innocent holiday snapshots, picture postcards, motoring maps and details provided by travel bureaux and tourist agencies contributed valuable material from which a vast store of knowledge was built up. A great deal of the material called for, of course, dealt with areas which were not selected for the invasion, but even if the invasion area had been decided upon, this would have been necessary in order to prevent our intentions from becoming common knowledge and reaching the enemy.

From all this information there were printed and held in readiness literally millions of sheets of maps, elevations and diagrams. These covered all parts of Western Europe which might be involved in forthcoming operations. To produce these, practically every firm in the country capable of map printing had to be employed, while at the same time elaborate steps had to be taken to ensure that no draughtsman or printer was aware whether or not he was dealing with a zone selected for attack.

Meanwhile there had been set up a very close working liaison between the planning staff and various civil administrative authorities who were indirectly but vitally concerned in the plans for " Operation Overlord."

Of these the Ministry of War Transport was obviously most closely concerned. Not only did it have to provide the merchant shipping required for the invasion, and do this with the minimum of interference with the normal flow of seaborne traffic, but it had to deal with the railway companies and the harbour authorities. The Ministry of Supply was concerned because it was that Ministry's responsibility to see that the interference with normal transport which was to be expected during the invasion did not lead to a slowing down of the whole of our war industries. The Ministry of Food was concerned that there should be equitable and sufficient distribution of food. The Ministry of Fuel and Power had to see to it that factories and power stations had sufficient stocks to tide over any interruption in fuel deliveries. The Ministry of Labour had to provide men and women at short notice for all manner of special work which had to be undertaken. The Home Office and the Ministry of Health had to contend with the problems arising out of the movement of large parts of the population in order to leave big tracts of country free of civilian inhabitants for the final battle-training of the assault troops for the invasion.

It is no exaggeration to say that the requirements of the invasion of Normandy impinged upon the private lives and work of every man, woman and child in the United Kingdom; and that one of the great wonders of "Operation Overlord" was that it was carried out with so little interference with the needs and convenience of the general population. That was one of the triumphs of the administrative planning of the invasion.

By January, 1944, the administrative planning was already fairly far advanced, not only as regards the preliminary work, but in relation to the actual facts and figures of invasion. This was because by that time three main questions had been settled.

It had been decided that the invasion should take place in the bay of the Seine.

It had been decided that the invasion would take place early in June, 1944.

It had been decided that the strength of the initial assault would be five divisions, with an immediate "follow up" of two divisions. These were the three concrete facts upon which it had been possible to press forward with the detailed administrative planning. An invasion is a gigantic operation in which all three Services are intimately concerned. In enabling the actual landings to take place the part of the naval forces is of paramount importance, but in the administrative planning stage the Navy must wait upon the Army. Only the military authorities can say what strength they consider essential, in men, equipment and stores, for the initial assault, the "follow-up," and the subsequent "build-up." Such decisions are, of course, made on the highest staff level, but once they have been made the naval and military planning staffs have to work together, and, in conjunction with the shipping administration, solve the problem of how the military commander is to be provided with all that he needs.

In solving these problems there have, of course, to be many compromises, for it is not in the nature of things that military ideals, shipping resources and naval operational considerations should match without difficulty. Here again, the initiative is with the military authorities. Given the three concrete facts regarding the invasion of Normandy enumerated above, the military Quartermaster-General's department produced what is known as the "Q Appreciation."

The "Q Appreciation" set out in detail the requirements of the military invading force in men, vehicles, equipment, ammunition, stores, rations and everything else that the fighting soldier would need. It formed the datum on which the administrative planning was carried out—a form of agenda for the hundreds of meetings at which every facet of the problem was minutely scrutinised, and mutually acceptable and feasible compromises evolved. The "Q Appreciation" was by no means concerned only with the far shore; in fact one of its main functions lay in dealing with the transport and assembly problems in this country and in ensuring that troops and cargoes were available at the right times at the ports where they were to be embarked.

In the administrative planning for the invasion of Normandy the object which had to be continually borne in mind was to synchronise the initial assault with an organisation capable of providing a smooth flow of reinforcements and supplies. Lack of "smoothness" in this flow would inevitably have produced "peaks" and "bottlenecks." Both would have been wasteful of shipping space, which it was essential to economise to the utmost. On a "peak" there would have been ships lying idle off the beaches, waiting their turn to unload, while in a "bottleneck" ships would have been lying idle in British ports waiting for cargoes.

The movement of modern armies, with their very heavy equipment, and arms which are quick-firing and, therefore, prodigal of ammunition, are matters requiring immense and widespread organisation.

It is an organisation, moreover, which has to be flexible and adaptable in order to meet unforeseen requirements or events. It must also be able

The Allied military high command for Operation Overlord, during a meeting in London. Seated from left to right: Air Chief Marshal Sir Arthur W. Tedder; General Dwight D. Eisenhower; General Bernard L. Montgomery. Standing from left to right: Lieutenant General Omar N. Bradley; Admiral Sir Bertram H. Ramsay; Air Chief Marshal Trafford Leigh-Mallory; Lieutenant General Walter Bedell "Beetle" Smith, Eisenhower's chief of staff.

to continue to function over a long period, during which the needs of the troops will inevitably fluctuate. It is all very well to say that there should, if the planning be good, be no unforeseen requirements or events. No man can plan his enemy's actions as well as his own. The most the greatest planning genius can achieve is a flexible organisation which takes into consideration every interference by the enemy or by the weather which can reasonably he expected, makes due allowances for meeting these, and still retains a degree of flexibility in reserve with which to meet the unexpected.

Steps had, of course, been taken over many months to build up in Great Britain a great invasion army and the vast accumulation of stores, vehicles and food that it would need on going into action. But these were in camps and dumps far from the ports at which they would embark for the invasion of France. An organisation had therefore to be evolved which would provide for the arrival of the men, vehicles, equipment and stores in the vicinity of the port of embarkation at the right time.

The task of organising this fell into four phases:

1. Formations, and all their requirements, would have to be concentrated in areas reasonably close to their embarkation ports. This would mean that large areas would have to be denuded of their normal military population; otherwise there would be bad overcrowding in certain areas and secrecy would thereby be jeopardised.

2. Once concentrated, and as close as possible to D-day, the troops would have to be moved into marshalling areas, where they would be divided into assault troops, first reinforcements to be kept as a floating reserve at sea off the beaches, and "follow up" troops. Then they would have to be split up into unit parties and loads for the various craft to be employed, having due regard to the principle that every load should be a "balanced" load of troops of every category needed for the initial assault, and with enough stores of the types required by the categories of troops employed during the initial assault period.

3. The embarkation of the assault troops, the "floating reserve," and the "follow up" wave, and the initial stages of the "build-up." In all of these the principle of "balanced" loads would have to be rigidly observed, for there could be no guarantee that these would not have to be put ashore under the same conditions as the first assault wave.

4. The force, having secured the beachhead, would have to be sustained and steadily built up by a harmonious and uninterrupted flow of reinforcements of men, material, ammunition and stores. In this phase the principle of "balanced" loads for every individual ship and craft could be ignored, but the need for a "balanced" delivery at the beachhead would remain a paramount consideration. Precautions would have to be taken to ensure that no act of God or the King's enemies could produce a situation in which one day's deliveries could lead to a glut of ammunition, forming a dangerous surplus, while the fighting men had nothing to eat.

To produce a steady flow of goods may at first sight seem a comparatively easy task. To a great extent it is what the distributive organisation of Britain does year in and year out, in peace as well as in war. But a vastly different set of circumstances ruled. In the first place the weight and volume of the material to be moved was enormous; and it would have to be moved first over an internal transport organisation already working to capacity. Secondly, the great weight of material and equipment would require, to a considerable extent, specialised rolling stock for its transportation. Thirdly, it would have to be moved quickly and within a short period in order that dumps of too great size and vulnerability should not be built up within easy reach of the *Luftwaffe*, thereby disclosing our intentions to the enemy and inviting retaliatory action.

Then there was the question of men. Even in peace time the transport system within Great Britain suffers from "rush hours." The assembly of the troops required for the first waves of invasion promised to produce a far greater "rush" traffic, and one which would be sustained over a much longer period. Moreover, troops have to be fed in transit and at their destinations, and the transport of their rations alone creates problems.

As an illustration of the need for absolute accuracy in administrative planning, particularly as regards transport, it may be noted that the addition of 50 men to the number to be carried in a particular troop train may have disastrous effects. Those 50 extra men will mean the addition of an extra coach to the train. With all the transport working to capacity, as it was before D-day, the addition of one coach to the train might well have made the train too heavy for the locomotive to pull—at least at the speed required to keep to a complicated but inflexible time-table. Thus those 50 men might have thrown out of gear a whole series of complicated movements, not only of railway transport, but also of ship-loading.

These initial problems are primarily military in cause if not in character, but they are all intimately connected with the planning of the maritime side of the expedition, for the arrival at the port of embarkation is but the first stage of the journey to invasion.

For the initial phase of invasion the ships can be "pre-loaded" that is, they can embark their troops and cargoes before the operation commences and be ready to sail at a moment's notice. This simplifies the initial problem, so far as the first wave of the assault, the "floating reserves" and the immediate "follow-up" are concerned; but pre-loading can only be used within a very limited time factor. To keep large numbers of laden ships lying in anchorages within striking distance of an enemy coast is to invite enemy action which may prove disastrous. It may also give the enemy invaluable clues pointing to the intentions of such concentration. It will certainly lead, after a very short time, to a deterioration in the physical and mental well-being of troops cooped up in crowded troopships, for there can be no question of disembarking them for exercise. The requirements of secrecy make it imperative that ships once loaded for an operation should be "sealed"—that is, they must have no communication with the shore.

It was for the maintenance of the invasion force, once successfully put ashore in France and in building up its strength, that the working out of time-tables and of schedules of the needs of the troops was of paramount importance. For the first wave of the assault, ships and landing craft were to be "pre-loaded" before the operation began. Their collection and loading, so that the fighting man should want for nothing even if a certain number of ships were sunk, was a difficult matter, but it was simple by comparison with the maintenance problem. For this, ships could not be "pre-loaded," for they would have to work a "shuttle service" backwards and forwards across the English Channel, and their tasks would only end with the end of the war.

The first steps in working out the maintenance problem was to predict, in the light of past experience, the probable needs of an expanding force, having regard to the estimated nature of the operation, in terms of both probable rate of movement and expected severity of the fighting. In launching an invasion in force against territory held by the enemy for four years this would seem to be "anybody's guess." But it was no guess. It was an estimate carefully worked out by the staff of the Force Commander in the light of the numbers of men, tanks, guns and vehicles which it was hoped to land day by day, and in the light of all available intelligence of the terrain and the disposition and strength of the enemy. The quantity of rations required was a simple calculation, but estimates of the probable expenditure of ammunition of each category, and of petrol, demanded highly expert judgment.

As the requirements for assault and for maintenance and "build-up" began to crystallise, steps could be taken to fit these in with the available shipping and loading facilities.

It had already been decided that coastal ships of small size and draught should be widely used both in the initial stages and during the "build-up." This decision, however, involved other problems. How much coastal shipping could be diverted to invasion duties without placing an intolerable strain on internal transport or depriving essential services of their necessary supplies? How many loading berths suitable for these ships were available at or near the main "invasion ports"? All this, of course, had to be dovetailed into the routeing arrangements for the various ships and convoys so that they could be given the maximum of naval and air protection during their voyages.

Thus the size, positioning, and routeing of the great fleet of ships of vastly differing characteristics was gradually determined. Then this had to be interpreted in terms of potential discharging capacity at the beachheads, with due allowance for possible loss or damage by enemy action or delay by weather. Allowance also had to be made for refuelling the ships themselves, and since they were of no homogeneous type or standardised performance, every ship had to be treated as a separate entity.

Small wonder that it was not until a very large number of elaborate calculations had been made, checked and re-checked, that it was possible to arrive at even an approximate figure of the numbers of men and tonnage of stores which could be brought to the vicinity of the beachhead on the heels of the assault. Even then, the rate of discharge depended to some extent upon a further factor—the carrying capacity from ship to shore of the DUKW's, barges and other ferry craft, all of which had to be procured and many adapted in advance.

The maintenance of one division of troops in face of the enemy demands a supply in the nature of 300-400 tons a day. We have seen that it was laid down as the immediate object of the invasion of Normandy that the lodgement in France was to contain a force of 26-30 divisions with a reinforcement by "follow-up" divisions at the rate of 3-5 divisions a month. This, be it noted, was the lodgement and the force estimated to be required "from which further offensive operations can be developed." Thus in the early stages of the invasion the overseas supply problem was for the delivery of between 8,000 and 12,000 tons of stores a day, irrespective of "build-up." Moreover, this commitment was to have a monthly increase of between 1,000 and 2,000 tons a day, to say nothing of the task of transporting the "follow up" divisions themselves.

Here was a problem in sea transport of greater magnitude than had ever before been considered in relation to any operation of war. It was immediately obvious that it could not be attempted unless there was exercised the most rigorous economy in shipping space and shipping time, so that every ton of shipping should be used to the utmost of its capacity, not only on each voyage, but in carrying out the maximum possible number of voyages in any given time.

The necessity for meeting these essential requirements produced the most detailed control of shipping that has ever been known. It was a control which concerned the actual loading of the ships, and the previous planning of their loading, as well as their movement at sea.

To say that the last thing put into a ship is the first thing to come out may seem obvious, but it is a truth which becomes really important only when dealing with the problems of invasion. The armies ashore would have to have "first things first," and that meant that the loading end of the cross-Channel ferry service would have to work on a basis of "first things last" as far as individual ships were concerned.

Another complication was the principle, to which reference has already been made, which has come to be known as "balanced loading." Basically, this is merely a means of ensuring that the soldiers get what they want when they want it. It means that a ship carrying motor transport must also carry the crews of the vehicles and the fuel for the vehicles. It means that if guns of a certain type are in one ship a supply of ammunition for those guns must be in

Hence "ETM5" would mean that the ship belonged to the 5th motor transport convoy outward bound from the Thames area. Similarly, a board with the legend "FWP3" would indicate that the ship belonged to the 3rd personnel convoy from France to the Isle of Wight area.

It will be noticed that the literal translation of the letters in the code gives the information in the reverse order to that used in ordinary parlance; but the order given in the code is the order in which it is required by the control organisation. For instance, the commanding officer of an escort group assembling an outward bound convoy could ignore all ships with legends beginning with the letter "F" without wasting time in reading the remainder of the legend.

Giles was a famous cartoonist for the *Daily Express* from the 1940s through to the 1960s. Two of his signature characters were Grandma and baby. This cartoon was published 30 December 1943 with Grandma character-swapped as Churchill, and Baby being the New Year.

CHAPTER V

MEN MUST BE TRAINED

*Shortage of officers—Special training—the Lochailort system—
Lessons of Dieppe—Bombardment requirements and training—
Rocket craft—Bombardment organisation—Air "spotters" and "weavers"—
The "V Scheme" for merchant seamen.*

While vast material resources were being harnessed on both sides of the Atlantic to the task of the invasion of North-west Europe, there was great acceleration in the training of personnel for amphibious warfare.

From the naval point of view this training was always an uphill struggle. It was for a long time a question of finding means of making the best possible use of very limited material and still more limited personnel.

The naval problem in amphibious training had been from its inception far more difficult of solution than that of the army.

The fundamental reason for this was that, from 1941 onwards the commitments of the military forces in the United Kingdom were small, whereas the Royal Navy was at full strength, fighting the Battle of the Atlantic, the Battle of the Coastal Trade Routes, and called upon at frequent intervals to mount important and large-scale operations in the Arctic, in the Mediterranean and even farther afield.

Nevertheless, two great training centres for naval officers and ratings who were to serve in landing craft during amphibious operations had been established. These were at Hayling Island, on the south coast of England, and at Inveraray, on Loch Fyne, on the west coast of Scotland. The former was known as HMS *Northney* and the latter as HMS *Quebec*.

There was a great difference between these two training establishments, to a great extent dictated by their geographical positions. There was every chance that the enemy would not become aware by his air reconnaissance of what was going on at Inveraray, but the reverse was true of Hayling Island. The Hayling establishment was, therefore, used only to give the landing craft crews their preliminary training in handling these queer vessels, both at sea and during the ticklish businesses of beaching and of "unbeaching." The Inveraray establishment became the base for advanced training for combined operations, where the Services worked together on exercises and where theories were put to the test and experiments carried out. Inveraray was, in fact, the first and most important Combined Training Centre, while Hayling Island continued to be a naval establishment for specialist training in much the same way as there were gunnery, torpedo and navigation schools in the Portsmouth area.

The naval commander at Inveraray, and the naval officer who was responsible for working out and superintending the whole of the combined training, was Vice-Admiral Sir Theodore Hallett. Admiral Hallett is a man of energy and of vision. Moreover, he had first-hand experience of some combined operations—albeit these had been concerned with the extrication of troops rather than in victorious invasion—and knew some of the difficulties of embarking and disembarking troops. He had served with tireless distinction as a beach commander during the withdrawal of the British Expeditionary Force from Dunkirk, and had also been at Namsos during the Norwegian campaign.

Under Admiral Hallett's direction and that of Brigadier Greenslade—his military "opposite number"—the work of the Combined Training Centre went rapidly forward. Not a minute was wasted. Every day officers and men practised embarking and disembarking men, vehicles and equipment. At the beginning of each course this was done by platoons. Then it was stepped up to companies and then to battalion and brigade landings. Moreover, these exercises were done both by day and by night.

Once the men were accustomed to embarking in their craft and to landing from them across beaches; assaults were practised with fire support using live ammunition. Thus before he had completed his combined operations training every man knew what it is like to storm a beach from landing craft with live shell bursting in the close vicinity and when he himself is using live ammunition.

The process of "stepping up" the scope of the training exercises was again carried out under these conditions, until finally each course carried out that was known as the "Brigade Exercise." In this a whole Assault Brigade was landed, with live ammunition and with live ammunition covering fire, under conditions which would approximate as closely as possible to those which would obtain during the actual operation against the enemy which was in prospect.

That is but a brief and sketchy outline of the work of the Combined Training Centre, but it is sufficient to demonstrate its thoroughness.

A problem which threatened for some time to retard training was lack of junior officers to command and to act as second-in-command of landing craft. This was not due to reluctance on the part of the Admiralty to part with young officers; there were barely enough of these available to commission the ever-increasing number of ships, particularly escorts and light coastal craft, at a time when the great emergency building programmes were turning out war vessels at a rate never approached in the war of 1914-18.

Thus, at a time when young officers were at a premium, the Combined Operations Command needed very large numbers to officer the ever-increasing number of landing craft which were becoming available. The situation was difficult, and it was aggravated by the fact that the proportion of officers to ratings required by the Combined Operations Command for the manning of landing craft bore no relation to the proportion of officers to ratings in the Navy as a whole. It thus became necessary for the Combined Operations Command to open a special cadet training establishment at Lochailort, near the western coast of Inverness-shire.

The officers trained at Lochailort for combined operations requirements were drawn from those who had already been selected for or begun their courses of instruction before being commissioned in the Royal Naval Volunteer Reserve. When they went to Lochailort they received the highly specialised instruction and training necessary to fit them to become officers of landing ships and craft during invasion. In order to allow them to receive this training and instruction in the time available, and to make a greater number of officer candidates available for the Lochailort training, the Admiralty waived, for the time being, certain general training and instruction which these men would normally have had to undergo before being commissioned as officers. The effect of this step, combined with the Lochailort training, was to produce a temporary but considerable acceleration in the commissioning of officers. This system successfully met the sudden and very large demand for officers of junior rank for the thousands of landing craft to be used in invasion.

It was agreed at the time that officers commissioned from the Lochailort establishment would hold commissions which were not applicable to the naval service as a whole. This was common sense, for the Lochailort officers had received special training at the expense of training in subjects which would be most necessary for them as ordinary naval officers. One of the subjects waived in the case of the Lochailort commissions was deep-sea navigation.

There is no denying that this system, while meeting the urgent demands for officers for invasion, did for the time being produce a specialist officer who was not a fully qualified officer in the general sense of the term. It was, however, a matter of necessity rather than of choice.

The peak requirement for officers for the Combined Operations Command was naturally around D-day and during the immediately succeeding weeks. As soon as established ports on the French coast began to fall into our hands and be rehabilitated, more orthodox shipping methods could be resorted to

For this reason, as well as to avoid giving the enemy premature warning of the sector of coast chosen for the assault, the timing of this first phase of naval bombardment had to be very carefully worked out. If it were too early it would give the enemy valuable information and allow him to recover before the "touch down" of the assault; if it were too late the vulnerable landing ships would inevitably suffer before the enemy batteries were silenced.

This first phase of naval bombardment in support of the invasion would be carried out partly with direct observation from the bombarding ships, and partly with aircraft spotting.

The second phase of the naval bombardment would follow immediately, the warships closing in to turn their attention on redoubts, pillboxes, the smaller batteries, mortar batteries and machine-gun posts, and concrete anti-tank defences. Most of this work would fall to the cruisers. Their work would be far more extempore than that of the heavy ships in the first phase. They would have to be here, there and everywhere, acting at a moment's notice on calls for counter-battery or supporting fire. They would be close enough to the shore to rely entirely on direct observation.

Then, as the assault forces approached the beaches, the "drenching fire" proper would commence. For this destroyers, special "landing craft, gun" (the modern equivalent of the floating batteries of past centuries) and other craft would literally "drench" every yard of the beaches with high explosive, laying a dense barrage behind which the assault troops would be approaching the beaches.

In order further to increase the density of the "drenching fire," rockets were to be used. These were to be fired from "landing craft, rocket"—vessels which had been tried out with great effect at Elba. The hull of these vessels is that of an ordinary tank-landing craft, but it is decked in, and along its broadsides it has batteries of rocket tubes. For purposes of short-range "drenching fire" one such craft has a fire-power equivalent to over 80 light cruisers or nearly 200 destroyers. The rocket tubes are fixed and the broadside is "aimed" by steering the vessel towards the target. The rockets generate such heat on discharge that the deck on which they are mounted becomes distorted. Decks are sprayed; but even so, men on deck have anti-flash clothing. The usual practice is for the personnel to go below decks before firing, leaving the commanding officer in a special heat-proof and blast-proof "hut" from which he can con the vessel and control the firing of the rockets. These are not all fired simultaneously as a broadside, but in groups with very short intervals between them. The effect is therefore that of a "ripple salvo."

Of the effectiveness of the new weapon for "drenching fire" there is no doubt. The rockets devastate whole areas, completely removing woods, villages, and any but the heaviest concrete defences which may have been set up in them.

In the case of the "drenching fire" accurate timing would again be absolutely essential. If it began too early the vessels concerned might well run short of ammunition, so high would be its rate of expenditure. If it began too late our assault troops might suffer at the hands of the enemy during the later stages of the approach to the beaches, and might even run into the "drenching fire" itself.

The third requirement of naval bombardment was that, in effect, the ships would be required to work as mobile artillery for the military forces. This form of bombardment might be expected to continue along the military front until the armies drew out of range of naval gunfire, but might have to continue on the flanks for much longer. It would be of great importance throughout, but it would be absolutely vital during the hours after the initial assault, when the ships' guns would be virtually the only artillery support available to the troops landed.

It is obvious that many special problems of fire control arise under conditions in which ships' gunfire must necessarily be under military control—for the guns must shoot when and where required by the military commanders in the field. Yet the mobility of the ships—and therefore the positioning of the guns—must remain under naval control, for this involves navigation, pilotage and other purely naval matters. There is, therefore, absolute necessity for some system approximating to "dual control"; but such a system must be as nearly instantaneous in operation as is humanly and materially possible. If the commander of military forces locked in battle requires an enemy strong point or concentration to be engaged or a barrage to be laid he must have the gunfire at once—not after an indeterminate interval, by which time his troops may have advanced and might therefore come under fire from our own naval guns.

The problem of controlling the fire of ships' guns firing in support of an army in battle had been studied on both sides of the Atlantic, and both the Americans and the British had evolved systems for such control. The American system consisted of landing a fairly large party of gunnery experts, known as the Shore Fire Control Party, which interpreted the artillery requirements of the military commanders into terms of naval gunnery and gave the orders for bombardment to the ships in naval parlance. The British system, on the other hand, consisted of having with the military commander, or in his immediate vicinity, a bombardment observer officer who was a military officer. This officer used to be known as the FOO—" Forward Observation Officer," but is now known as the FOB—"Forward Officer, Bombardment." The FOB relays the requirements of the military commander, as a purely military artillery requirement, to the BLO—"Bombardment Liaison Officer"—who is also a military officer, on board the bombarding ship and in close and direct personal touch with the gunnery officer of the ship. He interprets the military needs to the ship's fire control organisation.

This system was used very successfully during the invasion of Sicily and at Salerno and Anzio, but many improvements were made in the Organisation as a result of these experiences in the face of the enemy.

As has been said, time is a most important factor in this distant control of naval gunfire in support of troops, and time can always be saved, as well as mistakes avoided, by good training. To this end the BLO's and the FOB's were given special training, both at the Royal Artillery Establishment at Lark Hill on Salisbury Plain and at the Royal Naval Gunnery School at Whale Island, Portsmouth.

It was intended that, with ships engaging specific targets, the observation of the fall of shot and application of the necessary spotting corrections would normally be the duty of the FOB's. It was realised, however, that there would probably be occasions when he would not be able to do so, and arrangements were therefore made for aircraft to take part.

The spotting aircraft, which were to work during the first phase of preliminary heavy naval bombardment, also had other duties during the third phase of naval gunfire support. It was by no means intended that during this phase the guns of the ships should remain silent until fire was called for by the FOB's. The spotting aircraft were to search the country ahead of and on the flanks of the Allied military forces for likely targets, report these to the ships, and observe the result of their fire, passing corrections of range and deflection to the ships as might be necessary.

It was realised that to expect air observation and spotting from slow two or three-seater aircraft would be to invite their destruction by "flak" or the *Luftwaffe*, which would lose valuable lives and probably rob bombardments of their effectiveness at critical moments. It was, therefore, decided that the air spotting, as well as searching areas for likely targets for the ships' guns, should be done by fast fighter aircraft, and Spitfires and Mustangs were allocated for these duties. A team of fighter pilots was selected to fly these aircraft. There were 180 pilots, of which 15 were Americans and the remainder partly from the Fleet Air Arm and partly from the Royal Air Force.

In the normal course of events the duties of a fighter pilot are far removed from the tasks the men of this highly skilled team were called upon to carry out. They therefore had to undergo a special course of training. This was done in Scotland and lasted only a fortnight. The pilots had to learn the principles of gunnery and of spotting as well as perfecting their aerial navigation. They also had to learn how to recognise ships and types of army vehicles, distinguishing our own and the Americans' from those of the enemy. They also had to study methods of camouflage adopted by the enemy for various purposes in order to be able to penetrate its disguises, and they had to know a good deal about British and American army organisation so that they could tell by the formation and disposition of troops and vehicles whether they were friend or foe. Map-reading from various heights, too, was an important subject.

After this intensive course, the pilots moved to Lee-on-the-Solent, whence they operated during the invasion.

It had been found by experience that the best height at which to observe a bombardment and to spot the fall of shot is between 4,000 and 6,000 feet, and that, in clear weather, a pilot could observe efficiently from a position as much as five miles from the target. The best method of observing a bombardment is either to circle the target or to fly in a wide "figure of eight" over it. Pilots on spotting or searching duties went into the air with a squared large-scale map of the district and aerial photographs of the target to be bombarded or the area to be searched. They also had binoculars. It can be imagined that the pilot of a fast fighter would have his hands full in more senses than one, and could hardly be expected to keep a sharp look-out for enemy aircraft which might be manoeuvring to attack him. For this reason, every spotting aircraft had a partner called a "weaver." The "weaver" was another fighter, flown by a member of the specially trained team so that he should realise and appreciate what the "spotter" was trying to do, and his duty was to weave to and fro over the tail of the "spotter," keeping a sharp look-out for enemy aircraft and remaining in the best possible position to prevent an enemy from getting on the tail of the "spotter."

"Spotter" and "weaver" were partners who often flew together, taking it in turns to do the two duties, but they were not trained or regarded as partners. To have done so would have impaired efficiency in the event of casualties.

During the planning of the naval gunfire support to be given during "Neptune" it was early realised that the expenditure of ammunition would be so heavy that a special system of supply would have to be set up to ensure that no time was lost in re-ammunitioning ships, and that ships with full magazines and shell rooms were always ready at a moment's notice to take the place off the beach-head of ships which had to leave the assault area to replenish with ammunition. This would have been a comparatively easy task if numbers of ships could have been held in reserve, but such were the naval requirements of "Neptune" that practically every warship allocated to that great operation was urgently and constantly needed "at the front." Here again was a problem in which careful and detailed organisation could save time.

The system of ammunition supply evolved for "Neptune" was to keep at all likely ports lighters loaded with full "outfits" of ammunition for the types of ships likely to use those ports for re-ammunitioning. Thus, when a ship ran short of ammunition the naval commander informed the port that HMS —— was returning for ammunition and would arrive at such and such a time. As HMS —— entered harbour, with hatches open, derricks rigged and whips rove, there was immediately placed alongside her a lighter containing exactly the ammunition she required, in calibre, type and quantity. As HMS —— sailed, having re-ammunitioned, the lighter returned to the ammunition wharf and was replenished in readiness for the next call. As ammunition was loaded from the wharves into the lighters, the former were replenished from "dumps" inland, so that there was in effect a steady flow of shells and charges from inland "dumps" in England on to the German positions in Normandy.

The system and organisation were good, but to have lighters loaded with the ammunition requirements of different types of ship proved to be beyond the capabilities of the lighterage of the Naval Armament Supply Department. Additional lighters had, therefore, to be borrowed from the military.

The scale of naval support gunfire envisaged raised another problem. When the "fire plan" was examined it was clear that ships would wear out their guns during the operation, so arrangements had to be made for worn guns to be replaced without delay. New guns of the smaller and medium calibres were assembled in south coast ports, but replacements for the heavy guns were held in readiness in the north because to move a 15-inch gun weighing a hundred tons across England would have been more difficult than sending battleships and monitors to northern ports to change their guns.

The question of replacement of guns raised the problem of keeping berths under the big cranes free of other ships—and this at a time when berths would be at a premium, in the north as well as in the south.

While naval officers and technicians were grappling with the manifold problems arising out of the naval needs of "Neptune," the Ministry of War Transport was engaged on plans for the participation of the Merchant Navy. It was obvious that a very large number of merchant ships would be required for the invasion. For the manning of these merchant vessels for invasion purposes the Ministry of War Transport launched, in the late autumn of 1943, a volunteer scheme which was aptly named the "V Scheme." This invited officers and men of the Merchant Navy to sign on for invasion duties—which would be likely to subject them to even greater hazards than those to which they were accustomed.

It was characteristic of the unquestioning devotion to duty of the British merchant seaman and of his readiness to accept any risk while doing his job that more than 90 per cent of British merchant seamen who returned to this country after the inauguration of the "V Scheme" unhesitatingly signed the articles prescribed. Nearly all those who did not sign were deterred solely by reasons of age, health or special family responsibilities.

The number of merchant seamen becoming available under the "V Scheme" for duties in connection with the invasion enabled the Ministry of War Transport to work out a system of "reserve pools" of merchant seamen in the vicinity of the operational ports, ready to replace casualties or provide relief crews if necessary.

The part which the Merchant Navy would have to play in carrying out the operational plan for the invasion of North-west Europe was very closely studied in every detail by officials of the Ministry of War Transport, who worked in the closest collaboration at the highest level with the Service Planning Staff, the United States Army Transportation Corps authorities, and officials of the American War Shipping Administration.

The fact that the planning staffs and the outline plan had grown on the foundation of a great deal of exploratory and preparatory work proved of immense value. Among other things, this process of evolution had led to the collection on the staffs of men who were absolute experts in their various tasks.

A good story is told of an incident which arose from this fact. It happened at one of the many hundreds of meetings which had to be held to consider the loading and use of certain ships. As was inevitable, the Service representatives at the meeting asked that a quart should be put into a pint pot. The Ministry of War Transport officials said that it could not be done, but the naval officer present said that he thought the requirements of the military might be very largely met by making some adjustments to the method of loading. Argument developed along these lines, but showed no signs of getting anywhere when the naval officer was more than a little startled by one of the Ministry of Transport officials turning to a Brigadier in khaki and asking:

"Well, as a practical sailor, what do you say, Tom?"

The Brigadier was, in private life, the Marine Superintendent of the line to which the ship under discussion belonged!

A cartoon from the *Daily Mirror*, 2 May 1944.

CHAPTER VI

TO KEEP SHIPS GOING AND THE ENEMY GUESSING

*The repair organisation—The tug organisation—Repair ships
and repair parties—Surveying the French coast—Final planning—
Beach names—Misleading the enemy.*

In the very early days of considering the invasion of Northern France it had been realised that an offensive operation of such a nature would place a very heavy strain on the maintenance and repair resources, particularly those in the south of England.

The strain on the repair resources would not be caused solely by enemy action. It was to be expected that many landing craft would sustain damage by stress of weather, accidents, or faulty handling on and off the beaches. Landing craft are, by their very nature and the use to which they are put, certain to be damaged in considerable numbers during any landing operation. There is a risk which is inherent in running even specially designed vessels ashore in good weather—and the invasion weather could not be guaranteed. In even the slightest surf there is a marked tendency for any vessel, having taken the ground forward, to "broach to"—that is, be swung broadside on to the beach and to the sea. It is obvious that a vessel "broached to" is far more susceptible to damage than one which remains end-on to beach and sea. Not only does a vessel "broached to" offer a far greater area to the sea, by which she will almost certainly be bumped on the beach, but the sides of a vessel are very weak compared to the bows.

Even if landing craft do not "broach to," there is risk of their flat bottoms being damaged on the beach, where, apart from explosions and obstructions placed by the enemy, there may at certain states of the tide be boulders or outcrops of rock. The virtual certainty of damage if a landing craft "touches down" on an outcrop of rock or a boulder is increased by the rapid redistribution of weight in the vessel caused by the disembarkation of heavy vehicles, and even a very small boulder can do considerable damage when the bottom of a vessel "works" over it.

Another source of damage for which allowance had to be made was damage to screws and shafts through fouling wreckage. The nature of their tasks dictates that the screws of landing craft shall not be very deep, and it was to be expected that in a great invasion operation there would be much wreckage in the water off the beaches.

These hazards are normal and inescapable in what may be termed "amphibious navigation," and they are apart altogether from the hazards produced by enemy action or obstructions laid by the enemy, mined or otherwise, for the express purpose of destroying or damaging landing craft.

In order that every possible means of repairing, as well as maintaining, the landing craft and other vessels to be used in the invasion, the Admiralty set up Committees in the Home Commands. In the first instance these were set up at the Nore, Portsmouth and Plymouth, but later similar Committees were set up at the Western Approaches Command and at Rosyth.

The function of these Committees was the Co-ordination of Repairs, and their task became known as COREP from the initial letters of these words. The main committee in each of the Home Commands was composed of the Engineer Rear-Admiral representing the Commander-in-Chief of the Command, and representatives of the Director of Dockyards, the Director of Merchant Ship Repairs, and of other naval maintenance and repair bases.

These committees were known as "Command COREP Committees." At each of the outlying ports within a command there was set up a "COREP Committee" of somewhat similar constitution, the work of each one of which was closely co-ordinated by the "Command COREP Committee."

These Committees were charged with the preparation—and the operation during the invasion—of an organisation which would make the fullest possible use of all available repair and maintenance facilities within their areas. They were responsible that every dock, slipway, repair berth and workshop within their area—whether naval or belonging to a private firm—would be fully and properly used and that there would be no overlapping. The maintenance and repair of the invasion fleet was to take priority over all other work.

All these committees worked in very close co-operation with the Turn Round Control Organisation and with the United States naval authorities.

The initial data at the disposal of the "COREP Committees" concerned, of course, the facilities for repair and maintenance of ships and vessels of all types in their own areas. It was not long, however, before they received other data. The Combined Planning Staff were preparing an estimate of commitments; composition of assault forces; training and assembly; loading ports and schedules of sailings; and also an estimate of loss and damage likely to be sustained over a period of about three months after D-day. Thus the

"COREP Committees" soon had before them lists of the vessels of each type which would be using their areas, and an estimate of the loss and damage to be expected over a considerable period. They could then begin to make fairly detailed plans.

As the details of the repair and maintenance problem began to be filled in it became apparent that some co-ordination of the work of the "Command COREP Committees" was necessary, particularly in order to ensure the most effective and economical distribution of work between the various commands. In order to achieve this a "COREP Control" was set up under the Deputy Controller at the Admiralty, with representatives of every Technical Department and Ministry concerned.

The whole of this complex organisation of "COREP Control," "Command COREP Committees" and "COREP Committees" had scarcely been completed before casualties caused during training exercises and preliminary moves called for its services. The actual invasion followed rapidly upon these training exercises and preliminary moves. Never before had there been repair and maintenance problems of such magnitude, and the whole of the "COREP" Organisation was without precedence, yet it achieved mightily.

It was, of course, appreciated that the work of the "COREP" Organisation would be to some extent dependent upon the recovery of damaged vessels. So far as repairs on the British shore were concerned, this would obviously depend upon the availability and the work of tugs.

The recovery of damaged ships was not, however, the greatest towing commitment of the invasion. It was realised that this would be the transit to the French coast of the many components of the great artificial "Mulberry" harbours, and that if the tug fleet could carry out this feat it would be quite adequate for the work of recovery of damaged ships after the first few days of the invasion. In the first few days, of course, the two towing requirements would overlap, but there was no possible means of avoiding this contingency and it had to be accepted.

From the moment that approval had been given by the Combined Chiefs of Staff during the Quebec Conference for the construction of the great artificial harbours it had been appreciated that the provision of a sufficient number of tugs would be a matter of extreme difficulty.

The "Mulberry" harbours alone consisted of 400 components, amounting to about a million and a half tons. This meant, that if the plan was to be carried out to schedule, there would have to be 35 heavy tows every day from D-day to D plus 18, which was the planned completion date for the artificial harbours. There were also lighter tows, so that nearly 1,000 tows in all would be required. Even so it was appreciated that, in order to economise in tugs, the tows would have to be made as big as the tugs could possibly handle—the pier roadways, for instance, were made up into lengths of 480 feet to be towed across to France.

A census of all the tugs in the United Kingdom showed that there were not enough tugs to carry out the programme, even if tugs which had been built only for harbour work took to the open sea—as a great many did. It had been worked out that at least 160 tugs would be required, but it was soon realised that it would be impossible to provide so many. An emergency tug-building programme was put into effect on both sides of the Atlantic, but even so, there were available by D-day only 132 tugs, varying from large 1,500 horse-power ocean-going tugs to small 600 horse-power vessels usually employed only on harbour or river work. Nevertheless the plans went forward. The number of tows was cut down to the absolute minimum and it had to be accepted that the synthetic harbours, although they would provide shelter and considerable unloading facilities by D plus 18, would not be complete in every detail by that date.

The tug problem was such that a special organisation had to be set up to deal with it. This was called the Tug Control Organisation, with the short title COTUG. It had to deal not only with the provision of the tugs themselves, but with arrangements for their crews. The latter were complicated. Some tugs wore the White Ensign, some wore the Red Ensign, others belonged to various Dock and Harbour Boards and Salvage Companies—and the conditions of service and rates of pay of the crews of the various tugs varied accordingly. COTUG grappled with these manifold problems and brought to the south coast of England just before D-day a tug fleet which was extremely heterogeneous in the character and capability of the vessels and in the experience of their crews, but in which all worked together tirelessly and skilfully to the common aim.

The very varied characteristics and capabilities of the tugs called for much work on the part of COTUG, for the principle of economy of effort had to be rigidly observed in order that the best possible use should be made of every available tug—if possible on its homeward as well as its outward journey. A powerful tug would always have to have a heavy tow and a small tug a light tow, and steps would have to be taken to ensure that all the available tugs of one type did not accumulate, after D-day, on one side of the Channel—no easy matter with the heavy outward towing commitments imposed by the "Mulberry" components, the delivery of which to the French coast would have to be carried out against time.

The tugs which were mustered by COTUG, and which did such great work during the invasion of Normandy were not all British. Some of the biggest and most powerful were Dutch tugs which had for years distinguished themselves on rescue work in the Battle of the Atlantic and had saved a great many ships after they had been damaged by torpedo. There were also American and French tugs.

It was appreciated by the planning staff that the recovery of damaged craft from the far shore would not be solely a matter for tugs. There would almost inevitably be cases of coasters stranded on the beaches and unable to haul themselves off with their kedge anchors. Nor could tugs help efficiently in the case of assault and landing craft which might become "broached to" on the beaches. Yet the recovery of these vessels would be important, not only so that they could be put back into service, but also to clear the beaches. For this reason beach salvage parties were organised and trained. They were provided with tractors to serve as "land tugs" and bulldozers to help in pushing stranded craft back into the water.

The task of recovery and repair on the far shore was likely to be great, and for this reason strong beach repair parties were organised, and HMS *Adventure*, a minelaying cruiser, and HMS *Albatross*, a seaplane carrier, were fitted as special repair ships to work off the beaches.

Both the repair and the tug organisations had, of course, to work in the closest co-operation with the salvage organisation which was specially set up for the invasion. To run this organisation Admiral Sir Bertram Ramsay secured the services of the greatest salvage expert in the United Kingdom. This was Mr T. McKenzie, of Metal Industries, Ltd., who had handled the salvage in Scapa Flow of the scuttled ships of the German High Seas Fleet of the last war. Mr McKenzie joined the staff of the Allied Naval Commander-in-Chief on 15 January 1944, being gazetted a Commodore RNVR. The salvage organisation was also charged with the responsibility for wreck disposal. It was recognised that the wrecks of sunken vessels might obstruct the approaches to the beaches more effectively than enemy action during the critical "follow-up" and initial "build-up" periods, and that this was a danger which might well be exploited by the enemy.

From the beginning Commodore McKenzie's organisation was limited by shortage of heavy salvage gear, and above all by shortage of tugs. The latter caused Admiral Sir Bertram Ramsay no little anxiety. The towing commitments began some time before D-day owing to the need to assemble the components of the "Mulberry" harbours and the blockships for the "Gooseberry" shelter harbours, as well as all manner of dumb lighters and barges. He was aware that a great strain was unavoidably being placed upon the whole tug organisation, and particularly upon the crews of the tugs. At one stage prior to D-day representations were made to him that the available tugs were being greatly overworked. He replied: "Everyone must be prepared to work harder than they have ever had to work before. It cannot be helped. It has just got to be put up with."

One of the greatest technical achievements which was called for during the preparatory period was the waterproofing of many thousands of vehicles of great variety of type. This entailed experiment, manufacture of the special fittings required in order to "waterproof" the vehicles, and trial of the vehicles so fitted.

This waterproofing was no mere matter of making the mechanical and electrical mechanisms of the vehicles "splash-tight." They had to be *really* waterproof, for it was recognised that wave conditions might make it inevitable that vehicles would be almost totally submerged before they drove up the beach. The waterproofing of all these vehicles was not a naval commitment, except in so far as the navy was greatly interested and concerned in the experiments and trials, but it is worth recording the fact that for some months almost the entire tin-plate industry of the United Kingdom was engaged on the manufacture of the special shields and fittings required.

Meanwhile a great deal of surveying work was being done by the Royal Navy off the French coast. It must be remembered that such charts of the French coast as were in our possession were based upon surveys at least four years old. Shoals have a way of shifting, particularly in places where there is a large rise and fall of the tide. "Neptune" was an operation in which inches in the depth of water would be important. Nor was this all. A geological survey was also necessary to determine the nature of the beach and the sea bed below low-water mark. The components of the "Mulberry" and "Gooseberry" harbours had to be sunk in the correct depth of water, and it was also important to know the nature of the bottom in these positions. A "Phoenix" or a blockship would sink gradually down in soft mud, but would remain at a given level if settled on gravel or firm sand. Heavy vehicles, too, might get "bogged down" before reaching high-water mark if the beach was too soft.

To discover all these things surveys of the French coast were undertaken months before D-day. The very design of the "Mulberries" depended to a great extent on the results of the preliminary surveys.

It is no easy matter to survey the beaches and the sea bed close off a coast strongly defended and held by a determined enemy. It is even harder to do so and keep the enemy in ignorance of one's intentions. Surveying is an art which demands concentration and great accuracy if the results are not to be a menace. It is difficult enough by day in peace-time. Yet it was achieved on dark nights close under the guns of enemy shore batteries by some of the coolest heads that have ever worn naval caps.

Most of the work was done by RNVR officers in specially converted LCP's (Landing Craft, Personnel). The personnel space in these little craft was decked in and became a fairly large chart room and they were fitted with accurate compasses and echo-sounding machines. In their new guise they were called LCP (Sy)—the (Sy) indicating that they were specially fitted for surveying.

On every night during the dark periods of the moon when the weather was at all feasible these little craft worked close off Hitler's "Atlantic Wall," while others actually landed parties in dinghies to scoop up samples of the beaches from which the scientists could tell how they would stand up to the beaching of vessels and the passage of heavy traffic. In order to avoid giving the enemy any clue of the places in which we proposed to effect the main landing of the invasion, these surveys were carried out along most of the possible stretches of the French north coast, and one surveying party which was landed in the Pas de Calais area failed to return.

On the whole, however, the Germans paid practically no attention to these surveying activities. The reason for the immunity of the surveyors from enemy interference was the subject of considerable conjecture. It seemed impossible to believe that the German look-outs were so blind or their radar organisation so inefficient that they remained unaware of the presence of the surveying craft close off their coasts. Some would have it that the Germans had orders not to open fire since to do so would reveal the position of their batteries and strong points; others that the Germans were years behind us in the use of radar and employed it only for the control and ranging of their gunnery and not as a warning system.

Whatever the reason we may be thankful that our surveyors did not suffer heavy casualties.

The planning staffs had in the meantime pressed on with the planning of the details of the operation and with the preparation of the Operation Orders. As has been said, these Operation Orders for "Neptune" comprised a printed book of foolscap size nearly three inches thick. They were the most detailed operation orders ever issued. They left nothing to chance and covered every possible contingency. In the "build-up" section detailed orders were laid down for the sailing of the first 47 convoys after the initial assault. These 47 convoys were to sail to France by D plus 3, after which the three-day convoy sailing schedule would be repeated over and over again. In the operation orders there were included what were called "Mickey Mouse Diagrams." These were charts on which the positions of every convoy and every minesweeping, covering or bombarding force were plotted at a given time. There was one such "Mickey Mouse Diagram" for every hour during the approach phase, and by turning them over quickly one got the effect of a motion picture showing the movement of all the hundreds of groups of ships taking part.

The operation orders also detailed the actual beaches to be used in the Bay of the Seine area. There were to be five such beaches and assault areas off the beaches, and they were all given code names for rapid identification purposes.

To the west of the little harbour of Port en Bessin there were two beaches over which the United States troops were to land. These were called OMAHA and UTAH beaches. East of Port en Bessin there were three beaches, which were to be used by the British and Canadian troops. These from west to east, were called GOLD, JUNO and SWORD.

Thus there were five main beaches to be used in the initial assault. Each beach was to be assaulted by a division of troops, thus fulfilling General

Montgomery's requirement of assault on a five-divisional front. Each division of troops to be landed in the initial assault was to be transported across the Channel and landed by a separate naval assault force, which was known by the initial letter of the beach to be used. Thus "Force G" was charged with the landing on GOLD beach and "Force S" with that on SWORD. In addition to the five assault forces there were two "follow-up" forces, each carrying one division of troops for the immediate follow-up of the assault. The British "follow-up" force was called "Force L" and the American "follow-up" force was called "Force B."

The chain of naval command therefore became:

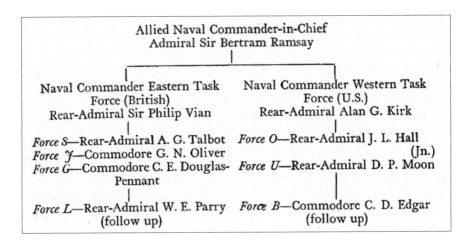

Allied Naval Commander-in-Chief
Admiral Sir Bertram Ramsay

Naval Commander Eastern Task Force (British) Rear-Admiral Sir Philip Vian	Naval Commander Western Task Force (U.S.) Rear-Admiral Alan G. Kirk
Force S—Rear-Admiral A. G. Talbot *Force J*—Commodore G. N. Oliver *Force G*—Commodore C. E. Douglas-Pennant	*Force O*—Rear-Admiral J. L. Hall (Jn.) *Force U*—Rear-Admiral D. P. Moon
Force L—Rear-Admiral W. E. Parry (follow up)	*Force B*—Commodore C. D. Edgar (follow up)

The operation orders for "Neptune" were ready for issue on 24 April 1944. That is not to say that they were by any means final. Again and again they had to be corrected or amended as new problems arose and their solutions were formed. This went on until shortly before D-day, when the operation orders were "frozen" by signal from the Allied Naval Commander-in-Chief. This step was necessary in order to ensure that no amendment would be issued so late as to be received by some of the forces taking part and not by others which might have already put to sea.

In so vast an undertaking as the preparation for the invasion of Normandy it was inevitable that a great many people should be "in the know," and that the number of these should increase rapidly as the plans and preparations advanced. Naturally, all possible steps were taken to ensure that nobody knew more than was essential to his job, but there is often much truth in Benjamin Franklin's dictum that "three may keep a secret if two of them are dead."

Secrecy—or "security," to use the Service term—was vital to the success of the invasion, and the fact that the place, time and strength of the invasion were kept so secret that tactical surprise was achieved in the assault must be considered a great triumph for the Security Executive, the Inter-Services Security Board, and all who served under them.

Men have for long cherished a belief that women can never keep a secret, yet many thousands of "Wrens" were engaged in the work of preparation for "Neptune," and they proved themselves at least as "secure" as naval officers of considerable experience and training. The naval commander of one of the assault forces wrote in his report: "Nor must the work of the WRNS officers and ratings be forgotten. In spite of working very long hours, they remained keen and cheerful, and I knew of no instance of even the smallest lapse of security in spite of the fact that the majority of them had access to all TOP SECRET papers from the beginning." It must be remembered that most of the cypher staffs dealing with 'most secret' signals, as well as the typists, teleprinter operators, and others were "Wrens."

The requirements of security for operation "Neptune" raised all manner of problems, many of which had never before been contemplated, and some of which demanded action which is normally repugnant to free and democratic peoples. There was, for instance, the necessity to "seal" ships and even camps and shore establishments so that there should be no communication between their inmates and the outer world. There was the need to empound all mails belonging to any of the forces to be engaged—a step which had to be taken about ten days before D-day. There was also the problem of the sick and the wounded. If a man from a "sealed" ship, who had been "briefed" and therefore knew the all-important secrets of when and where the invasion was to take place, was sent to hospital through sickness or injury; was the hospital, or the ward to be regarded as "sealed"? If a man was on the danger list, was access to his bedside to be denied to his relatives? Here was a direct conflict between the unfeeling ideals of security and the principles of common humanity. The Admiralty abided by the latter and directed that relatives should not be denied access to men seriously ill or injured, but the most elaborate precautions were taken to guard against any leakage of secret information.

At the same time it was desirable to mislead the enemy whenever possible regarding our intentions. In this various factors came into play. There was, for instance, the temporary sinking of the "Mulberry" harbour sections off Dungeness, opposite Boulogne; and the great concentration of British bombing in the Pas de Calais area prior to D-day.

Another important factor was the great, and quite fortuitous, concentration of shipping in the northern and north-eastern parts of Great Britain prior to D-day. This was inevitable, because all the southern ports from Harwich round the south coast to Milford Haven were so full of "invasion" shipping that all the ordinary shipping was forced to use the more northerly ports and caused an unusual accumulation of shipping in those ports. This concentration of shipping was known to the enemy, and added considerably to the German High Command's anxiety about a possible invasion of Norway. This was an anxiety which the Germans had felt for some time. It was still further increased by actions taken by the Allies shortly before D-day.

One of these was part of our pre-D-day mining campaign, which included an intensification of our mining of the Southern Baltic, the mining of the Sound, between Denmark and Sweden, and of the Kiel Canal. All these were, in fact, carried out for the greater protection of our projected invasion of Normandy, but they appeared to the German High Command to be an attempt to sever the German sea communications with Norway. We now know that the mining of the Kiel Canal was highly successful and forced the German High Command to take emergency measures for the regrouping of their slender shipping resources. At the same time there was considerable British minelaying activity on both sides of the Pas de Calais area, which might well have indicated that the Calais-Boulogne area was our objective.

Another Allied action which seemed to the German High Command to indicate that we were contemplating a descent upon Norway was the series of concentrated air attacks on U-boats off the Norwegian coast shortly before D-day. These attacks, which were highly successful, were in fact designed to prevent as far as possible, the U-boat squadrons in Brest and the Biscay ports being reinforced from Norway just before D-day, but they certainly helped to focus German attention on Norway.

All these factors helped to make the German High Command "take its eye off the ball" at the critical moment. The enemy was expecting feints before the invasion proper was launched, but the indications which reached him pointed either to Norway or the Pas de Calais area as the probable scenes of the main efforts of the Allies. Although he was very nervous about Norway, he believed it more likely, on the whole, that we would launch the main attack in the Pas de Calais area. This was partly due to the fact that he over-estimated our desire to assault the area from which the flying bombs were launched against London and southern England.

There were moments of anxiety regarding the security of the actual invasion plans, but the event was to show that this had been very good indeed, while the German High Command was "kept guessing" even after D-day and was reluctant to move reinforcements to Normandy during the first few days of the invasion.

CHAPTER VII

DECISION AND ANXIETY

*Assembly of the forces—Obstacles dictate daylight assault—Final exercises—
Preliminary actions—The British mining campaign—The minesweeping
problem caused by the change of tide—Anxiety about the weather.*

On 26 April 1944, the Allied Naval Commander-in-Chief and his staff
moved from London to his battle headquarters. This was at Southwick Park,
outside Portsmouth. It was a house which had already been taken over by
the Admiralty to house the Navigation School—known as HMS *Dryad*—
when that establishment had been forced to move out of its old quarters in
Portsmouth Dockyard owing to the blitz.

On the same day the assault forces assembled at their ports of departure as
follows:

Force S at Portsmouth.
Force G at Southampton.
Force J in the Isle of Wight area.
Force O at Portsmouth.
Force U at Plymouth.
Follow up Force L at the Nore.
Follow up Force B at Milford Haven.

The stage was set for "Operation Neptune." Yet, astonishing as it may seem,
neither D-day nor H-hour had then been definitely decided. It had not even
been finally decided whether the initial assault should take place in daylight
or during the dark hours or at what state of the tide the first wave should
"touch down" on the Normandy beaches. The two decisions were, of course,
interdependent.

During the initial stages of the planning of the invasion of Normandy
Admiral Sir Bertram Ramsay had been in favour of the initial landing taking

place in darkness, shortly before dawn. This preference he had formed as a result of experience in the highly successful invasion of Sicily, which he had planned and during which he had commanded the British Task Force.

As the planning progressed, however, Admiral Ramsay changed his view, for he realised that the advantages of an assault in darkness would, in the case of the invasion of Normandy, be outweighed by our unquestionable naval and air superiority, with ships and aircraft working from great bases in close proximity to the assault area. There was also another consideration: the vast number of ships and craft of all types to be deployed made it advisable that the assault should take place in daylight.

Having formed this considered opinion, the Naval Commander-in-Chief never wavered from his view that the initial assault should take place by daylight, but as early as possible in the day in order to give the maximum opportunity to our air forces and our naval bombardment forces. The military authorities, however, urged more than once that the plan should be altered to provide for the initial assault taking place in darkness. Moreover, the army wished to be landed dryshod at high water, which would, of course, have meant the stranding of many craft for six hours or more.

At the end of April, however, reconnaissances reported that the Germans were very largely increasing the number and effectiveness of the obstacles which they placed on the beaches between high and low water. An enormous number of aerial photographs of these obstacles were taken, many of them by aircraft which skimmed only a few feet over the water and the beaches in order to obtain photographs taken as nearly as possible horizontally. Reconnaissance parties were even landed on the beaches of France—chiefly in the Pas de Calais area—in order to make detailed examination of these obstacles.

It was at once obvious that these beach obstacles between high and low water marks were extremely formidable. They were of four main types. There were concrete pyramids to which were attached old French shells fused to act as contact mines; there were heavy timber ramps ten feet long specially designed to trap landing craft and fitted with Teller mines; there were thick stakes made of the trunks of young fir trees, eight or ten feet high and fitted with mines or fused shells; and there were "knife rests" made of railway line or angle girders, some of which were fitted with fused shells.

The appearance of these formidable obstacles quickly settled the problem of at what state of the tide the initial landing should take place and whether it should be in darkness or daylight. To attempt a landing at anything but low water would be to invite most serious loss among the landing craft and the troops and vehicles embarked in them, and would probably lead to the approaches to the beach becoming so encumbered with wrecks as seriously to impede succeeding waves of the assault. Moreover, daylight would be essential if the obstacles were to be avoided and removed.

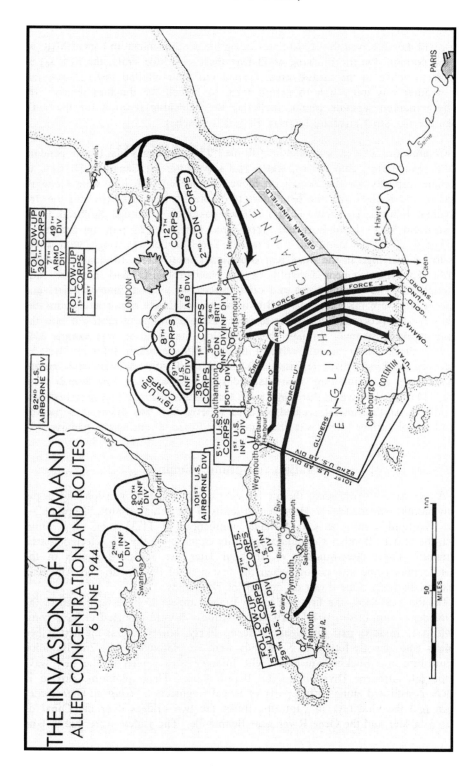

THE INVASION OF NORMANDY
ALLIED CONCENTRATION AND ROUTES
6 JUNE 1944

An aerial reconnaissance photograph showing obstacles on one of the beaches.

It was therefore essential that the initial landing should take place at or near low water and in daylight. This decision was taken at a meeting between General Eisenhower and Admiral Sir Bertram Ramsay on 1 May 1944. The decision, of course, narrowed down the choice of D-day and of H-hour, for there are not many days in the month when low water at any particular place occurs soon after daylight.

The appearance of these German beach obstacles led to other developments. The problem of finding the best way of dealing with them, and of training men in this work in the very short time available had to be faced and solved.

To this end similar obstructions were constructed and placed on a beach in the United Kingdom where the rise and fall of the tide was about the same as that in the Bay of the Seine; experiments were carried out, and men specially trained in the removal of these obstacles while working in water. These men were given the title of LCOCU's, which stands for "Landing Craft Obstacle Clearance Units." They have since become popularly known as "Frog Men."

In the weeks before D-day the enemy was very active in other ways, which is hardly to be wondered at since he was very nervous and his nervousness was being purposely increased by the Allies.

As early as March it had been noted that there had been a considerable increase in the enemy's mining activity, particularly by E-boats in the Channel. In April there had been a great deal of patrolling by E-boats, while the German destroyers normally based on Brest had also shown unusual activity. It was the E-boats which were to inflict the first losses on the Allied invasion

Coast Guard-manned LCI(L)-85 during a practice landing at Slapton Sands. The "85" would be pummelled by enemy fire during the invasion and sank in the English Channel on D-Day. It was at Slapton Sands that the enemy E-boats delivered there devastating attack during 'Exercise Tiger'.

forces. This was during one of the final exercises. On the night of 28 April, E-boats attacked a convoy of LST's (Landing Ship, Tanks) taking part in a rehearsal. Two American LST's were sunk and a third damaged. The loss of life was tragically high, over 600 men being killed, while nearly a hundred were wounded. It was ironical that the E-boats should have scored a bigger success against the Allied invasion forces during a rehearsal than they were ever to do during the invasion itself, but it is interesting to note that the E-boats were in complete ignorance of the fact that they had attacked a portion of the Allied invasion forces. This was shown by the fact that the Germans promptly broadcast the quite ordinary and usual claim that they had sunk three ships in convoy.

On the very next night the German destroyers put in an appearance and were in action with the Canadian destroyers *Haida* and *Athabaskan*. In this action HMCS *Athabaskan* was unfortunately torpedoed and sunk, but one of the German "Elbing" class destroyers was driven ashore in flames and became a total loss.

The Allied minelaying campaign designed for the general protection of our shipping in the Channel during the invasion, and more particularly for the protection of our assault and bombarding forces, was meanwhile being carried out. It had begun on 17 April, and by D-day nearly 7,000 mines had been laid in this campaign. They included many mines of a new type specially designed for use against small fast vessels such as E-boats. Forty-two per cent of the mines laid in this campaign were laid by the Royal Navy in no less than 66 operations, while fifty-eight per cent were laid by aircraft on 1,800 sorties. The scope of this minelaying campaign stretched from the Baltic to the Bay of Biscay.

The decision to deliver the initial assault as soon as possible after low water and as early as possible in daylight hours had a profound effect upon the minesweeping plan. The choice of D-day and H-hour meant that the sweeping of the ten channels to Normandy from the "Piccadilly Circus" of swept water south of the Isle of Wight would have to be begun with the tidal stream setting strongly to the eastward, while the tidal stream would have changed in direction to a strong west-going current before the sweeping of the approach channels could be completed. This problem of carrying out a minesweeping operation across the tide with a complete change of the tidal stream in the middle of the sweep had never before been mastered, for in nearly all minesweeping operations the time and state of the tide can be chosen to suit the minesweepers.

In "Neptune" the time factor was also a problem to the minesweepers. The minimum efficient sweeping speed of the minesweepers was 7½ knots. At slower speeds the sweeps would not ride out from the minesweepers and would not have enough power to cut the moorings of the mines. On the other hand, the maximum speed of many of the landing craft which were to lead the assault was little more than 5 knots. Thus, even if the first groups of landing craft left "Piccadilly Circus" immediately astern of the minesweepers, the latter would reach the French coast an hour and a half before the assault craft. For the minesweepers to wait about close off the French coast for an hour and a half in the growing light would obviously lead to heavy casualties and a complete; absence of surprise. It followed, therefore, that means had to be devised whereby the minesweepers could waste an hour and a half while still a reasonable distance from the French coast and before daylight. Minesweepers, however, cannot just stop and waste time in the middle of a sweep.

The problems of wasting time and of dealing with the change of direction of the tidal stream were solved together by the introduction of an intricate manoeuvre which had never before been attempted. In order to describe this manoeuvre it is necessary to give a brief outline of some of the principles of minesweeping which were involved.

The type of sweep which is almost universally used today is that known as the "Oropesa Sweep," because by its use only one vessel of a flotilla is in danger when sweeping through a minefield.

The Oropesa Sweep is a single sweep wire, serrated to saw through mine moorings, which runs out from one quarter of the minesweeper. At the outer end of the sweep wire is an "otter," which is a structure of inclined planes which carries the end of the sweep wire far out from the wake of the minesweeper when it is towed through the water. On the surface above the "otter" is the "Oropesa float" which marks the end of the sweep wire and thus the edge of the water swept by that particular minesweeper.

Minesweepers usually sweep in flotillas of six ships, with two spare minesweepers and danbuoy-laying vessels to mark the edges of the swept water. Each minesweeper keeps just within the edge of the swept water, which is traced by the Oropesa float of her next ahead. Thus only the leading minesweeper is in unswept and dangerous water. In practice the leading minesweeper is given a good measure of protection by being preceded by two shallow-draught motor launches, each with small Oropesa sweeps and sweeping a narrow lane for the leading minesweeper. The danbuoy-layers do not mark the actual edges of the swept water, but follow the second and the last minesweeper, so that there is a factor of safety on each side of the channel equal to the width of the swathe swept by one minesweeper. This factor of safety is necessary to allow for the sway of the danbuoys at the ends of their moorings in obedience to tide and wind. The spare minesweepers follow in the swept water with their sweeps "at short stay," ready to take the place of any minesweeper whose sweep may be cut by an exploding mine or anti-sweeping device.

The attached diagram shows the formation of a minesweeping flotilla while sweeping a channel.

Every ship at sea is affected by tidal streams and currents, and if a ship is to "make good" a certain course when steaming across a tidal stream she must make due allowance for it and "steam into it" to an extent dependent upon the relative speeds of ship and current.

No type of ship is as greatly affected by tidal streams as the minesweeper when sweeping, for the sweep as well as the ship is influenced by the movement of the element in which they are working, while for them accuracy in the course "made good"—not only by the minesweeper but also by the sweep—means the safety of the ships which are to use the channel. With an "Oropesa Sweep" the minesweeper can steer into the current or tidal stream and so make due allowance for it, but the "Otter" and "Oropesa float" at the other end of the sweep wire cannot, and so the outer end of the sweep will be carried "down stream." If the minesweeper is "up stream" of her sweep this is all to the good, for it will widen the swathe swept by the sweep; but if the minesweeper is "down stream" of her sweep the sweep will be carried in towards her wake and the strip of water swept will diminish—to vanishing point in the case of a strong cross-tide.

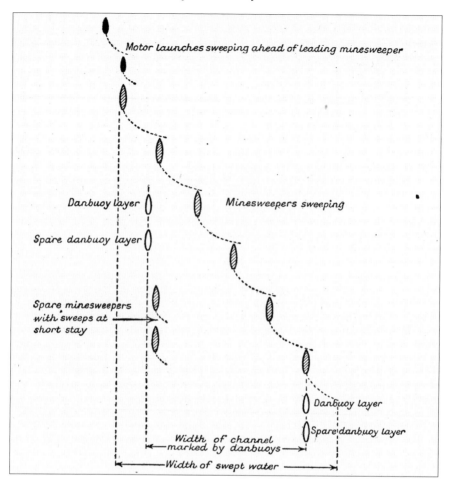

Motor launches sweeping ahead of leading minesweeper

Danbuoy layer

Minesweepers sweeping

Spare danbuoy layer

Spare minesweepers with sweeps at short stay

Danbuoy layer

Spare danbuoy layer

Width of channel marked by danbuoys

Width of swept water

It follows therefore that, when sweeping across a tidal stream of any appreciable strength, the minesweeper must be "up stream" of her sweep. In other words, when sweeping across a tidal stream running from port to starboard the sweep must be out on the starboard side of the minesweeper, and *vice versa*.

It has been said that the date and time of D-day and H-hour made it necessary for the sweeps from "Piccadilly Circus" to the assault area off the Normandy coast to begin when there was a strong east-going tidal stream and finish when there was a strong west-going stream. This meant that the minesweepers had to begin their tasks with their sweeps out on the port side and finish their tasks with their sweeps out on the starboard side.

This problem was not a simple one of getting in the port sweep and getting out the starboard sweep. It entailed changing the formation of each minesweeping flotilla from port quarter-line to starboard quarter-line.

Moreover, the whole operation had to be performed in such a way as to ensure that no minesweeper should enter unswept water and, above all, that no "holidays" of unswept water were left in the channels.

The working out of a manoeuvre which would meet all these requirements was indeed a puzzle, but it was solved in a most ingenious way, and in a manner which also provided the minesweepers with an opportunity of wasting time without risking the presence of unswept mines in the channels.

The solution was as follows. When the time came to reverse the sweeps the ships got in their port sweeps in succession, beginning with the last sweeper of the flotilla. As each sweeper got in its sweep it formed astern of the leader. The flotilla therefore reached a formation in which the ships were steaming in single line ahead, all protected by the sweep-wire of the flotilla leader, who was in turn protected by the two mine-sweeping motor launches ahead of her. There was now, of course, no "swept channel" in the accepted sense of the term—only the narrow lane swept by the flotilla leader. The end of the swept channel proper was marked by the last danbuoys laid just before the rear minesweeper hove in her port sweep.

Having reached this formation of single line ahead the minesweepers turned 180 degrees in succession, the rear ship being the first to turn. When it was the flotilla leader's turn to put her helm over she hove in her sweep. Thus the whole flotilla was steaming in single line ahead, the rear ship leading, back along the narrow lane of water previously swept by the leader, and so back into the swept channel proper.

Once back in the swept channel the minesweepers could steam back to the northward until they had wasted the necessary amount of time. Then they turned again on to a southerly course, streamed their sweeps on the starboard side, took up their sweeping formation, and continued to sweep the channel on from the last danbuoys placed before the manoeuvre was begun.

It was a complicated manoeuvre, and time was desperately short for practising it before it had to be carried out on the way to the invasion, with the lives of thousands of men dependent upon the accuracy of the minesweeping and the success of this unprecedented manoeuvre. That it was done, and done successfully, in darkness under "action" conditions, speaks volumes for the skill, seamanship and coolness of the men who commanded and manned the minesweepers.

On 3 and 4 May 1944 there took place the final rehearsal exercise for "Neptune." This was called "Operation Fabius," and it went off successfully without any interference from the enemy.

By that time the meteorological organisation was already hard at work. Stations as distantly separated as Spitzbergen, Iceland, Greenland, the Atlantic coast of North America, the Azores, and West Africa were sending in weather reports and data, and these were supplemented by reports and data provided by specially equipped weather-reporting ships stationed far out in the Atlantic Ocean. Time was when the Royal Navy had hunted down German weather reporting ships sent out to provide data for the forecasts which the *Luftwaffe* used in planning its big raids. Now we sent out weather reporting ships and there were no German surface ships and few U-boats to distract their attention from their instruments.

With all the data from these widely separated reporting stations the meteorological experts attached to the staff of the Allied Naval Commander-in-Chief were keeping a constant watch on the weather trends.

It was on 8 May that it was decided at a meeting between General Eisenhower, Admiral Ramsay, General Montgomery, Air-Marshal Leigh-Mallory and others that D-day was to be 5 June, with 6 June as a "spare day." It was laid down that 7 June could be used if this was absolutely essential, but there would be disadvantages of tide on that day which made it possible only as a last resort. If the invasion had to be postponed beyond 7 June it could not take place for another fortnight.

It was on 23 May that General Eisenhower, the Supreme Allied Commander, signalled to the naval, military and air commanders that D-day was to be 5 June. Everything was ready for the greatest inter-Allied undertaking in the history of warfare.

In the days before D-day the forces assembled to take part in "Operation Overlord" were visited by many distinguished persons. At the final "briefing" by the Commanders-in-Chief at No. 21 Army Group Headquarters on 15 May, His Majesty the King, Mr Winston Churchill and General Smuts were present, and all three of them addressed the senior officers gathered for that momentous meeting. On the previous day the British and Australian Prime Ministers had visited Admiral Sir Bertram Ramsay's battle headquarters.

On 21 May Mr A. V. Alexander, the First Lord of the Admiralty, visited the headquarters of the Allied Naval Commander-in-Chief at Southwick Park, near Portsmouth.

On 24 May His Majesty the King visited Rear-Admiral Sir Philip Vian's Eastern Task Force, and on the following day he visited the Western Task Force, which was the United States' naval component under the command of Rear-Admiral Alan G. Kirk.

On 28 May H-hour was fixed and signalled. It is, in fact, erroneous to speak of H-hour as if it was a touch-down time for the assault on all five beaches. Conditions of tide made it necessary to name five different H-hours—one for each beach to be assaulted, but these times were as close together as possible and were all between a few minutes before 6 a.m. and a few minutes after 7 a.m.

In those days before D-day the weather was the factor uppermost in the minds of all the high commanders, and it caused them no little anxiety. In

An artillery unit bound for Normandy loads equipment into landing vessels in Brixham on the southwest coast of England, 1 June 1944.

May there had been a long spell of quiet fine weather which had extended into the first days of June. By 2 June, however, the meteorological experts had begun to shake their heads and frown over the weather charts which they compiled from the reports of distant stations. There was no doubt that the prolonged fine weather system was beginning to break up. Would it give place to another fine weather system or would it yield to a period of uncertain and stormy weather? That was the vital question, upon the answer to which hung the fate of millions and maybe of nations. A long postponement of D-day would have consequences too appalling to contemplate. It would almost certainly jeopardise all security and make the task of invasion infinitely more difficult when it could be launched. It would have a most adverse effect upon the morale, not only of all the men who were anxiously awaiting the signal to

US Coast Guard Flotilla 10 tied up along with British landing craft somewhere in the south of England.

sail, but upon that of the forces of freedom all over the world. It would reduce the period available before the storms and rains of autumn set in and would therefore almost certainly greatly retard the march of the grand strategy of the United Nations.

Upon no man did the anxiety rest more heavily than upon Admiral Sir Bertram Ramsay, the Allied Naval Commander-in-Chief. His was the responsibility for taking the assaulting troops across the English Channel, thousands of them in small craft unsuited even to moderate weather, and for ensuring the delivery to our assault forces, once established on the far shore, a sufficient and rapid flow of reinforcements and supplies to enable them to defeat a determined and well-equipped enemy fighting in positions long prepared. There could be no "Overlord" without "Neptune."

Part Two

EXECUTION

CHAPTER I

TWENTY-FOUR HOURS' POSTPONEMENT

*Forecasts of deteriorating weather—The operations room at Battle
Headquarters—Historic meetings—The decision to postpone D-day—
The effect on ships at sea—The decision to invade on 6 June.*

As the chosen day for the invasion drew nearer the weather became more
uncertain, and any study of the weather charts during those anxious days
could not fail to cause grave concern. It became more and more certain that
the prolonged fine weather period of May was giving place to a system of
westerly weather, with all its uncertainties and threats of strong westerly
winds.

On 4 June the weather was bad and the forecast even worse. The wind in
the English Channel was blowing from west-southwest, force 5 to 6—which
is the Beaufort Scale numeral for a wind of 16-26 knots. The waves in the
Channel were 3-5 feet in height—nothing to a battleship or liner but a lot
to small assault craft crowded with troops. The sky was almost completely
overcast and the forecast stated that the cloud conditions would deteriorate
still further and that there was little prospect of them improving before late on
Wednesday, June, which was the last possible day of the period in which the
invasion could be launched and one which had many important disadvantages.
The forecast also stated that the wind would veer to the west-north-west and
decrease slightly in strength by late on the Wednesday—but late on Wednesday
would be too late to launch the invasion, even on the undesirable day.

It was hardly surprising that, at 2 o'clock on the morning of 4 June, the
Admiralty regarded the situation with considerable gloom, particularly since
they expected further deterioration in the weather before any improvement set
in. This view was confirmed when, at 11 o'clock on the morning of 4 June, the
Admiralty issued a gale warning affecting all the waters off the south coasts of
the British Isles.

During the night of 4 June 1944, the operations room at the battle headquarters of the Allied Naval Commander-in-Chief presented an historic scene. In the long, high room at Southwick Park there were about forty people. Most of them were naval officers or Wrens plotting positions on charts and dealing with the stream of signals which were carried in on the endless belt which came through a hole in the wall from the cypher office. There were also air liaison officers, military liaison officers, and American naval officers.

One end of the room, the walls of which were papered in white and gold, was covered by an enormous blackboard chart of the English Channel. Up and down in front of this moved a travelling step-ladder, used by the Wrens for plotting on the map the hour to hour positions of all units at sea. There were already plenty of these, for convoys had already sailed from the east and west coasts of Britain towards "Piccadilly Circus," while some of the blockships for the "Gooseberry" harbours and the first tows of the "Mulberry" harbours' were already at sea. Several minesweeping flotillas were also at sea, ensuring the safe passage of the convoys. In "Neptune" as in so many other operations, the work of the minesweepers began first and did not end until after the enemy had been decisively defeated.

In front of the big blackboard wall map, and to one side, sat the signal officer. Level with him, but near the centre of the room, sat Rear-Admiral George Creasy, Admiral Ramsay's Chief of Staff.

These two desks marked a line across the room about four yards from the wall map. That space was the "holy of holies," reserved for the Commander-in-Chief, his immediate staff and those who operated the wall map. There Admiral Sir Bertram Ramsay spent many long hours, his quick mind tirelessly and calmly taking in the Full import of every signal and every report and weighing its effect upon the problem to which he was applying all the lessons of his long experience and his tremendous singleness of purpose and moral courage.

On the afternoon of 4 June Admiral Sir Bertram Ramsay was visited at his battle headquarters by Admiral of the Fleet Sir Andrew Cunningham, the First Sea Lard and Admiral Ramsay's old friend. Sir Andrew Cunningham had, of course, been in the closest touch with Southwick Park throughout, and his visit on that Sunday afternoon was most heartening during a very anxious time.

To Southwick Park in the early hours of that Sunday morning came General Dwight Eisenhower, the Supreme Allied Commander. To discuss the problem of the weather and to make a decision which is historic. The decision was nothing less than whether or not to postpone D-day.

There had been previous meetings at Southwick to consider the situation created by the deteriorating weather conditions. The first of these had taken place on the morning of 1 June. There had been a similar meeting on the

Loading at a port somewhere in the south of England.

afternoon of 3 June, at which the Supreme Commander had decided to give the order for the first assault convoys to sail, for most of these had to put to sea that night if D-day was to be 5 June. These meetings were held in the library at Southwick Park.

At that fateful meeting at 4.15 on the morning of 4 June General Eisenhower presided as usual. He had with him his Chief of Staff, General Bedell Smith of the United States Army. All three of the Commanders-in-Chief were there, accompanied by their Chiefs of Staff. Thus there were present Admiral Sir Bertram Ramsay with his Chief of Staff, Rear-Admiral Creasy; Air Chief Marshal Sir Trafford Leigh-Mallory and his Chief of Staff, Air Vice-Marshal Wigglesworth; and General Sir Bernard Montgomery with his Chief of Staff, Major-General de Guingand.

Into the library came the meteorological experts—a Group Captain of the Royal Air Force, a Colonel of the American Army, and a British naval Instructor-Commander.

This "meteorological team" reported on the weather conditions and forecasts. They were pessimistic, but there was some hope of improvement on the following day. The experts then withdrew, and the Supreme Commander asked for the views of his Commanders-in-Chief. Then he made the fateful decision. D-day was to be postponed by twenty-four hours.

The decision to postpone D-day meant that all convoys at sea had to reverse their courses, otherwise there would be overcrowding and confusion at "Piccadilly Circus," and the convoys would be unnecessarily exposed to enemy observation and attack. The units at sea could not acknowledge receipt of the postponement signal, for they were keeping wireless "silence," yet it was essential to know that all units at sea had received the signal and turned back. And all the time there was that growing anxiety about the weather.

Boarding the ship in early June 1944. In the foreground two sailors from the Navy have customized their jacket. LCT "Channel Fever" transporting personnel and vehicles of the 1st Infantry Division US and the 741st Tank Battalion and 5th ESB.

Let it suffice to give two instances of the anxiety caused by the postponement of D-day when certain naval units, convoys and tows were already at sea.

The 14th Minesweeping Flotilla, commanded by Commander J. W. A. Irvine, RNR in HMS *Romney*, had been sweeping ahead of a convoy approaching "Piccadilly Circus" from the westward. Early in the morning of 4 June this flotilla found mines in a position roughly 30 miles south-south-west of The Needles, and at once began to clear this minefield despite the bad weather, which looked as if it would get worse.

Commander Irvine's flotilla had made a good start on clearing this minefield when the postponement signal was received. It could not be acknowledged owing to the necessity for maintaining wireless silence, and the presence and position of the mines could not be reported for the same reason. On the other hand, the mines were dangerous, for they were in one of the convoy channels leading to "Piccadilly Circus."

In the circumstances, Commander Irvine decided to complete the clearance of the minefield before putting back to port—a decision which was undoubtedly correct but which very nearly led to tragedy. The destroyers HMS *Campbell* and HMS *Hind*, which were in the vicinity, saw the 14th Minesweeping Flotilla apparently ignoring the postponement signal and thought that they had not received the signal. They therefore closed the minesweepers in order to pass the signal to them by semaphore. In closing the minesweepers the destroyers steamed into unswept water where the minefield had been discovered, and in a few minutes HMS *Campbell* was surrounded by floating mines, the moorings of which had been cut by the minesweepers. In the strong wind and fairly heavy sea the ship might easily have been carried down on to some of these mines. As it was, there was nothing for it but to stop engines and hope for the best. The best was accomplished by the minesweepers, which successfully extricated the *Campbell* from her very dangerous position. A PT boat—a fast American motor craft equivalent to the British motor torpedo boat—was then sent into harbour to report the mines and that the 14th Flotilla had swept most of them but was being forced to abandon the sweep owing to the weather.

When this message reached Admiral Sir Bertram Ramsay he had to decide whether the minefield discovered by the 14th Minesweeping Flotilla was likely to be extensive. If it was, it would mean re-routeing the convoys coming from the westward through water which had not been searched for mines.

The Allied Naval Commander-in-Chief decided in the light of all the evidence, that this was not a new German minefield purposely laid in that position, but a group of mines probably jettisoned by an E-boat which had been alarmed by one of our patrols. It was subsequently proved that this appreciation was perfectly correct, although one of the unswept mines in this field was to claim the first casualty of "Operation Neptune."

The other instance concerns the old French battleship *Courbet*, which had been earmarked as one of the blockships for a "Gooseberry" harbour.

The *Courbet* had no engines or boilers and therefore had to be towed to Normandy. Filled with concrete, she was cumbersome and could only be towed very slowly, so she had started early. She was south of The Needles and her tug was making rather heavy weather of it when the postponement signal was received. By dint of great efforts and magnificent seamanship the tug succeeded in turning the *Courbet* and towing her into the lee of Durlston Head. There, off Bournemouth, the old French battleship was safely brought to anchor. That was by no means the end of the anxiety about this ship, however, for she had no power to weigh her 7-ton anchor, so that she could only anchor once and would have to slip her cable when it was necessary for her to put to sea again. If she dragged her anchor or parted her cable in the bad weather it was doubtful if the tug would be able to save her.

Fortunately she did not drag her anchor or part her cable, and she was only required to anchor on that one occasion. She reached the Normandy coast

Frigate HMS *Dacres* Group HQ Ship for Assault Force S2, 'Sword Beach', lies at Portsmouth, outboard of the destroyer HMS *Onlsow*, 25 May 1944. HMS *Dacres* was laid down as USS *Duffy* (DE-268) on 7 April 1943 by the Boston Navy Yard and launched on 19 May 1943. Transferred to the Royal Navy and commissioned as *Dacres* on 28 August 1943. She was one of three Captain class ships (along with *Kingsmill* and *Lawford*) selected for conversion to headquarters ships for use during Operation Neptune. Her aft three-inch (76 mm) gun and all the depth charge gear was removed and the superstructure extended to provide accommodation for extra Staff Officers; two deck houses were built for communications equipment and a small main mast added to support more aerials. Four more 20 mm Oerlikons were fitted, and a number of radar sets installed.

safely and played a notable part in her last role as a "Gooseberry" blockship.'

On the afternoon of 4 June the meteorological experts at Admiral Ramsay's headquarters felt themselves able to give a forecast of the weather for 5 and 6 June.

This was that the wind would be from the west-north-west on 5 June and blowing with a strength of 5 on the Beaufort Scale—that is 12 to 16 knots—but would back slowly to the west and south-west and decrease in strength to force 3 to 4—7 to 15 knots. The waves in mid-Channel would be 6 feet high on the forenoon of 5 June, but would decrease slowly while the visibility would be mainly good. The further outlook was unsettled, with the westerly weather continuing, but some breakdown in this westerly system of weather could be expected.

Here was a much more cheering forecast, although those who had time to look out of the windows of the operations room might have been forgiven for doubting, for the weather at that time was indubitably much worse than that of the previous day, when the "met" experts had been so pessimistic. Admiral

Ramsay, however, had implicit confidence in his meteorological advisers, and in this he was to be proved fully justified.

In the light of the weather forecast, there was another historic meeting presided over by General Eisenhower in the library at Southwick Park. This meeting was held at 8.15 p.m. on 4 June, and at it the great decision was taken. "Operation Overlord" was to go forward; D-day was to be 5 June. There can have been few more momentous signals in the history of warfare, and this time the decision was irrevocable.

To say that the decision was welcome to all those who were to take part in the invasion would be an understatement. They had all been "on their toes" for some time and nearly all of them had already been cooped up for more than 24 hours in "sealed" ships with no communication with the shore. Inaction was the last thing that they were prepared for, and the crowded ships were far from ideal places in which gladly to suffer inaction.

Landing craft assembled along the quayside at Southampton, a few days before D Day.

CHAPTER II

THE LITTLE SHIPS WENT FIRST

Midget submarines as light-ships—Sweeping the assault Channels—
Minesweepers in sight of France before dark—German inaction.

And so the great armada of liberation, comprising 4,266 landing ships and
landing craft for the initial assault alone, and taking no account of the many
hundreds of warships, tugs, ferry craft and so on, sailed for the tortured land
of France.

As the first convoy of landing craft and ships of "Force S" steamed out
of Spithead, HMS *Largs*, the headquarters ship of Rear-Admiral Talbot,
commanding the force, hoisted a wisp of coloured bunting. The signal read:
"Good luck. Drive on." That was typical of the departure of the assault
convoys from their assembly areas in the United Kingdom.

Some tiny vessels of the Royal Navy were already off the Normandy beaches
and had already been there for some time. They had had to be in position on
the assumption that D-day was to be 5 June as planned, and the postponement
meant for them only a prolongation of great danger and hardship. They could
not leave their positions and return to harbour for a few hours' rest, and their
crews realised full well that much of the success of the initial assault might
hang upon the accuracy with which they held their positions close off the
enemy's shore defences.

These vessels were the "X Craft"—British "midget" submarines of the same
type as had penetrated Alten Fiord in September, 1943, and inflicted serious
underwater damage upon the great German battleship *Tirpitz* when she was
lying snugly behind net defences at the head of a thickly mined and closely
patrolled fiord 35 miles long.

These "X Craft" had been entrusted with the task of marking the limits of the
assault area, where an error in the approach might well lead to the first wave
of assaulting troops being landed in the wrong place. They were to fix their

an awkward predicament, but far more so when sweeping an all-important channel in which there must be no risk whatever of mines being left. There was only one thing to be done. The ships steamed out of the channel into unswept water although they knew that they were in a minefield. Then they cut away their sweeps clear of the channel, streamed new sweeps, and resumed their positions in the sweeping order. It sounds courageous but simple, but it was by no means simple, for steps had to be taken to ensure that not one square yard of the water in the channel was left unswept as a result of these manoeuvres.

A little later one of the motor launches sweeping ahead of HMS *Sidmouth*— it was *ML185*—"put up" a mine right ahead of the *Sidmouth* which would otherwise certainly have claimed her as a casualty. A sentence from Commander Thomson's report is worth quoting. He said: "All ships carried out their duties faithfully and exactly in circumstances where a mistake by one might easily have ruined the whole channel." There are no two better words to describe the work of minesweepers than "faithfully" and "exactly." What this exactness entailed may be gauged from the fact that Commander J. C. Richards, RN in HMS *Vestal*, commanding the 6th Flotilla, found that it was necessary at times to make an allowance in the course of as much as 20 degrees to allow for the tide.

The 14th Flotilla, commanded by Commander J. W. A. Irvine, RNR in HMS *Romney*, cut some mines and then had trouble of a different nature. The minesweepers were followed by a convoy of LST's (Landing Ships, Tanks), which was over eager to get to France and launch the assault. That convoy got nearly half an hour ahead of time and was pressing so hard on the heels of the minesweepers that Commander Irvine was forced to send a message by *PT500* (one of the American despatch boats) to the destroyer escorting the convoy telling him to slow down the convoy.

Both the 14th Flotilla and the 16th Flotilla had a most unpleasant and eerie experience on the evening of 5 June—"D minus 1." Both these flotillas were within sight of the French coast for some hours before darkness fell, yet they had to go on sweeping steadily towards the enemy-held coast.

Commander Irvine's 14th Flotilla found that the French coast was plainly visible by 7.40 p.m., with nearly three hours of daylight remaining. The flotilla carried on sweeping steadily towards France, expecting at any moment to be engaged by the German coast defence batteries—a prospect which was far from pleasant because the minesweepers' first thought had to be for the channel which they were sweeping, so that they would have been unable to take any avoiding action or to dodge the enemy's salvoes. Extraordinary as it seems, however, the enemy completely ignored the minesweepers, although by 9.45 p.m. the 14th Flotilla had approached so close to the land that individual features upon it such as houses could be plainly discerned with the naked eye. Not until 11.45 p.m. did Commander Irvine see any signs of activity from the enemy. Then there were some heavy gun-flashes from batteries in the neighbourhood of Fomenay and Roché de Grandcamp. So certain were the minesweepers that the batteries were shooting at them that their crews looked round for the shell-splashes, but they saw none and concluded that they could not be the target. Soon afterwards the men of the minesweepers had a "grand-stand" view of the heavy air attack on these and other coastal batteries, which fully engaged the Germans' attention and effectively, if only temporarily, silenced the guns.

The 16th Minesweeping Flotilla, commanded by Commander M. H. Brown, RN in HMS *Shippigan*, sighted the coast of France at 8.40 p.m. at a distance of 18 miles, and had to continue to sweep towards it until the flotilla was within 11 miles of the coast. Then, to Commander Brown's relief, came the time to carry out the manoeuvre of changing the sweep from port to starboard, which entailed steaming away from the land. As Commander Brown said in his report: "Having been described as the Lady Godiva of the party, who had to lead the parade, I felt remarkably naked at this time."

The reason why the Germans so completely ignored the approach of these two minesweeping flotillas remains one of the great mysteries of the invasion of Normandy. It is true that the attacks of the Royal and United States Air Forces had reduced the German radar network in that part of France to a mere one-tenth of what it had been, but radar is not necessary to detect the presence of groups of ships within a dozen miles of the coast in daylight and good visibility. Even if one accepts the theory that the Germans were so highly technical that they had come to rely upon their radar to the exclusion of ordinary and more simple precautions it is not easy to believe that the minesweepers were in fact unobserved. Even if no special look-outs or coast watchers had been posted—and it is almost impossible to believe that they had not been when the Germans knew very well that ninety per cent of their radar organisation was out of action—the ships must surely have been seen by anyone who gave even a casual glance to seaward. The 14th Minesweeping Flotilla was within sight of the coast by daylight for at least three hours, and the 16th Flotilla for about an hour. Before darkness fell the men of the 14th Flotilla could clearly distinguish individual buildings ashore. A ship, to say nothing of a group of ships, is far easier to distinguish than buildings ashore, where there is in summer nearly always an evening haze. Thus the most casual of sentries must surely have seen the minesweepers.

Yet the Germans did nothing to impede the work of the minesweepers. They did not open fire with their coastal batteries even when the ships were well within range. Nor did they send to sea any of the E-boats or R-boats which were known to be lurking in Cherbourg and Le Havre. Nor did the *Luftwaffe* put in an appearance.

Even more amazing is the fact that the Germans apparently took no warning from the approach of these minesweeping flotillas, for the Allied High

Command was quite convinced that complete tactical surprise was secured by the initial assault on the Normandy beaches next morning.

The only possible explanation would seem to be that the Germans thought that the appearance of the minesweepers was a feint, designed to "draw them." It is worth recalling in this connection that some twenty months before D-day we had "trailed our coats" close off Boulogne with ships laden with deck cargoes of motor transport and with hundreds of landing craft. The idea had been to "draw" the *Luftwaffe*, and our fighter squadrons had been massed for a great "killing." The Germans, however, had refused to respond and had not even fired a gun from a coast defence battery, although some of the ships were at one time within five miles of Boulogne in the middle of a bright, clear day.

The work of the minesweepers was far from over when they had completed the sweeping of the ten channels from "Piccadilly Circus" to the assault area off the Normandy beaches. At the ends of their swept channels they had to turn parallel to the beaches and sweep an area free of mines in which the infantry landing ships and transports could safely deploy and anchor while lowering their assault landing craft and disembarking their troops. Moreover, the areas in which the bombarding ships were to operate had to be searched for mines.

It was a matter of considerable difficulty to disengage ten minesweeping flotillas from the southern ends of their swept channels and to deploy them for the sweeping of the "lowering areas" and the searching of the "bombardment areas," but all the arrangements had been carefully worked out beforehand and there was no hitch although some flotillas were working within two miles of the coast, and in some cases flotillas were forced to diverge from their chosen sweeping courses by the crowds of landing craft making for the beaches. The latter would not stop or change direction for any man! This phase of the minesweeping was well described in his report by Commander R. E. H. Nicholls, RN, commanding the 1st Minesweeping Flotilla, when he said: "The story of the subsequent sweeping was largely concerned with efforts to dodge the hazards of the course in the shape of other sweepers, convoys, etc." It is noteworthy that interference by the enemy shore batteries was not mentioned as "one of the hazards of the course."

There was also much minesweeping work to be done in the channels leading to the Normandy beaches from "Piccadilly Circus." True, ten channels had been swept clear of mines for the initial assault, but these channels were narrow and, although so well marked, they were not sufficient to take the vast amount of shipping which would be plying to and fro across the English Channel during the immediate "follow up" and the early stages of the "build-up" period—during which the Allied Naval Commander-in-Chief had stated his determination to land the very maximum of men and material in France irrespective of the strain thrown on ships and their crews. The ten channels had therefore to be widened, and widened to the extent that the spaces between adjacent swept channels were cleared of mines so that one broad channel would take the place of two of the original narrow channels. So successfully was this work tackled that before D-day drew to a close the spaces between Nos. 3 and 4 channels and between Nos. 5 and 6 channels had been swept clear of mines by the 4th, 14th, 6th and 1st Minesweeping Flotillas.

No description of the initial work of the minesweepers before H-hour would be complete without quoting a sentence from the report of Commander J. C. Richards, RN, who commanded the 6th Minesweeping Flotilla which had swept channel No. 5 from "Piccadilly Circus" to the assault area. Commander Richards said in his report: "In the increasing light it was most satisfying to see powerful ships southbound in channel No. 5, apparently undamaged and finding no difficulty in following the channel."

It was the same in the other nine channels, but it was left to Commander Richards to find words to express the richly-earned satisfaction of the minesweepers in a most difficult and responsible job successfully done.

US troops in an LCI(S). At the same time as the LCI(L) was handed over for US development and production, the British reworked their need for a raiding vessel into something that could be produced natively without making demands on limited resources. Fairmile Marine had already designed a number of small military vessels that were built in wood and they produced the Fairmile Type H which was another prefabricated wooden design. This was taken on as the Landing Craft Infantry (Small) or LCI(S). These were made on a cottage-industry scale throughout the country.

The cruiser HMS *Belfast* bombarding German shore positions.

There was another factor which made the tasks of the bombarding ships more difficult. This was that the Germans had moved a great many of their guns after the pre-D-day air bombardments of the coastal defences. The result was that the guns were not where they were expected to be and the accurate bombing before H-hour had not caused as much damage as had been expected, except to the old and abandoned gun positions. It did, however, drive the guns' crews to cover, and this proved invaluable. Moreover, the German action in moving their guns—which had been done in both the British and American sectors—proved something of a disadvantage to the enemy, for the new emplacements and defences were not complete when we made our assault.

In the circumstances, it was somewhat surprising that, on the whole, the ships were able to keep the German batteries quiet. D-day was, in fact, said by an officer of HMS *Mauritius*, to have been a "crashing anti-climax." For a considerable time the ships thought that the Germans were "lying doggo" on purpose and suspected a trap. There was apparently no trap, and for this the bombarding ships and the support squadrons of LCG's and LCR's (Landing Craft, Gun, and Landing Craft, Rocket) were grateful, for in the initial stages there was a need to conserve ammunition in order that there should be plenty of seaborne gunfire to meet and break the expected counter-attack by German armoured divisions.

It was very soon after Rear-Admiral Patterson's eastern bombarding force had reached its bombarding positions to the east of the SWORD area that the enemy delivered the first—and last—attack on our big ships by orthodox surface forces. The incident appears to have been more in the nature of a German mistake than a planned attack.

Our aircraft had laid a smoke screen between the bombarding squadron and the Le Havre batteries. It would not worry the ships during their bombardment because they had aircraft spotting, but would almost certainly give them a high degree of immunity from the Le Havre batteries. It was one of the few deliberate smoke screens laid during the assault, although arrangements had, of course, been made for plenty of these in case they should be needed.

It is not known whether the Germans were making use of this smoke screen to hide their approach to attack the bombarding ships, or whether they were merely investigating it and were taken by surprise when they emerged from it and found themselves close to hostile heavy ships. The tactics and the rather flurried nature of their attack argues the latter.

Be that as it may, three enemy torpedo boats suddenly emerged from the smoke screen at about 5.30 a.m. on D-day. They fired torpedoes and then promptly beat a hasty retreat back into the smoke and towards their base at Le Havre.

Two torpedoes passed between HMS *Warspite* and HMS *Ramillies*. Another was seen to be approaching HMS *Largs*, the headquarters ship of Rear-Admiral A. G. Talbot, who was commanding in the SWORD area. HMS *Largs* only just avoided being hit by putting her engines to emergency full speed astern. The torpedo passed a few feet ahead of the *Largs* and stopped and then sank close to the destroyer *Virago*. A fourth torpedo scored a hit on the Norwegian destroyer *Svenner*. She was hit in a boiler room. There was a sudden cloud of steam and her funnel fell aft as the whole ship seemed to be lifted out of the water. Then those in the *Largs* could see the *Svenner*'s Norwegian crew falling in with perfect discipline on the forecastle and the quarterdeck. A moment or two later they had to jump for their lives as the ship broke her back and sank. Fortunately a large proportion of her ship's company were saved.

During the early part of the "fire plan" there was considerable anxiety in HMS *Arethusa* about the progress of a part of the Sixth Airborne Division— an anxiety which was experienced to a lesser extent by HMS *Mauritius*. Both these ships had as their main tasks the giving of gunfire support to the Sixth Airborne Division which had been dropped east of the River Orne to seize the bridges over the river and the Caen Canal, hold the bridgeheads to the east of these bridges, and neutralise some enemy batteries in that area. For a considerable time the naval supporting craft could get no reliable information which would enable them to give gunfire support to the airborne troops without risk of firing into our own men.

The anxiety caused by this shortage of information was most acute with regard to the Sallesnelles battery. This was a battery of 6-inch howitzers east of the River Orne. The plan was for its capture by airborne troops who were to make crash glider landings in its immediate vicinity. In fact, one glider crash-landed on the battery itself and the battery was duly captured. This, however, was unknown to HMS *Arethusa*, who was in a position to enfilade the German battery and so facilitate its capture. The trouble was that it was not known whether the battery was in German hands or in the hands of our airborne troops. The fact that the guns of the battery were silent was no criterion, for many of the German batteries had shown inability or disinclination to open fire. The *Arethusa* was told that she was to open fire at a certain time unless she received orders to the contrary. Then she was told not to open fire until she was certain that the battery was still in German hands. She never was certain and so she did not open fire. It was fortunate, for the battery had been quickly captured by our airborne troops after their crash-landings.

It is of interest in this connection to recollect that the Sixth Airborne Division, who fought so magnificently and successfully for so many days east of the Orne after capturing the river and canal bridges intact, stated positively that they would have been wiped out had it not been for the gunfire support which they received from the Royal Navy—the only artillery support which was available to them.

The batteries to the east of the River Orne fired chiefly at the bombarding ships, and HMS *Warspite* was straddled by the troublesome battery at Benerville. By 9.30 on the morning of D-day, however, all the main batteries facing the eastern sector of the Assault Area had been silenced, at least temporarily, although the beaches and anchorage in the SWORD area were being subjected to an increasing volume of shell fire from German mobile guns operating in the woods south of Franceville. These mobile guns were exceedingly difficult to locate and engage and they moved as soon as they came under accurate fire.

In the JUNO area the two main batteries were effectively neutralised by naval gunfire during the assault and were subsequently captured by our troops before they had been able to "come to life" sufficiently to interfere.

In the GOLD area Commodore Douglas-Pennant's headquarters ship HMS *Bulolo* was engaged and straddled by Longues battery shortly before 6 a.m. HMS *Bulolo* had to shift berth to avoid being hit, but the battery in question had been effectively silenced by 6.20 a.m. In this area, however, German field batteries of medium calibre continued to engage destroyers and landing craft with intermittent and inaccurate fire from the hill west of Arromanches until about 9.30 a.m.

The deliberate bombardments of enemy batteries and prepared defences by the cruisers and larger warships was only the opening phase of the "fire plan."

Despite the virtual invulnerability of the bigger batteries and the fact that the enemy had moved many of his gun positions, the combined effect of the air and the first part of the naval bombardment had the effect of silencing, temporarily at least, nearly all the fixed German batteries from the mouth of the Seine to Cape Barfleur. This was done, according to plan, just before the landing ships came within their range. It is true that a certain amount of intermittent trouble was experienced with some batteries, particularly those of Le Havre, but each time they opened fire they were engaged again by the ships with such accuracy that they again lapsed into silence.

As soon as the more formidable of the German coastal defences had been neutralised, the cruisers of the bombarding forces turned their attention to the other German defences, such as pillboxes, redoubts, anti-tank defences, and machine-gun posts, while the heavier ships stood ready to re-engage any heavy German battery which might reopen fire. The cruisers were, of course, able to operate much closer inshore than the heavy ships and could therefore bombard the enemy positions at short range with direct observation from the ships. It was this phase of the naval "fire plan" which saw to it that the troops and tanks of the first waves of the assault were not held up by such obstacles as had been encountered undamaged at Dieppe.

While the cruisers were still engaged on this work, which, of course, further encouraged the German defenders to "keep their heads down," the landing craft carrying the troops of the assault wave were approaching the beaches. It was time for the third phase of the naval "fire plan" to come into operation.

This was the "drenching" of the beaches and their immediate approaches from landward by the guns of the destroyers and the LCG's (Landing Craft, Gun). Seventy destroyers mounting 4.7 and 4-inch guns, and a great collection of other craft ranged up and down the beaches, literally "drenching" every square yard of them from water line to vegetation line with high explosive shells. Behind that curtain of fire the landing craft laden with the assault troops made for the beaches.

Accurate timing of the naval "fire plan" was of paramount importance. If the "drenching fire" had begun too early ships might have expended all their ammunition before the assault "touched down" on the beach. As it was one ship—the Hunt class destroyer *Tanatside*—expended all her ammunition by 8 a.m. on D-day. If the "drenching fire" had been too late the enemy might have been able to "keep his head up" long enough to do terrible execution among the landing craft packed with troops as they approached the beaches.

The timing of the naval "fire plan" on D-day was excellent. That is not to say that the landings were made unopposed. It had never been expected that such could be the case, but it is a fact that they met with far less opposition than had been expected (except in the OMAHA sector), and there is no doubt that this was very largely due to the efficacy and timing of the naval "fire plan."

As the landing craft with the first wave of the assault neared the beach and "touched down," the "drenching fire" was lifted to the vegetation line and just beyond. It was, in fact, a development of the "creeping barrage." And to the guns there were added the "mattresses" of rockets from the LCR's (Landing Craft, Rocket). A big LCR could have a most devastating effect upon any defences not built of thick concrete.

Many were the tributes paid by both naval and military authorities to the accuracy and effectiveness of the naval gunfire. Commodore Douglas-Pennant, who commanded in the GOLD area, where the 50th Northumbrian Division delivered the assault, put it on record that: "The accurate fire support given by the cruisers of the Tenth Cruiser Squadron, the Dutch ship *Flores*, the 50th Destroyer Division and four "Hunt" class destroyers contributed largely to the success of the assault. The determination shown by the close support craft in closing the beach defences to almost point-blank range was one of the decisive factors in this phase."

It was HMS *Ajax* which neutralised Longues battery on this sector after Commodore Douglas-Pennant's headquarters ship had several times been "near-missed" by shells from its guns. The Longues battery was very troublesome and was in a position to do much damage. Its neutralisation by the 6-inch guns of HMS *Ajax*, which had spoken so decisively at the Battle of the River Plate, was therefore a matter of great importance. It was, moreover, due to some "exhibition" shooting on the part of the *Ajax*, which will long be quoted as an instance of amazing gunnery by a ship against a shore battery.

The German battery at Longues consisted of four 155 mm guns—roughly equivalent to 6-inch—mounted in reinforced concrete casemates. The Ajax fired 114 rounds at this battery from her 6-inch guns at an average range of 12,000 yards—6 sea miles. When the battery was occupied by our troops it was found that the Ajax's shooting had had the following results. Number 1 gun was undamaged. The casemate of Number 2 gun had been hit and damaged. Number 3 gun had received a direct hit on the gun itself which had put it completely out of action. Number 4 gun had been completely destroyed by more than one shell which had passed into the casemate between the sides of the aperture and the gun barrel and had burst inside the casemate.

HMS *Orion*, sister ship and squadron mate of the *Ajax*, was probably the most experienced ship in bombarding in support of invasion. She had distinguished herself off Sicily and off Salerno and Anzio. On D-day off Normandy, however, she did not fire a shot after the completion of the part of the pre-H-hour "fire plan" which had been allotted to her. This was because she was kept in reserve, it being deemed unwise to allow all ships to expend a large proportion of their ammunition in the opening phase of the invasion. Instead of allowing all ships to use a high proportion of their ammunition and so risk running short at the same time, arrangements were made that some ships of each class in each area should fire off all their ammunition before the next ships began firing. This, of course, was a principle rather than an order,

HMS *Ajax* was launched in 1934 and entered service in 1935. On 13 December 1939 *Ajax* along with other cruisers *Exeter* and *Achilles* engaged the German pocket battleship *Admiral Graf Spee* in the South Atlantic. *Ajax* was hit seven times by the Germans: X and Y turrets were disabled, structural damage was sustained and there were 12 casualties including 7 killed. The *Graf Spee* was scuttled off Montevideo on 18 December 1939, the German captain believing he was likely to be up against vastly superior Royal Navy forces.

As part of Force K, *Ajax* bombarded Gold Beach during the D-Day invasion (The battery at Longues gave some trouble but was silenced by 6-inch shells through the embrasures of two of the four casemates).

for the latter had to be left sufficiently elastic to allow all available ships to take part if the situation demanded. There was only one area in which this became necessary. That was in the American OMAHA area, where the assault troops were held up for many hours by encountering an unexpected German field formation which had just moved into the area for anti-invasion exercise. There all available ships joined in the bombardment without hesitation, and their timely interference proved decisive.

On D-day the bombarding squadron on the eastern flank approached their bombarding position down a swept channel two cables wide to a buoy and then had to steam round and round the buoy while bombarding, as this was the only water then swept clear of mines. On that night the ships anchored as close inshore as possible in SWORD area. This they did because it was fully expected that some of the ships would be sunk, for the Germans were expected to react far more strongly and quickly to the invasion than they actually did, and it was deemed wise to be in as shallow water as possible to facilitate salvage. Moreover, there was the possibility that the guns of a ship sunk in shallow water could still be brought to bear on the enemy.

In retrospect and in the light of the enemy's comparative impotence this may appear as a somewhat defeatist attitude. In reality it was just the reverse. It demonstrates the risks which were taken and the lengths to which the navy was prepared to go to ensure support for the invasion troops. There was nothing defeatist in anchoring close inshore to facilitate salvage of a ship if she was sunk, for that would be the last thing the Royal Navy would do if it expected a reverse which might lead to the ship becoming readily salvable by the enemy.

By next day the minesweepers had cleared a fairly large pear-shaped area between the eastern limit of SWORD area and Le Havre, which gave the ships of the eastern bombarding squadron more sea room in which to operate; and twenty-four hours later this had been joined to the swept area of SWORD by a broad expanse of mine-free water. The bombarding squadron made good use of the greater freedom of movement accorded to it—though it did on one occasion cut straight across a known minefield in pursuit of some German ships reported to be leaving Le Havre.

The mere fact that the initial phase of the invasion went so perfectly "according to plan" made life in the bombarding squadron somewhat uneventful and tedious after the first few hours. The ships' companies were always expecting some strong and determined action by the Germans, but they saw very little action apart from their rather dull bombardment routine, for our minesweepers and patrols proved more than a match for the German reactions. Nevertheless, they played a most important part and fired a prodigious amount of ammunition which gave invaluable support to our troops during their assault across the beaches and subsequently as they battled their way far inland. In the first few days of the invasion British warships alone fired more than 72,000 shells from guns ranging in size from the 15-inch guns of the battleships and the monitors to the 4-inch weapons of the "Hunt" class destroyers.

Millions of rounds were also fired from the smaller quick-firing weapons. During the seven months from D-day to the end of the year 1944 Allied warships fired well over 190,000 rounds, varying in calibre from 16-inch to 4-inch, in general support of the invasion armies, while a further 8,000 rounds were fired in special bombardments such as those of Cherbourg, Brest and Walcheren. In the first eighteen days of the invasion United States warships alone fired 44,000 shells varying in calibre from 15-inch to 4-inch, while a further 5,000 shells were fired by British and American warships in their bombardment of Cherbourg. In the centre and on the eastern flank naval bombardment and supporting fire was necessary for a longer period, and here rather more than 97,000 shells varying in calibre from 16-inch to 4-inch were fired by British warships before the break through and the German retirement to the east.

As the Allied troops advanced inland the naval bombardments altered in character. Instead of engaging enemy batteries they were called upon to give supporting fire to our troops, often many miles inland. This they did with great success thanks to the accuracy of their shooting and the efficiency of the specially trained FOB's (Forward Officers, Bombardment) and BLO's (Bombardment Liaison Officers) and the aircraft spotting.

Cruisers were able to give "deep support," as this fire at targets far inland was called, at ranges between 20,000 and 24,000 yards—between 10 and 12 sea miles—while battleships supported our troops with gunfire at ranges up to 17 miles. On more than one occasion a German commander assembling his armoured vehicles for a counter attack found his force suddenly shattered by heavy shells coming apparently from nowhere. German prisoners have borne witness to the serious moral effect of this unexpected heavy naval gunfire, with the shells coming over the hills from the sea, and many ships received the special thanks of the military units to which they gave this supporting fire. Among the British ships to receive special congratulations from the Army were the battleships *Nelson* and *Warspite*, the monitor *Roberts*, and the cruisers *Orion* and *Argonaut*.

It was an unorthodox form of naval warfare, and many unusual targets were engaged by the ships. Ten per cent of the shells fired in the first month by the big guns, for instance, were fired against enemy infantry, while 28 per cent of the shells fired from medium guns in the same period were fired at enemy tanks and motor transport. It is interesting to note that the ammunition expended on counter-battery fire by the ships amounted in this first month of the invasion to roughly one-fifth of the total rounds fired by heavy, medium and light guns.

Naturally, many ships wore out their guns during the invasion and had to have new guns fitted. Even before the fall of Caen the battleships *Warspite* and *Ramillies* and the cruiser *Orion*, as well as a number of other ships, had to change worn-out guns for new. It was one of the triumphs of the organisation of the invasion that even the big operation of changing the guns of a battleship did not lead to any temporary reduction in the naval fire power available off the Normandy coast. Another triumph of organisation was that of ammunition supply, which was carried out in such a way that no ship was ever delayed for a moment and no ship left the Assault Area with magazines empty or nearly empty without having been replaced by a similar ship with magazines and shell rooms full.

On the eastern flank there remained for a long time the necessity for bombardments other than those giving "deep support" to our troops far inland. The batteries east of the River Orne and the big gun batteries at Le Havre were for ever coming to life and having to be neutralised anew. This could not always be done, particularly in the case of the German mobile batteries east of the River Orne, where the contours of the land were such that they militated against accurate fire from low trajectory naval guns. The result was that the anchorage in the SWORD area had to be abandoned as it was considered that ships lying there would be exposed to unjustifiable risk from enemy shell fire.

The Germans also produced one or two other most annoying innovations. One of the most infuriating of these was a heavy gun on a railway truck mounting. The Germans used to keep this gun in a railway tunnel behind Houlgate, east of the Orne. At intervals they used to trundle it out, fire a round or two into our anchorage, and trundle it back again into the shelter of the tunnel just before our retaliatory shells arrived. This infernal jack-in-the-box was more annoying than harmful, but it was not silenced until our troops had cleared the enemy from the area.

For the most part it was all work and no play for the ships' companies of the larger bombardment ships, particularly when the troops had advanced well inland. They did not see the enemy or the positions at which they were firing when they were carrying out "blind firing" bombardments or providing "deep support" for the armies, yet they had always to be ready to act within a split second of receiving a message saying "Snap Map Reference such and such." The lives of many soldiers and the success or failure of some unknown military operation would depend upon the speed and accuracy with which that call for immediate support was answered.

Accuracy as well as speed had to be the watchword of the bombarding ships, and this meant not only accurate setting of the gun sights and accuracy in making allowances for wind, gun wear, temperature, and even the amount which the earth would turn during the time of flight of the shells, but also accuracy of navigation. A navigational error in the position of the ship would, of course, affect the accuracy of the gunfire when firing at map references, to say nothing of the fact that it might take the ship into mine-infested waters.

The accuracy of naval gunfire during the period when it was providing "deep support" at long range for the troops fighting far inland was phenomenal. Over one period in which the results were carefully analysed it was found that the average range at which the bombarding ships had been firing was 17,000 yards—eight and a half sea miles—and that the average distance of the first ranging shot from the target was only 146 yards—an error which was promptly made good by the spotting correction passed to the ship by the Forward Officer, Bombardment, or by aircraft.

This bombarding and provision of deep artillery support called for great endurance on the part of the officers and men of the bombarding ships. When they were in the Assault Area or its vicinity they had to be ready for action at an instant's notice both day and night. Many of the officers in these ships did not take their clothes off for seventeen days and nights, yet the enemy never tried to profit by their weariness, which he could easily have deduced. It was also very trying to the nerves. Imagine being in a ship which fired one 15-inch or 16-inch gun regularly once a minute, as did the battleships *Nelson* and

Above and below: US PT boats crossing the channel, 6 June 1944.

Ramillies when they bombarded Caen throughout the night of 12-13 June. They ensured that the Germans got no rest, but the crews of the ships got no rest either.

Some of the British Forward Officers, Bombardment, and the American shore fire control parties had a very bad time during the assault. Ensign E. A. Fehlig, USNR, for instance, was one of a shore fire control party attached to an infantry regiment. The whole party had to wade ashore under shell fire and Fehlig was badly wounded. He was lying face down and could not rise because of the weight of his pack, so that he was, although conscious, about to be drowned by the rising tide when somebody noticed his plight and cut his pack off. Without his pack he was able to crawl clear of the water, but the enemy shell fire was so intense that the wounded could not be taken off the beach and had to be collected in the shelter of an overturned landing craft.

Chief Water Tender W. Venable of the American destroyer USS *Glennon* also had a close call. The *Glennon* was badly hit by shore batteries and her stern fell away and anchored the ship so that she became a sitting target for the German guns. Her commander, Commander C. A. Johnson, USN, ordered all but fifteen men to abandon the ship. After dark a repair crew of forty men went on board to try to salvage the ship, but at dawn the German 155 mm guns opened fire again and hit the ship, setting her on fire aft. Venable was working below and thought the German shells were the *Glennon*'s guns firing. Although slightly wounded he went on working, unaware that the order to abandon ship had been given. When he was finally rescued from the burning wreck by a PT boat all he had to say was "We got 600 pounds of steam, let's get this son of a gun outa here," and was highly indignant at having to leave the ship.

General Eisenhower on D-Day plus one, on his way to Normandy on HMS *Apollo*, a fast minelayer, Abdiel class. He is accompanied by Major General Ralph Royce, General Omar Bradley, [unknown], Admiral Bertram Ramsay, and Petty Officer Ames on right.

CHAPTER IV

INTO NORMANDY

The Germans keep their heads down—The first wave goes into the beaches—The Germans come to life—Clearing the obstacles—Casualties and damage—The Battle of OMAHA beach—The Le Hamel strongpoint—Gallantry and determination—Beach commandos.

The initial blow in the invasion of Northern France was, of course, delivered by the air forces of Britain and the United States, and so heavy was this blow in the hours immediately preceding the landing of the first wave of the assault troops that it was estimated that between midnight and breakfast time there were about 31,000 Allied airmen in the air over France, not counting the airborne troops which were dropped east of the Caen Canal and in the Cotentin Peninsula.

The proportion of this air blow which was delivered against the German coast defences, and particularly the heavy gun batteries of Le Havre and the Cape Barfleur neighbourhood, was designed as part of "Operation Neptune." Apart from the assistance rendered by the air forces to the Allied navies and the shipping in their charge, there was the all-important fighter "umbrella" over the assault area and the convoy routes from Britain. So effective was this that the *Luftwaffe* made no attempt at daylight attack during the approach or the assault. In fact, Allied fighters ranged as much as 75 miles inland in France without encountering any air opposition.

The two initial successes of "Operation Neptune" were that our great and heavily laden armadas were not bombed in their ports of assembly in Southern England, and that they were not subjected to air attack on their way to the assault area. For both these successes the thanks of the maritime forces and of the troops embarked must go to the Allied air forces.

The troops, particularly in the smaller craft, had good reason to be thankful that they did not have to contend with enemy air attack as well as the weather. Although a distinct improvement on that of the previous day, the weather was

Small landing craft going into the beaches. In the background is USS *Augusta*, flagship of Rear Admiral Alan G. Kirk, USN, Commander Western Naval Task Force.

Senior US officers watching operations from the bridge of USS *Augusta*, 8 June 1944. From left to right: Rear Admiral Alan G. Kirk, USN, Commander Western Naval Task Force; Lieutenant General Omar N. Bradley, US Army, Commanding General, US First Army; Rear Admiral Arthur D. Struble, USN, (with binoculars) Chief of Staff for RAdm. Kirk; and Major General Hugh Keen, US Army.

Probably the most iconic photograph taken on D-Day. "The Jaws of Death." A photograph by CPHOM Robert F. Sargent, USCG. A Coast Guard-manned LCVP from the USS *Samuel Chase* disembarks troops of Company E, 16th Infantry, 1st Infantry Division on the morning of 6 June 1944 at Omaha Beach.

such that the smaller types of landing craft had a very wet and uncomfortable passage. The engines of four LCT's (Landing Craft, Tanks) were swamped on passage. Three of these were successfully got under way again, but one LCT was broached to by the seas, swamped and foundered, and a high proportion of the heavily-equipped troops lost their lives.

The crews of the landing craft experienced great and to some extent unaccustomed difficulties in landing their craft in the weather conditions prevailing, but they never faltered. "Force S" had been trained in the stormy waters of the Moray Firth, a fact for which their commander was thankful during the approach to France, but many of the landing craft crews had had far less experience of handling their craft m rough weather. Nevertheless, they rose to the occasion magnificently.

Rear-Admiral Sir Philip Vian, commanding the Eastern Task Force, is not a man lightly to give praise, but he reported: "Conditions of wind and sea

Troops and crewmen on a landing craft approaching the beach.

on the day of sailing were, in my appreciation, unexpectedly severe for the launching of an operation of this type, and imposed a high test on the landing craft crews. Their spirit and seamanship alike rose to meet the greatness of the hour and they pressed forward and ashore, over or through mined obstacles in high heart and resolution; there was no faltering, and many of the smaller landing craft were driven on until they foundered."

Rear-Admiral Vian's reference to landing craft being driven on until they foundered did not refer to the passage to Normandy, but to the assault on the beaches, when a great many of the smaller landing craft were damaged by the mined underwater obstacles.

The weather in the assault area on the morning of D-day was cloudy, with a cloud ceiling at 10,000 feet but some cloud at 1,000 feet. The wind was westerly, blowing at 15 knots, and the waves were 3-4 feet high, with surf on the beaches.

The greatest enemy of the troops in the smaller landing craft proved, during the approach, to be seasickness. All the troops had been given anti-seasickness pills before sailing, and these may well have helped, but no man has ever yet discovered a real preventative for seasickness, and most of the troops in the smaller craft were very seasick. There are few maladies more quickly lowering to morale than seasickness, and the fact that the soldiers in the small craft

Commandos of 1st Special Service Brigade landing from an LCI(S) (Landing Craft Infantry Small) on 'Queen Red' Beach, Sword Area, at la Breche, at approximately 0840, 6 June 1944. The brigade commander, Brigadier the Lord Lovat can be seen striding through the water to the right of the column of men. The figure nearest the camera is the brigade's bagpiper, Piper Bill Millin.

were in such good heart and high spirits at the end of their trying ordeal was no mean tribute to their determination.

The spirit in which the men went in towards the beaches in the smaller landing craft was illustrated by the case of one LCA (Landing Craft, Assault), which had a bugler on board. As it passed the headquarters ship HMS *Largs* on its way in to the beach the bugler sounded the ceremonial "general salute." The salute was acknowledged by Rear-Admiral A. G. Talbot commanding "Force S" and Major-General T. G. Rennie, commanding the 3rd British Infantry Division, who were standing side by side on the bridge.

In the assault area off SWORD beach, too, the passage of the landing craft towards the beach was enlivened by a motor launch, the young commander of which had conceived the idea of playing a portable gramophone and broadcasting the music through his "loud hailer." Unfortunately his supply of records appeared to be very limited indeed, but "Roll out the Barrel" was one of them. To this the irrepressible bugler in the LCA replied by sounding "Come to the cookhouse door, boys" over and over again!

On the whole, the opposition on the beaches was much less than had been anticipated, but there was, nevertheless, considerable opposition. The scale of this opposition varied. On some beaches it was almost negligible during the initial stage of the assault, while in others it was extremely stiff, notably in the case of the American OMAHA beach.

That the opposition was not equally determined on all beaches was due to the terrific "softening up" process which had been begun by the bombing of the Allied air forces and continued by the naval bombardments. These, and particularly the short-range naval gunfire and the "drenching" fire produced by the destroyers, LCG's (Landing Craft, Gun) and LCR's (Landing Craft, Rocket) dazed and numbed the defenders of most of the German strong points during the critical period of the "touch down" of the first wave of the assault. To escape the fury of the bombardment the Germans had been forced to abandon their defence positions and take cover underground. The short time which it took them to recover and to get back to their weapons and their defence positions was fully exploited. It was in that interval that the craft carrying the troops of the first wave of the assault dashed in to the beaches.

It was indeed fortunate that the bombardments did have this effect upon the enemy and that the assault was able so successfully to profit by the period in which the Germans were "keeping their heads down" as a result of the terrific volume of fire to which their positions had been subjected. It had never been considered possible that either air or naval bombardment could achieve the destruction of the enemy's prepared defence positions. In fact, Rear-Admiral Sir Philip Vian, who commanded the Eastern Task Force, stated categorically that the German beach defences were not suitable targets for naval gunfire, and this was aggravated by the fact that many of the enemy pillboxes were so sited that they derived considerable protection from the lie of the land against low trajectory fire from seaward, while the almost straight nature of the coastline made it impossible for the ships to direct enfilading fire on these positions.

Rear-Admiral Vian reported to Admiral Sir Bertram Ramsay: "Except for the considerable moral effect of naval fire, which in many cases so demoralised the occupants of the concreted defences that the assaulting infantry captured them with little opposition, this type of beach defence was not a legitimate naval target." And again, writing of the German shore batteries: "The considerable effect on the morale of the enemy gunners was the main factor contributing to this success. Following the heavy air bombardment on the majority of the coast defence batteries the accuracy and intensity of the naval bombardment broke the enemy's nerve and no accurate return fire was experienced during the assault period."

An LSR — Landing Ship Rocket in a peaceful view.

A spectacular broadside from an LSR.

This demoralisation of the defending enemy lasted only a few minutes, but those were the all-important minutes while the first wave was going in to the beaches, and during which there would otherwise certainly have been serious casualties among the landing craft and the troops huddled together in them. As it was, the leading groups of landing craft in most areas were within 3,000 yards of the shore line before they met with any opposition at all, and even then the resistance was at first spasmodic.

On some beaches the enemy opposition was even less, and the coxswain of an assault landing craft returning from the first trip to SWORD beach sang out to the craft on their way in: "It's a piece of cake!"

Even on that beach, however, the lack of opposition was of short duration. The Hun soon came to life and there was a lot of mortar and machine-gun fire on the beaches and in the water close off the beaches. To some, who had found the initial absence of enemy resistance somewhat uncanny, this was almost a relief. Certainly it did not for one moment deter either sailor or soldier, but rather spurred them to even greater efforts. Rear-Admiral Talbot, who was commanding the assault on this beach, reported of the effect of the beginning of this enemy opposition: "But to soldiers and sailors alike, the vast majority of them under fire for the first time in their lives, if they ceased to joke it was because this was more as they had visualised an assault to be, and they only drove on the harder.',

The Allied Naval Commander-in-Chief, Admiral Sir Bertram Ramsay, felt after D-day that there was some danger of the magnitude and hazard of the operation, and of the courage and determination of those who took part, becoming minimised in the public mind simply, because it was so successful. This he stressed to the Lords Commissioners of the Admiralty in his letter accompanying his official report, and added: "That the operation proceeded smoothly and according to plan was the result of the hard work and foresight of the many thousands concerned in its preparation and of the determination and courage of the tens of thousands in the Allied Navies and Merchant Fleets who carried out their orders in accordance with the very highest traditions of the sea."

At most of the beaches it was found that the worst difficulty in the initial assault, and the cause of the majority of the casualties, was presented by the mined obstacles set up between low and high-water marks, and even in some cases below low water mark. The LCOCU's (Landing Craft Obstacle Clearance Units) did magnificent work, but the speed of the assault was such that they had insufficient time to neutralise or demolish many of the obstacles. The armoured bulldozers which were landed with the first wave of the assault also did great work in demolishing these obstacles. On the whole, however, the majority of the obstacles were cleared by the simple method of the larger and heavier types of landing craft charging the beaches and crashing their way through the obstacles. At the same time the smaller types of landing craft threaded their way in between the obstacles.

Support troops of the 3rd British Infantry Division assembling on 'Queen Red' Beach, Sword Area, near la Breche, Hermanville-sur-Mer, at 0830 on 6 June while under intermittent enemy mortar and shell fire. In the foreground and on the right, identified by the white bands around their helmets, are sappers of 84 Field Company Royal Engineers, part of No.5 Beach Group. Sappers Jimmy Leask (left, glancing up at the photographer), Cyril Hawkins of No. 1 Platoon, whilst on the right, walking towards the camera past the medical orderlies is Sapper Fred Sadler of the same Platoon. All three survived the war.

Vehicles unloaded from LCTs on a British beach.

Royal Navy beach commandos near Courseilles directing traffic by loud hailer.

Opposite below: The British 2nd Army. Infantry waiting to move off 'Queen White' Beach, Sword Area, while under enemy fire, on the morning of 6 June. The first landings on Sword were made by the British 3rd Infantry Division, 27th Armoured Brigade and Royal Marine and Army Commando units from General Crocker's I Corps. By nightfall the British had 28,850 men ashore and the Orne bridge had been seized.

Some of the underwater obstacles cleared from Juno.

Naturally, the method of charging through the obstacles with the heavier types of landing craft led to damage and to casualties, but no other method could have been so successful without delaying or reducing the momentum of the first wave of the assault, and thereby failing to profit to the utmost from the brief period in which the enemy was incapable of putting up any effective resistance.

The following eye-witness report, compiled on board HMCS *Prince David*, of the landing of the Canadians near Bernières-sur-Mer on JUNO beach, is eloquent of the trouble caused by the mined beach obstructions:

"HMCS *Prince David* landed her first body of invasion troops exactly on schedule on the beach at Bernières-sur-Mer. The soldiers, members of a French-Canadian regiment recruited from the lower St Lawrence, were ferried from the parent ship by the landing craft flotillas, commanded by Lieutenant R. G. Buckingham. It was not until the assault infantry and tank landing craft were practically on the beach that they ran into trouble in the form of mines. The small assault boats were the heaviest sufferers. The boats rode in with a stiff wind that sent the surf crashing on the beach. Their way lay through a section of crossed scantlings which gave this piece of water the appearance of a field filled with stumps. These were the mine supports. First Lieutenant

HMCS *Prince David* was one of three Canadian passenger liners converted for the Royal Canadian Navy; first to Armed Merchant Cruisers at the beginning of the War, then to Infantry Landing Ships (Medium). For three years, they were the largest ships in the RCN.

HMCS *Prince David* at Normandy, landing US Service Corps troops after the initial landings.

J. McBeath's boat was mined; then Lieutenant Buckingham, Lieutenant Beveridge and Leading Seaman Lavergne had their craft smashed by mines. It was a wild scramble for shore, but every one made it with the exception of two French-Canadians in Lieutenant McBeath's boat. They were killed outright by the mine which their boat hit. While our boats were emptying their men, others were taking punishment from mines farther up the beach. Chunks of debris rose a hundred feet in the air and troops, now hugging the shelter of a breakwater, were peppered with pieces of wood. The bigger landing craft did not escape, but they could take it."

The American equivalent of the British LCOCU's is the Naval Combat Demolition Unit. These units did magnificent work in clearing the mined obstacles in the OMAHA and UTAH areas. Typical of their exploits was that of a unit whose men had to crawl on their stomachs under heavy fire and dragging the explosives with which to blow gaps in the obstructions for the landing craft. J. L. Comfrey of this unit described his experiences as follows: "The Jerries started pouring lead at us right off the bat. They used everything they could muster, 88 mm guns, mortars and machine guns, and the snipers were busy too. But we managed to wire our charges to the obstacles, which were pyramids of railway iron with mines attached, and blow the gaps. We worked on those things all day and for the next two days with the Jerries

Canadian troops in heavy seas heading for Juno Beach after having left HMCS *Prince Henry*.

Canadian troops landing at Juno Beach.

Canadians landing at Bernières-sur-mer, Juno Beach.

Obstacles on the beach to be dealt with by LCOCU.

working on us all the time with their 88 mm's. As soon as we heard them go off we'd try to make it to foxholes, but often we didn't have time, so we'd just hit the deck and hope."

Another case of a United States Naval Demolition Unit which accomplished its task in spite of being almost wiped out by the enemy's fire was that of which Seaman E. Corvese was the only survivor. The group was pinned down on the beach for fifteen hours by very accurate German fire from 88 mm guns and the entire crew except Corvese became casualties. Nevertheless, as soon as the German fire slackened a little Corvese pressed on and blew up the obstacles for the destruction of which his unit had been made responsible.

The losses of landing craft off the beaches were almost negligible by comparison with the number of craft employed, but a great many landing craft were damaged off the beaches.

The actual numbers of landing craft damaged during the assault phase of the invasion were as follows:

Landing craft, Tanks	131
Landing craft, Assault	117
Landing craft, Infantry (small)	22
Landing craft, Infantry (large)	21
Total	291

US troops disembark from a landing vehicle on Utah Beach on the coast of Normandy, June 1944. Carcasses of destroyed vehicles litter the beach.

D-Day + 1. American troops land in about two feet of water from an LCI(S) on 7 June 1944. On the beach ahead are a DUKW and several jeeps, a smoke screen provides some minor coverage.

The great majority of these were, of course, repairable. Some of these craft were damaged by enemy shell or mortar fire while on the beaches, and a considerable proportion of the damage caused to the smaller craft was due to the weather and the surf on the beaches, but most of the damage to the larger type landing craft was caused by the mined obstructions off the beaches.

While things were going well on the beaches in the British and Canadian sectors—on these, beaches the assault and reserve companies of troops were through the exits from the beaches by about 10 a.m. and the beaches were no longer under direct fire from small-arms, machine-guns or mortars—the same could not be said of the whole of the American sector. That was no reflection upon the skill, determination and courage of the American personnel. Had the American sailors and soldiers not possessed these qualities in full measure matters would have been far worse.

On UTAH beach the landings had gone according to plan, but on OMAHA beach the American assault troops found themselves unexpectedly opposed by a full-strength division of German field troops.

This was the 352nd Field Division of the *Wehrmacht*, and its presence in the assault area of the invasion came as a complete surprise to the Allies. It was the only occasion on which the Allied intelligence organisation proved at fault, and this was hardly to be wondered at, for the division had only moved into

An amphibious vehicle approaching a beach in an early dawn phase. An uncomfortable night crossing, cold, constant water ingress, were minor compared to the mixture of fear and adrenalin.

A radio unit in on Utah Beach. The Crosley Corporation of Cincinnati, Ohio manufactured the Signal Corps Radio set SCR-284 that consisted of the BC-654 and associated support equipment. The BC-654 was introduced in Africa during Operation Torch and was the first radio set used for communications from the beach to the US Fleet to coordinate naval gunfire and beach radio networks. More than 50,000 BC-654s were produced and delivered in support of Operation Overlord generator. Power is produced by a hand-crank generator.

Tanks on Utah Beach shortly after H hour.

Vehicles and men of LCT-524 landed at Utah Beach. The large sign on the right and small sign on the left have been painted out by a censor.

Utah Beach is full of materials of all kinds. Most men wear the helmet of the 1st ESB, (Engineer Special Brigade), the 'blue arcs'.

the area two or three days before D-day in order to carry out anti-invasion manoeuvres. It was subsequently established beyond doubt that its presence in the invasion area was quite fortuitous and not due to any prevision on the part of the enemy or leakage of the Allied plans.

That, however, did not help the Americans assaulting OMAHA beach. Not only did they find themselves opposed by an overwhelming superiority in manpower, but the Germans were in very strong prepared defensive positions. As Rear-Admiral Kirk stated in his report, the defensive system, at OMAHA beach was "highly organised, strongly built, and skilfully designed." To make matters worse, the initial pre-H-hour air attack on this particular sector had not materialised. It was a tragedy that this was the only part of the assault area where the preliminary "softening up" had not been carried out according to plan.

Nor did the Germans reply to the naval bombardment and so give any indication of their strength or of the formidable nature of their defence positions. As the Germans have done on so many occasions, they lay low until the first wave of the assault "touched down" on the beaches, and only then did they open fire.

The German defensive system at OMAHA beach consisted of strong points constructed in and on the cliffs to landward of the beach, with others at the foot of these cliffs. There were many pillboxes, partly buried in the slope and therefore gaining extra protection from their surroundings. These pillboxes were so sited that they could give a volume of fire across the beach to seaward and also provide cross-fire on the beach itself. Nor were these pillboxes isolated strong-points. They were connected by underground passages and were provided with an elaborate inter-communication system of zinc voice-pipes. Moreover, the beach and its seaward approaches were thickly mined, while all the possible landward exits from the beach were blocked by ditches or walls and barbed wire. Along the 7,500 odd yards of OMAHA beach there were:

8 Casemated batteries with guns of 75 mm or larger calibre.
35 Pillboxes, with guns of less than 75 mm calibre and automatic weapons.
4 Field artillery positions.
18 Anti-tank gun positions with guns of between 37 mm and 75 mm
6 Mortar pits.
38 Rocket pits, each with four 38 mm rocket tubes; and
85 Machine-gun posts.

The mere fixed defences of OMAHA beach made it a very tough proposition indeed, and it must be remembered that these defences were manned, not by elderly and indifferent coast defence troops diluted with foreign conscripts, but by a fresh German Field Division.

Part of the first wave to go into the heavily defended Omaha Beach.

A scene of desolation and destruction at low tide on Omaha Beach; the vast number of underwater obstacles clearly visible.

As the landing craft carrying the first wave of American assaulting troops "touched down" on OMAHA beach the 352nd German Field Division opened a murderous fire from their strongly armed positions. This fire knocked out the majority of the tanks which had accompanied the first wave of the assault, and caused very heavy Casualties among the troops. Moreover, as a result of this fire the initial wave was only able to clear five lanes through the beach obstacles instead of the sixteen lanes which had been planned, a fact which, of course, hampered the landing of the subsequent waves.

Despite the terrific odds against them the remnants of the first wave of American assault troops clung to their small and precarious footing on the beach, and they continued to hang on, thus forming a tiny but invaluable beachhead for the landing of their reinforcements.

As soon as Rear-Admiral J. L. Hall (Jr.), who was in command of "Force O" charged with the assault of OMAHA beach, saw the degree of opposition being met by the first wave of his assault troops, he called an Rear-Admiral Alan G. Kirk, the commander of the Western Task Force, for support. Rear-Admiral Kirk was quick to appreciate the situation and to act, but even so his orders were forestalled by some of the warships in the immediate vicinity of OMAHA beach. The commanders of these ships displayed great initiative and determination that nothing that they could do to support their hard-pressed troops should be left undone. Battleships, cruisers and destroyers were soon deluging the strong positions of the German 352nd Field Division with short-range gunfire, while the air forces were also quickly on the spot to add bombs and rockets to the shells of the ships. In the last resort, however, the honours of the struggle on that beach must go to the soldiers who held on to a small portion of beach with magnificent tenacity in face of withering fire, and to the succeeding waves of troops who flung themselves ashore in support without a moment's hesitation. It must be remembered that these troops were not veterans; the great majority were under fire for the first time.

Rear-Admiral Kirk thus summed up that critical period on the beach: "The initial check on the beach was overcome because of the initiative displayed by gunfire support ships, the assistance of the air force, and the intrepidity of the infantry on the shore line." He went on: "The performance of battleships, cruisers and destroyers in support of the landing was magnificent."

For all the troops could do and the support of the ships and the air force, the struggle for OMAHA beach did not end until about 1 o'clock in the afternoon. By that time the German Field Division had been decisively defeated and the beach and its exits were in American hands, with armoured bulldozers demolishing the obstructions on the beach and in the beach exits. For nearly six hours that bitter struggle had waged, which will surely go down to history as "the Battle of OMAHA Beach."

A view out to sea from Omaha Beach with wounded and dead in the water.

Rescuing the wounded in the surf at Omaha.

Three Engineers prepared a rope to retrieve survivors standing on the wreckage floating in the sea at Omaha Beach. In the background mist stands the cruiser USS *Augusta*, flagship of Rear Admiral Alan G. Kirk on board with General Omar Bradley.

Landing Craft USS LCI(L)-83 was built by the Consolidated Steel Corp, Orange, Texas, and launched, 13 December 1942. It took art in the North Africa landings, Sicily, Salerno, and after Normandy went to the Pacific where it was at Okinawa finishing a busy war. It was part of Flotilla 10 at Normandy.

D-Day + 2, 8 Jun 1944. American assault troops of the 3d Battalion, 16th Infantry Regiment, 1st US Infantry Division, having gained the comparative safety offered by the chalk cliff at their backs, takes a "breather" before moving onto the continent at Colleville-Sur-Mer, Omaha Beach. Medics who landed with the men treat them for minor injuries.

D-Day + 2, 8 Jun 1944. Reinforcements and artillery press inland from Omaha Beach two days after the initial invasion. Within a week of D-Day, more than 300,000 Allied troops and 2,000 tanks had arrived, but the beachhead remained pinched and crowded.

A busy scene on Omaha Beach a few days after D-Day.

American and German dead await burial in a makeshift morgue behind Omaha Beach. The 4,700 US casualties at Omaha, including wounded and missing, accounted for more than one-third of the Allied total on D-Day.

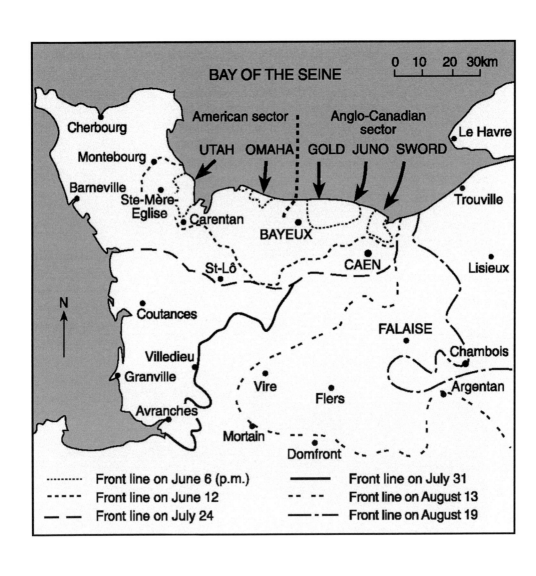

BAY OF THE SEINE

0 10 20 30km

American sector

Anglo-Canadian
sector

Cherbourg

Le Havre

Montebourg

UTAH OMAHA   GOLD JUNO SWORD

Barneville

Trouville

Ste-Mère-
Eglise

Carentan

BAYEUX

St-Lô

CAEN

Lisieux

N

Coutances

FALAISE

Chambois

Villedieu

Granville

Vire

Argentan

Flers

Avranches

Mortain

Domfront

·········· Front line on June 6 (p.m.)   ———— Front line on July 31

- - - - - Front line on June 12   - ·· - ·· - Front line on August 13

— — Front line on July 24   — · — · Front line on August 19

Although on the British and Canadian sectors there was no pitched battle on the beach to compare with that on OMAHA beach, there was plenty of bitter fighting, mostly inland from the actual beaches. Behind SWORD beach there was a very strong German position in the village of Le Hamel. This had been engaged for some time by three destroyers, but the German strongpoint was partly in "dead ground" protected by the contour of the land against low trajectory fire from seaward. Nevertheless, the ships' gunfire was far from being useless. Unfortunately, however, they stopped shelling this strongpoint at the time appointed on the plan, and the naval authorities received no intimation that any further fire was required. They could not, of course, reopen fire on their own initiative on a point which might well have been by that time overrun by our advancing troops.

In fact, Le Hamel had not been overrun by our troops. The Germans were still obstinately resisting in their strongpoint and not only holding up our advance but also inflicting heavy casualties upon our troops. The reason why the navy received no request for further gunfire against Le Hamel and in support of our troops attacking that place was that both the commanding officer and the second-in-command of the troops attacking Le Hamel—the 1st Battalion the Hampshire Regiment—had become casualties early in the fighting. In these unfortunate circumstances it was not until after 4 o'clock in the afternoon that the 1st Hampshires finally cleared Le Hamel of the enemy.

We are here concerned with "Neptune" and the naval component of "Overlord," but no account of any part of the invasion of Normandy would be complete without some reference to the epic deeds of the 6th Airborne Division. This Division was dropped from aircraft and landed in gliders to the eastward of the River Orne and the Caen Canal. They seized bridges intact and held on to their bridgeheads day after day in the face of the worst that German armour, artillery and infantry could do. Moreover, their work had an important effect upon the naval side of the invasion, for among their first objectives were batteries close east of the Orne and the Canal, the guns of which could command the sea off the assault area at close range. These batteries the airborne troops faithfully liquidated in the first hours after they landed. One glider, in fact, "landed" on top of one of the German batteries.

"Neptune" was the greatest offensive operation of the war, in which the navy played a vital part in the van of the assault. It was by far the most hazardous undertaking in the face of the enemy ever carried out. Yet it resulted in no award of the Victoria, Cross to a naval officer or man. In fact, there was not a single recommendation for a VC. That is not so strange as it at first sight appears. "Neptune" was a triumph of organisation and collective determination and courage rather than an operation giving scope for extempore feats of individual bravery. There were certainly a very great many instances of great fortitude and magnificent courage, but it is small

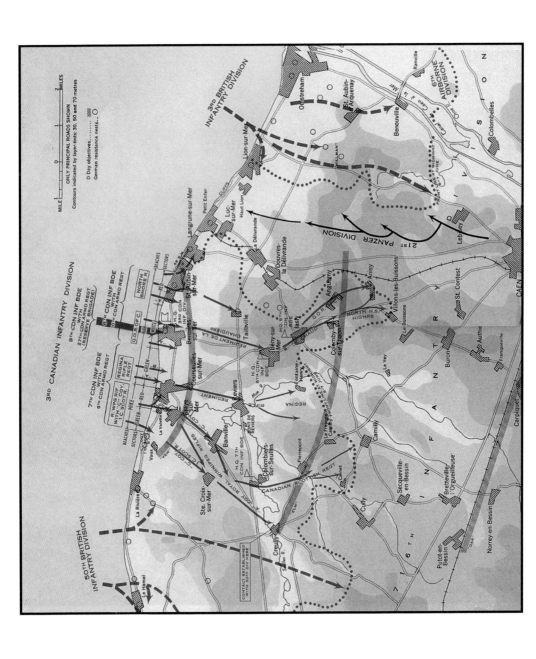

wonder that, with all achieving so mightily, commanders could not single out individuals for the special distinction of the highest award for bravery in the face of the enemy.

It is possible here to outline only a very few of the instances of great courage and fortitude displayed by the crews of the landing craft and other small vessels during the assault of the Normandy beaches.

Sick Berth Attendant Emlyn Jones was in LCI(L) 111, which was engaged in bringing wounded off the beach. The craft was just leaving the beach when it was hit below the water-line by a shell and holed. The troop-space, in which Jones was attending the wounded, at once began to flood rapidly. There were seven serious casualties and these were in danger of drowning. These Jones saved, and continued to work on the wounded in the partially flooded troop-space. He was only a Sick Berth Attendant, not a fully qualified and experienced doctor, but in those almost impossible conditions and under fire he coolly carried out three emergency operations for the amputation of shattered legs.

It would be difficult, too, to match the fortitude of Able-seaman George Wells of LCT 898. Wells was wounded by a shell just as his landing craft "touched down" on the beach, but he carried on with his work without even mentioning it. A few minutes later he was again wounded by another shell. This time he was dreadfully injured, but still he remained cheerful and concerned only for the welfare of his messmates, some of whom were also wounded. He even found heart to joke about it while one of his shattered fingers was roughly amputated with a pair of scissors.

One of the men who earned a Distinguished Service Medal during the assault on the Normandy beaches was Corporal George Tandy, Royal Marines, and the manner in which this decoration was earned is eloquent of the spirit in which the crews of the landing craft discharged their responsibility of putting the troops safely ashore. Corporal Tandy was coxswain of LCA 786. The craft was lowered from an infantry landing ship seven miles off the beach, but before the LCA could get clear in the sea that was running, the block on the after lowering fall crashed into the wheel and engine-room telegraph, smashing them both. In calm weather it is possible to control and to steer an LCA by manoeuvring the engines, but it was impossible to control the craft in this way in the heavy sea. Nevertheless, Corporal Tandy was determined that the troops entrusted to his charge should be duly landed. Without hesitation he slipped over the stern of the craft and stood with one foot on the rudder guard rail and the other on the rudder itself, while he hung on to the beading and a cleat. In this way, steering the craft by controlling the rudder with his foot, he took the LCA into the beach, threading his way through the mined obstructions. It would have been a skilful feat in calm weather, but in the weather prevailing off the beaches on D-day it required courage, strength and endurance as well as skill. In that following sea he was high out of the water one minute and submerged to his armpits the next, and he was considerably buffeted by the sea, so that it was a wonder that his leg was not smashed against the rudder guard rail. It was seven miles to the beach, but in this way Corporal Tandy took his craft in under fire and landed the troops in his charge at the right place and only three minutes after the schedule time of the "touch down." Then, having landed the troops, Corporal Tandy set out to take his craft back to its parent ship in the same manner. This was for him an even worse ordeal, for with wind and sea against the blunt-nosed little craft she was pitching badly and it took two and three-quarter hours for her to cover the seven miles back to the ship. When he arrived alongside Tandy had to be hauled out of the water. He was badly bruised and spent the next two days in the sick bay, but all he had to say about his exploit was: "There were thirty-two soldiers' lives at stake in that boat apart from the sailors manning her. Any one of them would have done the same as I did if they had had the opportunity."

It is traditional in the Royal Navy that midshipmen are usually endowed with considerable resource and an even greater fund of "cheek." Midshipman Charles Fowler, the First-Lieutenant of one of the LCT's (Landing Craft, Tanks) was no exception. As this LCT, came into the beach she came under heavy fire, and as luck would have it one of her own guns jammed at the critical moment. The commanding officer of the LCT made a dash for the disabled gun in order to help clear the jam, but he fell mortally wounded before he reached it. Midshipman Fowler took command, but as he did so the steering gear of the LCT was shot away. Nevertheless, he held her into the beach while the tanks disembarked. All this time the LCT was under heavy fire. A mortar bomb landed on the LCT but fortunately did not explode. Without a moment's hesitation Leading Stoker Gamble picked it up and hurled it back among some Germans in a slit trench, where it exploded. Nevertheless, the casualties in the LCT were mounting—two of the crew had been killed and three were wounded.

After completing the unloading, Midshipman Fowler tried to leave the beach, but found that she was stuck on the sand. With true "snotty's nerve" he went ashore and found an army bulldozer, the driver of which he persuaded to come and push his craft back into the sea. Thus he got the LCT clear of the shell-swept beach and set out for England, where he arrived safely some hours later, demanding an ambulance for his wounded, repairs to his steering gear, and another load of tanks. Midshipman Fowler had only been in the service a "dog watch," he had never before handled a vessel, and the LCT had no steering gear, but it never occurred to him to ask for assistance in handling his "first command."

Sub-Lieutenant Douglas Jones was another LCT commander who fended for himself and refused to complicate the tasks of others by asking for assistance although he was placed in very difficult circumstances. Sub-Lieutenant Jones's craft—LCT 8854—had just "touched down" on the beach when a German mortar shell landed in the after end of the hold and started a fire among the vehicles. This soon assumed serious proportions and the ammunition with which the vehicles were laden began to explode. Sub-Lieutenant Jones took LCT 8854 to the assistance of another craft which was having difficulty in getting off the beach against the wind and sea. This craft he successfully towed off, and finally he succeeded in getting the fire in his own craft under control with only three of the vehicles burnt out.

Another notable instance of devotion to duty on the part of a wounded man was provided by LCI(S) 505 (Landing Craft, Infantry, Small). The LCI was on the beach and her decks were being swept by enemy fire. She embarked some wounded and then tried to leave the beach. It was found that the craft was firmly held because the life-saving "scrambling" nets over her sides had become foul of some of the beach obstructions. The First-Lieutenant of the craft shouted to Wireman Arthur Martindale to cut away the nets. The crew of the craft were lying down in order to present the least possible target to the enemy fire, and when the First-Lieutenant gave this order he was unaware that the wireman had been wounded in the face. Despite this, Martindale obeyed the order without a second's hesitation. He leapt to his feet, climbed over the side of the craft, and cut the nets free. Then he clambered on board again and was later found dressing the wounds of the wounded men who had been embarked. He had made no attempt to have his own wound attended to.

It would be quite impossible, even today, to list all the deeds of gallantry which were performed on and off the Normandy beaches. There were occasions on which commanding officers were themselves killed before they had any opportunity to report the deeds of those serving under them, and other occasions in which no officer or man has survived to testify to an act of bravery deserving of special mention. All that can be done is to detail a few such acts and to stress the fact that they were representative of the spirit animating all. Thus the cool, calculating courage of Lieutenant J. G. Clarke of the United States Coastguard Service is representative of the dauntless devotion to duty of the members of that Service, whose craft plied hither and thither on all manner of errands and allowed no amount of enemy fire, air attack or minelaying to interfere with their duties.

The cutters of the United States Coastguard Service are boats about 80 feet long. Their engines use high-octane petrol which is the most volatile and inflammable of fuels. This is a fact well appreciated by their officers and men, but they have never been known to allow the knowledge to set any limit to their service or to the dangers which they are prepared to face.

So it was with Lieutenant Clarke. His cutter was in the vicinity when a British landing craft carrying high-octane petrol in to the beach was hit and

The 83-foot cutters *83401*, renamed USCG 20, and the *83402*, renamed USCG 21, were two of the sixty Coast Guard cutters sent to England to serve as rescue craft off each of the invasion beaches during the Normandy Invasion.

blew up. The burning spirit spread at once over the surface of the water and made it literally a sea of flame. Although he fully appreciated the danger to his own craft, with the same volatile fuel in her tanks and engines, Clarke drove his cutter through the flames and rescued the survivors of the landing craft. For this service Lieutenant Clarke was subsequently decorated with the DSC by Admiral of the Fleet Sir Andrew Cunningham, First Sea Lord.

It would be difficult to find an instance of bravery to rival that of Paul Kozub, Motor Machinist's Mate, First Class, USNR. Kozub was serving in a landing craft which was damaged by mines and mortar fire and had to be abandoned while it was still 160 yards from the shore line. He helped to get the wounded ashore and to tend them despite heavy fire from the enemy. Then he saw another landing craft disabled 150 yards off the beach. There were bodies to be seen on the after part of this landing craft, and Kozub saw that there was movement among them. Some of the men were only wounded, yet they would surely have been drowned if they had been left, for the tide was rising rapidly over the wrecked landing craft. Kozub searched about on the beach under withering fire until he found a line. With this round him he plunged without hesitation into the water and succeeded in rescuing the wounded men from

USCG Rescue Flotilla, cutter No. 1 was under the command of Lieutenant Commodore Alexander V. Stewart Jr. Here it is typing up against an LCT(S), which itself is by the side of a much larger vessel from which the photograph was taken.

the landing craft despite the surf and the machine-gun fire of the enemy. For this act of extreme gallantry Paul Kozub was decorated with the Navy and Marine Corps Medal.

While the work of the landing craft in bringing the troops and their equipment into the correct positions on the beaches was being carried out with such determination and skill, the organisation of the beaches themselves was proceeding apace. This was a matter of tremendous importance. If the beaches had not been properly organised they would have quickly become "bottlenecks" in the system of supply and reinforcement to the troops who had fought their way inland. Moreover, the beaches would quickly have become choked with men, equipment, vehicles and stores, thus impeding further unloading in addition to presenting valuable and vulnerable targets to the enemy. The task of organising the beaches would have been difficult enough even if there had been no enemy opposition whatever.

The officers and men who had to control the beaches were landed with the first wave of the assault. They had to begin their work from "scratch" under fire and be prepared for an ever-increasing flow of men, vehicles and stores. The officers in charge of reinforcements had to be shown the way to the units they had to join. The drivers of vehicles had to be guided. Landing craft had to be shown where to "touch down" in the sectors which had been cleared of obstructions. The moment landing craft had been unloaded they had to be got away from the beaches to make room for their successors of the following waves. Landing craft which had "broached to" in the surf or which had been so damaged that they could not put back to sea had to be hauled out of the way by tractors or pushed out of the way by bulldozers. Notices and direction posts had to be put up. Above all, efficient communications had to be established at once with ships and with the headquarters of military formations fighting their way off the beaches and inland.

The task of organising the beaches was one demanding an instantaneous grasp of a rapidly changing situation, tireless energy, and almost unlimited patience, coupled with tremendous driving force. It was a task which, in the initial stages, fell almost entirely upon the Royal Navy Beach Commandos, although the army beach parties were soon on the scene to lend a most welcome and efficient hand.

In planning "Operation Neptune" the Allied Naval Commander-in-Chief had given great thought to the problem of organisation on the beaches, and this was well repaid by the way in which the Royal Navy Beach Commandos dealt with their manifold problems. They worked under the direction of a Naval Officer in Charge of each beach. On the British and Canadian sectors these officers were:

SWORD beach	Captain W. R. C. Leggatt, RN
GOLD beach	Captain G. V. M. Dolphin, RN
JUNO beach	Captain C. D. Maud, DSO, DSC, RN

In the Royal Naval Beach Commandos there were many officers and men who were specially trained signalmen and wireless operators familiar with military as well as the naval technique of signalling. Some of these were attached to the military beach parties, and it is for this reason that one sometimes saw, say, a Sub-Lieutenant of the RNVR wearing the "RN Commando" flash on the shoulder of his khaki battledress, below his RNVR shoulder-straps, and below that the coloured insignia of a corps or division of the British Army.

D-day drew to a close with the armies of liberation firmly established inland from every beach assailed, and with more men, vehicles and stores being constantly landed on every beach. In that day an average of over 21,000 men had been landed an four of the five beaches—the exception being OMAHA beach where the rate of landing had been slowed down by the bitter opposition and the long struggle for the beach. On that day, too, 3,200 vehicles and 2,500 tons of stores had been landed on one beach alone JUNO beach, where the Canadians had been landed. Admiral Sir Bertram Ramsay's determination to land the maximum in the minimum of time was being amply fulfilled, and three successes had already been scored—the invasion armadas had not been bombed in their ports of assembly; they had not been attacked on passage; and they had not met crippling opposition on the beaches. "Operation Neptune" was going "according to plan."

The Front page of *The New York Times*, 6 June 1944. With Britain being on war-time double-summer-time, the East Coast time was six hours behind, enabling the press to achieve a same-day scoop.

CHAPTER V

THE ROYAL MARINE COMMANDOS

Landing under fire in a seaway—Battle for the Langrune-sur-Mer strongpoint—Battle for the Lion-sur-Mer château—a long march through enemy-held territory—The battle for Port-en-Bessin— The struggle east of the River Orne.

Royal Marine Commandos played a most important part in the assault on Europe. They were allotted various tasks, all of them exceedingly difficult of achievement, but they achieved them all, although unhappily they suffered heavy losses in so doing. Of the major tasks which fell to them in what may be termed the initial coastal phase of the invasion two were concerned entirely with primary naval requirements, while another was of importance to the navy as well as to the army. To the Royal Marine Commandos goes the honour of having reduced and destroyed one of the worst of the German "hedgehogs" of defence along the coast of the Bay of the Seine, and also of having captured the first French port to fall into Allied hands.

All four of these feats of the Royal Marine Commandos during the initial coastal phase were entirely separate operations. It is convenient, therefore, to consider them one by one, while bearing in mind the fact that they were all in train at the same time. Nor must it be forgotten that these Royal Marine Commandos, once put ashore, were dependent upon themselves alone, although they did, in fact, get assistance from naval bombardment an from the military authorities in the areas in which they operated.

In the SWORD area—that on the eastern flank of the Allied landings, the Canadians were to land on the Bernières—St Aubin-sur-Mer beaches and press on inland at their best speed. The Third British Infantry Division were to land in the Lion-sur-Mer—Ouistreham area and were also to press inland as fast as possible. These two military forces would therefore leave a gap along the coast some 5 or 6 miles in length, and any enemy coast defence in this area which had not been destroyed by our bombardment or which subsequently "came to life" would thus be by-passed. The Royal Marine Commandos were to clear this coastal strip and liquidate any German positions or defences encountered.

To this end 48 Royal Marine Commando, under Lt-Colonel J. L. Moulton, RM, was to land at St Aubin-sur-Mer and clear the coastal fringe eastward through Langrune until they met 41 Royal Marine Commando, under Lt-Colonel T. M. Gray, RM, who were to land at Lion-sur-Mer and advance westward in the coastal area. It was planned that the junction of these two Commandos should take place a little to the west of the fishing village which rejoices in the name of Le Petit Enfer. That area was to live up to the name of the village it contained.

The troops were thoroughly "briefed" for their tasks before leaving England, but in the interests of security this was done using maps with bogus place names, and the real names of the objectives were not revealed to them until after they had embarked for the voyage to Normandy.

Both 48 and 41 Royal Marine Commandos crossed the English Channel in LCI(S)—(Landing Craft, Infantry, Small). These small craft are far from ideal for a sea voyage in weather which left a great deal to be desired. All the men were heavily laden with packs and equipment, and they also took with them some bicycles, motor cycles and hand carts.

Canadian troops ashore on 6 June 1944 at 'Nan-Red sector' (Saint-Aubin-sur-Mer). This beach was the objective of the North Shore (New Brunswick) Regiment, 8th Brigade 3rd Canadian Infantry Division on the morning of D-Day, with support from Shermans of the Fort Garry Horse (10th Armoured Regiment).

Canadian troops plod ashore, some with bicycles.

The six LCI(S) with 48 Royal Marine Commando on board began to close the shore at St Aubin-sur-Mer at about 7.30 a.m. As the craft drew in towards the beach it seemed as if the landing was to be unopposed, for there was no sign of life from the enemy.

Suddenly, however, when the craft were within a few hundred yards of the beach, the German strongpoint at St Aubin-sur-Mer opened fire with machine-guns. This strongpoint was almost directly ahead of the port wing craft. This machine-gun fire seemed to be the signal to other strongpoints and batteries, for in a moment or two the landing craft were also under mortar and shell fire. The landing craft replied to this fire with their Oerlikon guns, and some 2-inch mortar smoke shells were fired by the craft carrying the headquarters personnel, but the smoke did not prove dense enough to afford much cover. The landing craft carrying Z Troop was hit amidships, but struggled on towards the beach.

Worse was to follow. Two of the six landing craft struck underwater obstacles while still 150-200 yards off the shore. The obstacles held them and they were unable to get free and go in to the beach. These two craft carried Y and Z Troops, and the Marines of these two troops had to swim for the shore. Many of them, even strong swimmers, failed to master the very strong undertow and were drowned, while others were carried far down the coast.

Marines of 48 (RM) Commando coming ashore from landing craft at St Aubin-sur-Mer on Juno Beach, 6 June 1944.

Troop Sergeant-Major Travers, for instance, was carried far to the eastward and succeeded in reaching the shore over a mile away only to find himself right under the guns of the German strongpoint at Langrune.

The landing craft carrying the headquarters also struck a submerged obstacle, but she was close in to the beach before doing so, and the troops which she carried were able to wade ashore. The men of the three other troops—A, B and X Troops—also had to wade ashore as the ramps of the LCI(S) proved useless in the seaway. Either they were shaken loose by the sea or their outboard ends floated, making them impossible for heavily laden troops to negotiate.

Other craft in the vicinity were quick to come to the rescue of the Royal Marine Commandos in the LCI(S)'s which were stranded on the obstacles offshore. One LCA (Landing Craft, Assault) under a stout-hearted young Leading Seaman, made two trips to the beach, landing men of Z Troop. A number of men of Y Troop, however, fell victim to one of the most infuriating episodes which can ever have happened. About 50 men of this troop were rescued by an LCT (Landing Craft, Tank) from their own wrecked craft, only to find that the LCT was under orders to proceed at once to England—so to England those Royal Marines had to go, despite their energetic protests. To their bitter disappointment at "missing the party" was added the realisation that their Commando was now not up to strength. As a result of this, and the losses sustained by both Y and Z Troops, these two troops were amalgamated into one after reaching the shore.

Once ashore, the men were sheltered against the enemy's small arms fire so long as they kept close under the sea wall and the low earth cliff on the landward edge of the beach, but any movement away from this shelter was promptly greeted by machine-gun fire. At the same time the whole beach area was under constant German shell and mortar fire. The beach was a shambles. It was narrow and was congested with tanks, self-propelled guns, and other vehicles. Some of them were trying to find a way to move inland. Others were wrecked. The strip of sheltered ground under the sea wall and earth cliff was a jumble of men from many different units, among whom there were many dead and wounded.

Within a few minutes, however, reconnaissance revealed that there was a gap in the minefield along the shoreward side of the beach. This gap was only about 200 yards to the westward, and the Royal Marines infiltrated through this gap singly and in small groups and reached the appointed Assembly Area a short distance inland. This Assembly Area was fortunately fairly quiet.

The Marines mustered in the Assembly Area and contact was made with the Canadians and orders were then given for the advance to the eastward to begin. B Troop moved straight to the beach defences immediately to the east of St Aubin-sur-Mer. B Troop was soon able to report their section of the

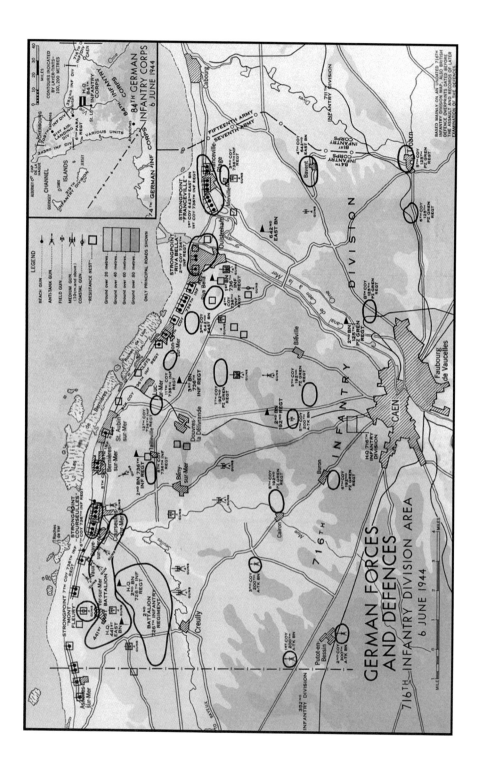

GERMAN FORCES AND DEFENCES
716TH INFANTRY DIVISION AREA
6 JUNE 1944

beach defences cleared of the enemy, and X Troop was sent ahead to clear up the next sector of the beach defences. Meanwhile, an advance guard formed of men of A Troop moved eastwards a short distance inland and this occupied the inland portions of the village of Langrune without incident.

Langrune-sur-Mer, however, contained a German strongpoint on the sea front which was well designed and strongly held and gave 48 Royal Marine Commando a great deal of trouble.

For their strongpoint the Germans had selected a block of houses and buildings between the sea front road and the parallel street next inland, and between two adjacent streets running down to the sea front. The sea wall itself was surmounted by concertina barbed wire and backed by trenches dug in the sea wall road. Both approaches along the sea front road were blocked—the wide road from the west by a mass of wire and mines stretching for fifty yards, and the narrow road from the east by anti-personnel mines.

To the westward the next road inland was blocked by a concrete road block with mines and barbed wire. At each of the two cross roads where this street intersected the two streets running down to the sea front there were machine-gun posts, centrally placed so as to be able to fire down any of the intersecting streets. These machine-gun posts were sunk in the roadway, had concrete cupolas, and were connected to the adjacent reinforced buildings of the strongpoint by underground passages. The other defences consisted of machine-guns and 5 cm anti-tank guns in emplacements firing to seaward, a number of mortars, and snipers and grenade throwers. All the buildings had doors and windows bricked up, and the easterly road running down to the sea front was blocked by a concrete wall 5 feet 6 inches high and 4 feet thick. This was backed by trenches. The whole length of the wall along the road parallel to the sea front was faced and topped by tangled concertina barbed wire.

The Langrune-sur-Mer strongpoint was, in fact, a very tough nut indeed, for all the fixed weapons were well-sited and gardens and streets gave these and the snipers good fields of fire.

X Troop of 48 Royal Marine Commando, having cleared their sector of the beach defences immediately to the westward of Langrune-sur-Mer, tried to advance into the village along the sea front road and that running parallel to it some 50 or 60 yards inland, but they soon found themselves held up by machine-gun fire from the area of the cross roads. This was, of course, one of the westerly defences of the German strongpoint. Unable to work their way eastward they began to work round inland and then tried to attack towards the sea along the westerly street leading to the sea front, but were again held up by machine-gun fire from the cross roads.

For the sake of simplicity in describing the ensuing battle this street will be alluded to as "Street No. 1," and the easterly street leading to the sea front as "Street No. 2."

When Lt-Colonel Moulton received the report that X Troop had been unable to make headway, either to the eastward along the lateral street or along "Street No. 1," he decided to ask for a naval bombardment to encourage the Germans to "keep their heads down" and to follow this without delay by two probing movements.

The naval bombardment was duly carried out by LCG's (Landing Craft, Gun), and was lifted at 3.30 p.m. The Royal Marines at once began to advance towards the sea front, X Troop down "Street No. 1" and B Troop down "Street No. 2." Both X and B Troops reached and crossed the railway, but both were then met by machine-gun fire from the cross-road positions, sniping down the streets, and mortar fire from the gardens.

X Troop in "Street No. 1" very soon ran into thickly sown mines. The troop lost a number of men as a result of these mines and the machine-gun fire from the cross roads ahead of them, and they consequently did not succeed in progressing far down the street.

B Troop succeeded in making slow progress down "Street No. 2" and by 6.15 p.m. they were only about 50 yards from the machine-gun post at the cross roads. At that time, however, Captain Perry, the Commanding Officer of this troop, was killed by a sniper. Second-Lieutenant Rubinstein at once took over command and pressed on slowly to within 20 yards of the cross roads and machine-gun position. Here, however, B Troop reached the edge of a cleared area, where the Germans had demolished a building in order to give themselves a better field of fire, and the Royal Marines met such intense cross-fire as well as fire down the street that Second-Lieutenant Rubinstein had to report that he and his men were held up and unable to advance farther.

At this stage in the proceedings one Centaur light tank of the Royal Marine Armoured Support Regiment was sent to back up each troop. The one which reinforced B Troop in "Street No. 2" did a good deal of damage to the houses around the cross-roads, but its high explosive shells could make no impression on the anti-tank wall across the street on the far side of the cross-roads or upon the reinforced buildings immediately to the eastward of it.

Under cover of this tank fire B Troop again attacked. Some men actually succeeded in getting across the cross roads and into two of the damaged houses on its north-west corner, but they could not get across the anti-tank wall or into the reinforced buildings east of it. Meanwhile a steady flow of stick grenades came over the wall, but these did surprisingly little damage. Since they could make no progress, however, the Marines were withdrawn from the two houses on the north-west corner of the cross roads, and the troop began to consolidate in the demolished buildings on the south-west corner of the cross roads. By this time the Centaur tank had run out of ammunition and had withdrawn. It had been replaced by another, but this ran into a mine and broke a track about 30 yards short of the cross roads. This tank blocked the

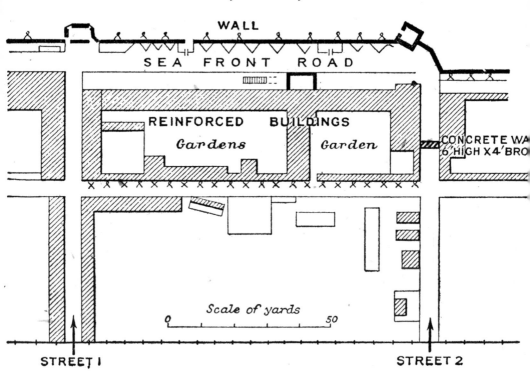

street and made it impossible for another tank to come up, but it did provide some shelter up the street from the machine-gun post at the cross-roads.

At 9 p.m. Lt-Colonel Moulton received information that a German counter-attack from landward was to be expected at dawn next day. This news placed him in a most awkward predicament. Two troops of the depleted force of 48 Royal Marine Commando were heavily committed in the battle for the Langrune-sur-Mer strongpoint; all his men had been fighting throughout a long day after a long and rough sea passage and a landing under heavy fire which had been anything but dryshod, officers and men were consequently very tired, and if a strong counter-attack should come from landward they would be between the counter-attacking enemy and the Langrune-sur-Mer strongpoint. It was not a pleasant prospect, but it had to he faced. Lieutenant-Colonel Moulton disengaged B and X Troops from the attack on the strongpoint and consolidated the whole remaining force of the Commando in the outskirts of the village, covering all approaches from landward. There the Royal Marines snatched such brief rest as they could consistent with watchfulness and instant readiness for the threatened counter-attack. Fortunately, the counter-attack never materialised. The Germans must either have been too preoccupied with the general situation or unwilling to accept the opportunity which was offered to them.

Next morning—that of D plus 1—the battle for the Langrune-sur-Mer strongpoint was resumed at 11.30 a.m., by which time all danger of a German counter-attack from landward had passed.

This time Lieutenant-Colonel Moulton concentrated his attacks on the cross-roads of "Street No. 2" and the lateral street between the railway and the sea front. He was determined that the anti-tank wall should be demolished so that a tank could reach the sea front, and he had arranged for the support of an "M.10" Special Anti-Tank gun to breach the anti-tank wall and the reinforced buildings.

First the minefield on which the Centaur tank had been wrecked the previous day was counter-mined by a "Bangalore Torpedo," which detonated the mines. (A "Bangalore Torpedo" is a long tube filled with explosive which can be pushed into a minefield or barbed wire entanglement and then fired.) The wreck of the Centaur tank was then moved and the "M.10" got through. Little further trouble was experienced with the cross-roads machine-gun post, and the "M.10" began to hammer away at the concrete anti-tank wall.

For an hour and a half the special anti-tank gun hammered away at the concrete anti-tank wall, and at the end of that time it had exhausted all its ammunition. The wall, however, was by that time far from being its former self, and the top half of it had been breached. Having fired all its ammunition the "M.10" then withdrew, and its place was taken by a Sherman tank of the Royal Marines Armoured Support Regiment. The Sherman then "had a go" at the wall, but it still proved to be an anti-tank obstacle.

At this stage A Troop advanced over the cross-roads and secured two houses on either side of the wall. Under the protection afforded by A Troop in these houses, B and Z Troops came up armed with picks, shovels and explosives. They further demolished the wall, blew up a house, and used the rubbish from this to build a causeway over the remains of the wall for the Sherman tank and to fill up the trenches on the sea side of the wall. No praise can be too high for the men who devoted themselves to this task with battle raging all round them.

Thus the Sherman tank was able to cross the obstacle at about 3 o'clock in the afternoon. It reached the terrace along the sea front, but while turning to go along this it ran a track into a communication trench. The tank was ditched and immobilised, but fortunately it was in such a position that it could rake the sea front with machine-gun fire.

Meanwhile A Troop had been fighting its way westwards from the No. 2 Street cross-roads, through the houses along the north side of the street. These houses were, in fact, part of the German strongpoint. It was a house-to-house struggle, entailing breaching the walls between one house and the next or one garden and the next, but the Royal Marines made rapid progress despite the difficulties and the continuous mortar fire, sniping and grenade throwing.

The Germans, faced with the progress of A Troop through their southern

defences, with their northern defences swept by machine-gun fire from the
Sherman tank and their eastern defences largely demolished, decided to
surrender.

The battle of the Langrune-sur-Mer strongpoint was over. It had been
difficult and costly, but it had long been appreciated that the reduction of
such strongpoints, prepared over a term of years and usually manned by
picked German troops, would constitute one of the major difficulties in the
initial stages of the invasion. Thirty-one German prisoners were taken in the
Langrune-sur-Mer strongpoint. The arms captured included a 5 cm anti-
tank gun, three machine-guns, a "Bazooka" type gun, several 5 cm mortars,
an anti-tank rifle and a number of small arms. Inspection of the strongpoint
demonstrated the thoroughness with which the Germans had built these
prepared positions. The trenches and gun emplacements and mortar pits were
lined with concrete, and ranges and other data were painted on the walls of
the gun emplacements and mortar pits so that fire could be directed against
any point without any German having to expose himself. Outlying positions
such as the machine-gun posts on the cross-roads were connected to the main
strongpoints by underground passages. It is not without interest that the
Royal Marines who finally reduced this "fortress" in the built-up area had
been trained for such fighting in the ruined streets of the most-bombed areas
of London, as had many other men of the Royal Marine Commandos.

It will be remembered that the plan was for 48 Royal Marine Commando
to advance eastwards from St Aubin-sur-Mer and meet 41 Royal Marine
Commando, advancing westwards from Lion-sur-Mer, in the neighbourhood
of Le Petit Enfer.

Lieutenant-Colonel T. M. Gray, commanding 41 Royal Marine Commando,
had decided to divide his Commando into two forces. Force I, consisting of P
and Y Troops was to be under his command and would assault the known
German strongpoint in Lion-sur-Mer. One company of the South Lancashire
Regiment was to be available to support this force if necessary. Force II,
consisting of B and X Troops, was to be commanded by Major D. L. Barclay
and was to drive straight for the château to the west of Lion-sur-Mer—suspected of being a German strongpoint or headquarters—and capture it.

Forty-one Royal Marine Commando crossed the English Channel in five
LCI's (S) (Landing Craft, Infantry, Small). Shortly before 8 a.m. on D-day a
signal was received that the beaches at which the Royal Marines were to land
were not under fire. They may not have been at that time, but by 8.30 a.m.,
at which time, the craft were approaching the beach, it was painfully evident
that no such happy state of affairs existed. Shells and mortar bursts were seen
to be crashing down in unpleasant profusion on the beach, which was littered
with dead and wounded and with burnt-out tanks and vehicles. Shells also fell
around the craft, close enough to cause damage but fortunately causing no

casualties.

The LCI's "touched down" at 8.45 a.m. about 200 yards from the surf line and, unhappily, about 300 yards to the westward of the correct beaching position, where the enemy fire was not so intense.

P Troop, commanded by Captain B. J. B. Sloley, moved quickly to the eastward immediately on landing and got clear of the beach in a few minutes. Five minutes later A Troop, led by Captain C. N. P. Powell, DSO, followed, and these two troops moved inland to the first lateral road to await the other two troops. Eventually about a dozen men of X Troop arrived. They had had a bad time disembarking and on the beach and their commander, Captain H. E. Stratford, MC, and about 25 others had become casualties. The majority of the men of Y Troop arrived, but they reported that Major Barclay had been killed.

Lieutenant-Colonel Gray then decided to push on with the force at his disposal, and P, Y and A Troops accordingly moved into Lion-sur-Mer. Civilians in the village stated that the Germans had left at about 7 a.m., so Lieutenant-Colonel Gray ordered P Troop to occupy the strongpoint, followed by Y Troop.

Soon after this contact was made with B Troop, and it was learnt that the Commander of the Troop—Captain H. F. Morris—had become a casualty on the beach.

In Major Barclay, Captain Morris and Captain Stretford, the intended Force II had lost its commander and both troop commanders. In these circumstances Lieutenant-Colonel Gray decided to take the intended Force II, consisting of B and X Troops, under his own command.

No sooner had Lieutenant-Colonel Gray effected this change of plan than news was received that the enemy were still in parts of Lion-sur-Mer. P Troop reported that it was held up by snipers and machine-gun fire from houses on each side of the German strongpoint, and the South Lancashires also reported that the strongpoint was holding them up. The information given by the civilians had proved incorrect. The Germans had not left; they had merely been lying low.

The situation was not easy. Supporting fire from the Royal Navy could not be called for as one of the wireless sets for this purpose had been destroyed on the beach, when all the signalmen attached to the Forward Bombardment Officer had been wounded, and the only other wireless set had been damaged. P Troop was held down, and the South Lancashires were having casualties from machine-gun and mortar fire.

In these circumstances Lieutenant-Colonel Gray ordered B Troop, under Lieutenant Sturges, up the road towards the château to make contact with the South Lancashires and outflank the strongpoint, while Y Troop was sent to back up the South Lancashires and assault through them if possible. Y Troop was supported by three tanks which had just arrived.

Y Troop moved up behind the tanks and were within 100 yards of the strongpoint when the Germans opened fire with a 50 mm anti-tank gun. At almost point blank range this gun knocked out all three of the tanks within five minutes. At the same time heavy mortar fire came down on Y Troop, whose commander, Captain P. T. H. Dufton, was killed, and a number of other casualties inflicted.

B Troop also came under heavy mortar fire and shell fire from an unidentified mobile gun. This troop suffered casualties and was forced to report that it had been held up before making contact with the South Lancashires and could not advance unless some fire support was given in the neighbourhood of the château; but no support of any kind could be given, as all 3-inch mortar ammunition had already been used against the strongpoint.

Just after 1 p.m. A Troop reported having reached the houses immediately south of the strongpoint, but being under mortar and rifle fire from their left flank. Captain C. N. P. Powell, commanding A Troop, had been wounded. At the same time B Troop reported that the Germans were counter-attacking on the left flank with about 60 men supported by an infantry gun and mortars.

Lieutenant-Colonel Gray was quick to realise that this counter-attack might become general, in which case the situation of the Marines and South Lancashires, heavily committed and pinned down as they were, would became desperate. He accordingly made a difficult but courageous decision and withdrew all troops to a line east of the Lion-sur-Mer strongpoint.

In the early afternoon the situation improved. A jeep with a wireless set enabled contact to be made with the naval ships offshore and a bombardment by destroyers of the strongpoint and the château was arranged, At the same time strong army reinforcements were sent, a battalion of the Lincolnshire Regiment and a battalion of the Royal Ulster Rifles being detailed to complete the perimeter round the strongpoint and château.

The bombardment by destroyers lasted from 4 p.m. to 6 p.m., during which time there was intermittent shell and mortar fire from the enemy.

Next morning—D plus 1—three Heinkels with Spitfires on their tails suddenly swooped out of the clouds and dropped, or jettisoned, three sticks of bombs. As luck would have it all these bombs straddled the headquarters of the Royal Marine Commando, which had been set up in an orchard. They killed the Forward Bombardment Officer and two men and wounded Lieutenant-Colonel Gray, the chaplain, and nine men.

Soon after this unhappy incident the Lincolnshires and 41 Royal Marine Commando successfully reduced the strongpoint and the château, and that evening the remainder of 41 Royal Marine Commando pushed on to Luc-sur-Mer and made contact with 46 Royal Marine Commando. It had originally been intended that this Commando, under the command of Lieutenant-

Colonel C. R. Hardy, should carry out raids on the enemy batteries at Houlgate or Beneville to the east of the River Orne. They had been embarked in two LSI (Landing Ships, Infantry) and, in view of their special task they carried specialised equipment such as climbing stores, demolition charges and pistols rather than battle equipment. They were consequently under a handicap when the raids on the batteries were cancelled and they were told to land at Luc-sur-Mer in an infantry role on the morning of 7 June—D plus 1.

The landing of 46 Royal Marine Commando, in contrast to those of 48 and 41 Commandos, was successfully carried out without casualties at 9 a.m. The first task was the capture of the German strongpoint at Le Petit Enfer. This was known to be formidable, but naval gunfire and tank support was available and an attack in three waves from the westward by the Royal Marines successfully reduced the position and led to the capture of 65 prisoners.

One of the most important tasks allocated to the Royal Marine Commandos during the assault on Normandy was the capture of Port-en-Bessin.

Port-en-Bessin lay just at the western limit of GOLD area, where the naval component commanded by Commodore C. Douglas-Pennant landed the 50th Northumbrian Division, commanded by Lieutenant-General G. C. Bucknall. To the west of Port-en-Bessin lay the American OMAHA area, and Commodore Douglas-Pennant had attached to his force some squadrons of American LST's (Landing Ship, Tank) commanded by Commander L. F. Teuscher, USN, one group of American LCT's (Landing Craft, Tank) commanded by Lieutenant-Commander W. Leide, USNR, and a squadron of American LCI(L)'s (Landing Craft, Infantry, Large) commanded by Lieutenant-Commander W. T. Patrick, USNR, as well as a Canadian flotilla of LCI(L) commanded by Lieutenant-Commander L. S. Kyle, RCNVR.

Port-en-Bessin is the port of Bayeux and a railway terminus. The harbour is sheltered by two long curved breakwaters, and the port itself lies at the north of the Dromme river in a deep cleft between two high hills. It was known that Port-en-Bessin was very strongly defended against frontal assault from seaward. It was for this reason that the capture of this important place had been entrusted to 47 Royal Marine Commando, commanded by Lieutenant-Colonel C. F. Phillips. The Royal Marine Commando had been trained for this task in the Dorset hills.

The plan was to assault the Port-en-Bessin defences from the landward side and thus take them in rear. It was realised that in order to do this the Royal Marines would have to make their way through about ten miles of enemy held territory after having been landed on a beach to the eastward of Port-en-Bessin. For this reason all weapons and supplies had to be carried on the back—the average weight carried by each man being 88 pounds.

The Commando was to land from fourteen LCA's (Landing Craft, Assault) close to the westward of Le Hamel, but when the flotilla was off Le Hamel it came under shell fire from a German strongpoint in that village—this was a

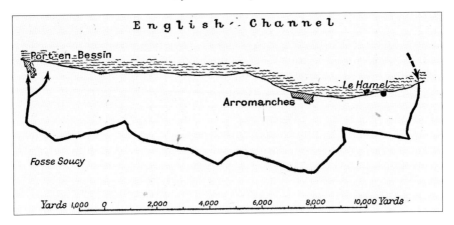

strongpoint which caused trouble until late in the afternoon of D-day. This shell fire, coupled with the fact that no activity could be seen on the beach, where there were a number of burning tanks, led to the decision to beach farther to the eastward.

Thus 47 Royal Marine Commando landed at 8.25 a.m. about one and a half miles to the east of Le Hamel. The final run into the beach of the LCA's was made exceedingly dangerous by the rough sea and the mined obstacles off the beach. Four of the fourteen LCA's struck these obstacles and were blown up about 400 yards from the beach. Many of the men in these craft were able to struggle ashore, but in most cases they lost their equipment in the process.

The beach was under mortar fire and the road inland from it was under machine-gun fire as well as mortar fire, and it became apparent that the military assault forces had not progressed as far inland as had been expected. The advanced rendezvous arranged was in the hamlet of La Rosière, a short distance inland, and it had been expected that this would be clear of the enemy by the time the Royal Marines arrived. This proved to be far from the case. On the way to the rendezvous the Marines had one brush and two small battles with the Germans, while La Rosière itself had to be fought for. It was taken by B Troop, which attacked under cover of smoke.

The difficulty of the landing and the subsequent clashes with the enemy had all led to delay, and it was not until 7.45 p.m. that the Commando was ready to resume its march. Good use had, however, been made of the time by re-equipping the men who had lost everything when they landed. This was done from German equipment which was captured in La Rosière.

After fighting another battle with a German detachment, and crossing a small river, the Commando arrived on "Hill 72," a prominent hill immediately south of Port-en-Bessin. There they dug in for the night. They were in a dangerous position, between the defences of Port-en-Bessin and a fortified German camp at Fosse Soucy, about a mile south of "Hill 72." The Germans, however, seemed to be quite unaware of the Commando's presence, despite the fact that the latter had found an enemy casualty station on the hill, where they had captured two doctors and four wounded men.

With the first light of D plus 1 patrols were sent out in all directions. It had been hoped that one of these would make contact with the United States forces to the westward but it failed to do so. Other patrols reported that the fortified camp at Fosse Soucy was deserted, and no enemy was encountered south of Port-en-Bessin. It was obvious, however, that the assault on Port-en-Bessin could not take place without gunfire support, and the task of arranging for the navy to supply this, as well as making contact with all the military authorities in the neighbourhood, fell upon a single wireless set, the other three having been lost during the landing.

The defences of Port-en-Bessin were disposed roughly in a triangle. There were powerful strongpoints on the heights east and west of the port, and a third smaller position immediately to the south of the town. The assault was planned to take place at 4 p.m., under cover of smoke provided by field artillery, and preceded by a naval bombardment beginning at 3 p.m., followed by air attacks on the three strongpoints ten minutes before the attack.

When some naval ships opened fire on the port at 2 p.m. it was feared that the timing had gone awry, but this preliminary bombardment turned out to be in the nature of a "bonus," for punctually at 3 p.m. the 6-inch gun cruiser HMS *Emerald* opened fire. Then, at 3.50 p.m. the rocket-firing fighters of the Air Force came in and plastered the three German positions with extreme accuracy. Then, according to plan, the smoke shells arrived from the 25-pounders, firing from away beyond Arromanches.

It all seemed most encouraging, but the Royal Marines had the unpleasant experience of being fired on from an enemy position behind them as they began their advance.

The small strongpoint south of the town was soon disposed of, and by 8.30 A Troop reported that they had taken the German position on the height to the west of the port. They had, however, been fired on from the rear by two German flak-ships lying in the harbour, and this fire had cost them eleven killed and fourteen wounded before the flak-ships were to some extent subdued by Bren gun and mortar fire. The attack on the eastern strongpoint was not progressing so well, having been held up by confused street fighting in the town.

At about this time the Germans to the south of Port-en-Bessin suddenly came to life and put in a fairly strong counter-attack on "Hill 72," where the headquarters of the Commando had been established. The Royal Marines unfortunately mistook the Germans at first for Americans, who were expected to arrive at any moment. As a result of this counter-attack the Germans overran the position on "Hill 72," capturing about 20 Marines and releasing some of their own prisoners. Most of the Marines subsequently regained the Allied lines.

It was becoming very doubtful if the strong position on the height east of the town could be taken that night, but Captain T. F. Cousins said that he had found and reconnoitred a zigzag path up the hill and thought that he could get up to the German position with twenty-five men by that route.

Captain Cousins was given between forty and fifty men and set out. It was like a miniature replica of the storming of the Heights of Abraham at Quebec by General Wolfe. At dusk Captain Cousins and his men reached the skyline and they at once assaulted the German defences. These they penetrated, while at the same time another troop attacked from the extreme right. This troop also penetrated the German defences, and captured the German commandant in his dugout. The German commandant was induced to lead the Marines forward through the mines and summon the remainder of the German garrison to surrender, and this they did.

It was found that the whole top of the hill was honeycombed with dugouts and trenches. Mopping up was therefore a slow business and Captain Cousins unhappily lost his life in the process.

Over a hundred prisoners were taken from the strongpoint on the hill to the east of the port, and during the night the two flak-ships in the harbour also decided to surrender. Port-en-Bessin was in Allied hands.

Away to the eastward, on the extreme left flank of the invasion of Normandy, another Royal Marine Commando landed on the morning of D-day. This was 45 Royal Marine Commando, under Lieutenant-Colonel N. C. Ries, which formed part of Brigadier Lord Lovat's 1st Special Service Brigade. The task of the Royal Marine Commando was to get across the River Orne and try to secure the eastern side of its estuary, or at all events to form a hard front against the enemy on that flank to the east of the seaward reaches of the river.

Forty-five Royal Marine Commando landed safely at La Brèche, on the western outskirts of Ouistreham, at 9.10 a.m. on D-day. Ouistreham is on the western side of the mouth of the Caen Canal, and it was intended that the Royal Marines should cross the canal and the River Orne in rubber dinghies in order to seize positions on the east bank of the river.

So well, however, had the 6th Airborne Division done their work that the bridges between Benouville and Ranville had been captured intact. The Royal Marine Commando consequently crossed the canal and the river by these bridges. On the way to the bridges, however, snipers made themselves a nuisance and Lieutenant-Colonel Ries was wounded, so that Major N. M. Gray assumed command.

After crossing the River Orne the Commando swung northwards, but on entering the village of Sallesnelles it came under fire from a German strongpoint near the river and north of Sallesnelles. As time was getting on Major Gray decided to by-pass this position and push on to Franceville, to the east of the river mouth, but a message was received from the Brigade Headquarters that the Royal Marine Commando was not to go beyond Merville, about halfway between Sallesnelles and Franceville, but were to dig in there for the night.

It was already apparent that the scale of German resistance east of the River Orne was considerably greater than had been anticipated, a fact which led to the belief that German Field Formations had recently moved into that area for exercises, as had proved to be the case in the OMAHA area.

Next morning—D plus 1—45 Royal Marine Commando was ordered to withdraw from Merville and dig in south of Sallesnelles. There it came under fire from mortars in the vicinity of the strongpoint which it had bypassed on the previous day.

In the early afternoon orders were received to push on again towards Franceville, but as soon as the Royal Marine Commando began to move it came under heavy shell fire. Rear-Admiral Sir Philip Vian, commanding the Eastern Task Force, alluded to the troublesome German mobile guns firing from the woods south of Franceville, and of the difficulty in locating these.

Under cover of fire from a 6-pounder gun and some machine-guns, however, the Commando continued to push slowly forward. Sallesnelles was passed, and 5.5 p.m. the attack of Franceville was launched. Two troops succeeded in fighting their way into the northern end of the village, but at 9 p.m. the Germans counter-attacked strongly, supported by mortars and machine-guns. The Royal Marine Commando had by this time lost its 3-inch mortars and its radio set as a result of casualties. It could therefore neither provide any support itself nor call for support from other units of the 1st Special Service Brigade. It was consequently forced to fall back again to Merville, where it spent the night while three men were sent to the Brigade Headquarters to report the situation. These three men returned in the morning with another wireless set and orders that the Merville position was to be held at all costs.

Next morning—that of D plus 2—the general position in the Merville area deteriorated. Two heavy attacks on the positions held by the depleted ranks of 45 Royal Marine Commando were driven off, but the Germans had brought up an anti-tank gun and were continuously shelling and mortaring the Commando's positions. At about 5 p.m. that day the Commando was ordered to fight its way back through the German lines and rejoin the remainder of the 1st Special Service Brigade in the Amfréville area. The Royal Marines had a very hard fight to get back, but they finally broke through by about 8 p.m., silencing two German machine-gun positions and capturing one 81 mm mortar on the way.

That night the survivors of 45 Royal Marine Commando rested in the church at Amfréville before taking up the defensive positions which they were to hold for several weeks, during which they drove off enemy attacks and repeatedly asserted their moral superiority over the Germans by the audacity of their active and offensive patrolling.

CHAPTER VI

THE GERMANS REACT

Air attacks on the anchorage—The German mining offensive—Killing the U-boats before they could attack—the U-boats try the "schnorkel."

During dark hours opportunity was taken to open fire on enemy aircraft with close-range weapons." That laconic sentence is taken from the official report of the Sixth Minesweeping Flotilla, commanded by Commander J. C. Richards, RN in HMS *Vestal*. It referred to the night of D-day. The operative words in that sentence are undoubtedly "dark hours." The air cover put up by the Allies air forces over the Assault Area during and after the invasion was such that strong enemy air attack, which might have done tremendous damage among the crowded ships and craft in the anchorages off the beaches, did not materialise. That is not to say that there were no enemy air attacks by day. There were sixteen such attacks in the first twenty-four days—up to 30 June—but they were all of the "sneak" raid variety, carried out mostly by single German aircraft which came in low, either under the protection of low cloud or the fog of battle and smoke of burning buildings. Day after day the Allied fighter patrols not only gave protection to the Assault Area, but ranged inland over France to a depth of seventy-five miles—yet it was seldom indeed that they encountered German aircraft in the air by daylight.

The "sneak" raids, nevertheless, had considerable nuisance value, for the usual air raid alarms were sounded for them and, to begin with, those on the sea and in the beachheads found it impossible to believe that no major German air attacks could develop.

On one occasion only did a daylight "sneak" raid have more than a nuisance value. That was at 6 a.m. on D plus 1, when HMS *Bulolo*, the headquarters ship of Commodore C. Douglas-Pennant, commanding in the GOLD area, was hit by a 250-kilo phosphorous bomb. The bomb blew a hole in the forward bulkhead of the operations room, and there is no doubt that if it had pitched a few feet farther aft the entire operations staff would have been wiped out.

As it was, the efficiency of the ship in controlling the area was not impaired, although three officers and one rating were killed.

The "nuisance value" of these "sneak" raids ironically recoiled upon the Allied air forces which precluded the enemy doing anything more, for the ship and craft and the men on the beaches were prone to regard any aircraft coming in low as necessarily enemy.

The personnel of the Royal Observer Corps embarked in ships and craft for "Operation Neptune" did wonders and performed great feats of endurance, but so many of the personnel engaged in the invasion had little experience of aircraft recognition in circumstances where an instant's delay might mean death or the loss of a ship and messmates, that one can hardly blame them if their instinct was to shoot first and ask questions afterwards. To use the colloquialism of the day, they were "trigger-happy."

Authority, however, was quick to put a stop to a state of affairs which was leading to our own aircraft being fired on when proceeding "upon their lawful occasions" over the Assault Area, and the strictest orders were issued to all craft that no aircraft were to be fired on during daylight hours.

At night it was very different. Until the final break-out of the beachhead not a night passed without German aircraft coming over the anchorages. The night fighter and intruder patrols were increased and they certainly took toll of the enemy, but they were unable to put a stop to the nightly raids.

These German aircraft robbed a great many men of the few hours of rest that they might have been able to snatch, but that was the least of their achievements. Each night some of the German aircraft used to bomb ships, and attack craft by cannon and machinegun fire whenever opportunity offered; but it very soon became obvious that the main German air effort was being devoted to minelaying in the anchorages and the approaches to them and to the beaches, and that the bombing attacks were by way of being diversions, or hopeful incidentals.

One of the best descriptions of a German aircraft engaged on one of these night bombing attacks was written just after the event by a Royal Marine who was coxswain of one of the smaller landing craft—one of the many thousands of Marines who manned these vessels for the invasion. The aircraft was attacking a warship which was firing streams of tracer at it. "The plane seemed to be diving into a jet of fire. She came screaming down with two headlights on like an infuriated owl. She had no chance of getting away with it. She spouted flame, fell off her course, and came heading straight for our craft out of control. Waiting for the crash I had just time to realise that this was no film, when the plane canted to port, slipped into the water well short of us, and blew up."

Any number of aircraft up to fifty used to come over the anchorages every night, and the great majority of these were employed on minelaying. There was no doubt that the main counter to invasion being employed by Admiral Krancke—who commanded the German naval forces in the west under von Rundstedt—was a concentrated mining campaign for which he had secured the use of practically the total force of German bombers available in the west.

On the night of D-day there were a great many enemy aircraft over the Assault Area, and some ships saw parachute mines falling into the sea. The enemy mining activity at this juncture was directed chiefly against the American sectors, particularly in the UTAH area and the neighbourhood of Cardonnet. In these areas no less than thirty ground mines were detonated on D plus 1. Unhappily these mines claimed seven ship casualties, including two American destroyers and the United States Fleet Minesweeper *Tide*. Thereafter, however, the centre of gravity of the German minelaying effort appeared to move to the eastward to the British sector, although the American sector was by no means left free. In the British sector, for instance, the 31st Minesweeping Flotilla, which was manned by Canadians and commanded by Acting Commander A. J. G. Storrs, RCNR in HMCS *Caraquet*, detonated 19 mines on D plus 2 and no less than 42 mines on D plus 3.

Strong action had to be taken without delay to counter the threat posed by a minelaying campaign of such intensity in the limited area and shallow waters of the Bay of the Seine. The work of the minesweepers, and particularly of the flotillas of small minesweepers, known as BYM's, which were capable of working in the shallow waters close inshore, had to be redoubled. A mine-watching organisation had also to be set up to watch the fall of the parachute mines and mark their positions for the next day's sweeping.

All this entailed a mounting strain upon the minesweepers. They were sweeping all day and at night some of them had to take their place in the defence lines around the anchorages while others had to take up their positions for the nightly task of mine-watching, a task requiring great watchfulness and accurate plotting of the positions of the mines. Their daily task of sweeping, had, moreover, to be done against time and often against weather conditions, while the traffic in the anchorages did nothing to make their task easier. There could be no question of waiting for the right tide and weather or for the line of the sweep to be kept clear of shipping.

They felt, moreover, that any and every delay in their sweeping, either due to weather, to sweeps being carried away, or any other cause, could only mean that the concentration of mines would be increased during the next night and that the odds were consequently piling up against them. It was clear that the Germans were well aware of this, and they did everything possible to delay the minesweeping and to make it more difficult.

It had long been maintained that the Italians were the greatest adepts at mine warfare, but the Germans surpassed any tricks which the Italians have been known to use. The German has always been ingenious in the making of mechanical and electrical toys and contrivances, and when he combines this ability with devices to prevent or hinder minesweeping he is capable of almost anything.

Thus, the minesweepers had to contend with magnetic mines and acoustic mines. Others embodied both the magnetic and acoustic properties at the same time. Others, again, were fitted with clocks which made them unresponsive to anything for a day or more, so that they could be swept over without result and the area pronounced "clear of mines" before they "came to life." Some of the German mines had to be swept over many times before they became "alive."

Practically all these types of mines required different treatment from the minesweepers. The Germans knew this and they cunningly mixed them all up. Moreover, they also sowed all sorts of anti-sweeping devices, carefully devised to put the sweeping gear of the minesweepers out of action—usually just before they passed over a particularly unhealthy patch of mines.

The men of the minesweepers, with their irrepressible humour, used to speak of their ships "being de-bagged" when they were robbed of their sweeping gear by one or other of the German devices, and this "de-bagging" of the ships proved to be one of their major troubles. Not only did it demand constant work in repairing the sweeping gear, but it made prodigious demands upon the supply organisation for replacements. Fortunately neither the supply organisation nor the endurance of the minesweepers' crews proved unequal to the great demands made upon them.

As an instance of the trouble caused by the German anti-sweeping devices one may quote the experience of the 14th Minesweeping Flotilla, commanded by Commander J. W. A. Irvine, RNR, in HMS *Romney*. On D plus 2 this flotilla encountered a great many of these anti-sweeping devices. Eleven mines were swept and no less than 25 anti-sweeping devices were encountered. Seven of these "de-bagged" sweepers but—a great triumph—one of the German anti-sweeping devices was recovered intact and sent to the Admiralty for investigation.

The small minesweepers working close inshore had yet another problem with which to contend. This was due to the amount of wreckage and other flotsam off the beaches, which was apt to damage the screws of the small shallow-draught BYM's. This problem did not, however, become really acute until after the great gale of D plus 13 to D plus 16. After that gale Lieutenant-Commander J. H. Butler, RNVR, commanding the 165th Minesweeping Flotilla, composed of BYM's, reported that six of his ten ships had damaged screws owing to drifting wreckage and ropes' ends. It was, nevertheless, a very real problem for these little minesweepers from D-day onwards. Later on, the flotsam in and around the anchorages became a nuisance and a danger on a different count—because it was so apt to be confused with the large numbers of novel and ingenious German decoys and booby traps dropped in the area or floated down by the tide in order to confuse the defences and create general "alarm and despondency."

In order to deal with the menace Captain A. F. Pugsley, who was Captain of Patrols guarding the anchorages, instituting "scavenging days," on which every craft under his command had to hoist every two hours flags denoting the number of bits of wreckage and flotsam recovered. Captain Pugsley rewarded the winning craft at the end of the "scavenging day" with an issue of "Mars bars"—a chocolate confection very popular with the sailors. On one "scavenging day" a certain craft omitted to hoist her two-hourly total and it was thought that she had not "scored" at all, while at the end of the day another craft proudly hoisted the figure 149 and "stood by" to receive the prizes of "Mars bars." Within a minute or two, however, the craft which had omitted to hoist two-hourly totals hoisted a figure of well over 200! Captain Pugsley duly fined this vessel for not making the two-hourly reports, but even so he found that he had not got enough "Mars bars" to go round—an incident which, needless to say, was taken in good part by all concerned.

Apart altogether from the valuable work done in clearing floating wreckage and jetsam from the anchorage—it was landed at the end of each "scavenging day"—the rivalry which the system produced among craft working day and night in what Captain Pugsley afterwards described as "the most bloody awful corner in the world" (the north-eastern corner of the British Assault Area), proved of tremendous value to the morale of the crews.

In the eastern—the British—sector of the Assault Area the German minelaying effort continued to mount steadily for nearly a fortnight after D-day. So far as enemy action was concerned, the German mining campaign was the only source of the major anxiety felt by Admiral Sir Bertram Ramsay, the Allied Naval Commander-in-Chief. Admiral Ramsay was always confident that the mine menace would be overcome in the end, but he was acutely conscious of the great strain under which the crews of his minesweepers had to work day and night almost without interruption for long periods, and that as time went on more and more of these little ships began to show signs of requiring repair. All manner of defects were becoming apparent as the result of the frequent explosion of mines in close proximity to their hulls. Singly, these defects mattered little, but they threatened to have a cumulative effect. The repair and maintenance organisation on the far shore did wonders, and to the officers and men of this organisation must go much of the credit for keeping not only minesweepers but a host of other craft in running order when none of these could be spared to visit a British dockyard.

The concentration of mines in the Assault Area was such that on one occasion when a Minesweeping Flotilla of BYM's switched on the electrical impulse gear one morning to begin sweeping for magnetic mines, no less than

23 mines "went up" in their vicinity within a few seconds. It was, as one of the officers feelingly said, "One hell of an explosion," for the smallest of these mines contained seven hundred pounds of high explosive. There were several other occasions on which nine or ten mines detonated as soon as the electrical impulse gear was switched on preparatory to sweeping.

In order to cope with the situation produced by the large scale German mining offensive it was necessary for risks to be taken which would in other circumstances have been deemed unjustifiable. Moreover, everything possible was done to try to reduce and restrict the number of ships off the beaches and therefore in the danger area. So gigantic and rapid was the build-up of the strength of the invasion armies and of their requirements in equipment, vehicles and stores, that the average number of ships in the Assault Area was between three and four hundred. This was reduced to some extent during the height of the German mining offensive, but it could not be greatly reduced without effecting a corresponding reduction in the scale and the rate of the build-up of the Allied armies. Against this Admiral Sir Bertram Ramsay most resolutely set his face. Come what might, the armies should get all that they required both for maintenance and for reinforcement. Other means would have to he found to eke out the naval resources so that the difficulties imposed by the German mining should be overcame. The only "other means" possible entailed a further increase of the burdens of danger and responsibility imposed upon the minesweepers, but they responded without question. Even so, it was found to be quite impossible to keep the Assault Area swept and at the same time maintain all the wide swept channels leading to it which had by this time replaced the ten narrow swept channels running south from "Piccadilly Circus." The anchorages had to be kept swept, so the minesweepers on this endless task had to be reinforced by some of those which had up till then been engaged in widening the cross-Channel routes and keeping them clear by daily sweeps. This meant a narrowing of the swept channels running across to Normandy from England. This was a serious matter, for the daily traffic in these channels amounted to sixteen convoys, with an average number of fifteen ships in each convoy—a total of nearly 150 ships a day exclusive of warship traffic and groups of landing craft. Nevertheless, it had to be accepted as the lesser of two evils.

By D plus 16 more than 90 ground mines had been accounted for in the eastern area alone, and on three of those sixteen days minesweeping had been quite impossible owing to the great gale. And in that time three ships had been sunk and twelve damaged by mines in the eastern area—an astonishingly low dividend for the German minelaying effort. It must be borne in mind that a ship sunk in the Assault Area did not only mean the loss of ship and cargo, but might well produce a navigational obstruction which would greatly impede and even endanger the movement of other ships. Such a contingency had to

be perpetually borne in mind, for it could not but lead to a slowing down of
the rate of the build-up of the armies. For this reason a special wreck-disposal
organisation was in constant readiness to tackle and move or destroy any
awkward wreck.

The severity of the German mining campaign in the Assault Area is
illustrated by the following three extracts from the log of one of His Majesty's
ships in the Assault Area on the morning of 24 June:

> 07.30—HMS *Swift* (destroyer) blew up on mine on port bow.
> 07.40—Motor-transport ship blew up on mine on starboard beam.
> 08.10—Unidentified ship well astern blew up on mine.

If one examines the German minelaying campaign off the Normandy
beaches as a whole, one finds that there was not very much difference between
the degree of concentration in the German mining in the British and American
areas. One would have expected rather more mines to be laid in the eastern
area than in the western area because the former was slightly nearer to the
main airfields used by the German aircraft employed on minelaying, and this
proved to be the case—at least in so far as the number of mines accounted for
was concerned.

From D-day to D plus 27 (3 July) the total number of mines accounted
for in the Assault Area was 552. Of these 291 had been accounted for in the
eastern, or British Assault Area, and 261 in the American or western area.
In the British Assault Area 95 moored mines and 177 ground mines were
accounted for between these dates, while there had been 19 ship casualties due

HMS *Swift* sinking off Normandy, 24 June 1944.

to mines in the area. In the American Assault Area in that period 91 moored mines had been swept, 146 ground mines accounted for, and there had been 24 ship casualties due to mines. Among the ships mined in the British area in this period was the cruiser HMS *Scylla*, which was wearing the flag of Rear-Admiral Sir Philip Vian, commanding the Eastern Task Force. HMS *Scylla* had just reached her night patrol area on the north-east corner of the British Assault Area when she was mined at 10.56 p.m. on 23 June. Fortunately she was only damaged and was able to reach a British dockyard for repair, and Rear-Admiral Vian, who was unhurt, transferred his flag to HMS *Hilary*, which had been serving as headquarters ship to Commodore G. N. Oliver in JUNO area.

The German minelaying campaign did not end on 3 July, but there was no doubt that its back had been broken by that date. Later, the Allied Naval Commander-in-Chief in alluding to the German minelaying effort and the strain which it had laid upon our minesweeping resources, stated that in three months in the Assault Area off Normandy the numbers of mines swept amounted to rather more than 10 per cent of the total number of mines swept in all theatres of war in five years. When one reflects upon the great German and Italian mining campaigns, one begins to appreciate the degree of concentration of the German mining campaign in the comparatively small Assault Areas of "Operation Neptune."

While the mining campaign was undoubtedly the Germans' main and most important counter to the invasion of Northern France, Admiral Sir Bertram Ramsay, as Allied Naval Commander-In-Chief, had to take many other possible German moves into account and take steps to counter them. He certainly could not work on the assumption that the German Admiral Krancke would put all his eggs in one basket—even if the "eggs" were particularly devilish types of mines and the "basket" were the Assault Area. It had, of course, long been realised that one of the chief dangers to the anchorages and to the lifeline of invasion across the English Channel might come from U-boats. There was no doubt that Germany had several hundred of these craft at her disposal, and it was reasonable to suppose that the German High Command would appreciate that the defeat of the Allied invasion of Northern Europe would be essential to the future of the Third Reich, and would therefore attack its sea lines of communication with the utmost force. Moreover, the Germans had good and long prepared operational U-boat bases on the flank of the invasion lifeline in Brest and the Biscay ports. The Allied Naval Commander-in-Chief had, in fact, worked out on the basis of all available intelligence that up to 200 U-boats might attack the western flank by D plus 19, considerably over half that number being available to attack during the preceding ten days. It had also been known that the main reinforcements for the U-boat flotillas based at Brest and in the Biscay ports came from the Bergen and Trondheim areas of Norway.

It had been for this reason that Coastal Command of the Royal Air Force had been asked to concentrate a considerable force on anti-U-boat operations off the southern part of the Norwegian coast for some time before D-day, and some anxiety had been lifted from Admiral Ramsay at the very gratifying results of this offensive. The anti-U-boat offensive by Coastal Command of the Royal Air Force off the Bergen and Trondheim areas of Norway began on 16 May. By the end of May there had been no less than twenty-two sightings of U-boats. Aircraft had been able to attack on thirteen occasions, and it was estimated that at least six certain "kills" had been obtained. Between the end of May and D-day the operations were hampered by weather, but other promising attacks were made and probable "kills" listed.

These results told Admiral Ramsay that the Germans had, in fact, been trying to send reinforcements to the U-boat flotillas in the west to operate against the invasion, which the Germans must have known by that time to be imminent. They also indicated that such a high rate of certain loss and probable damage had been inflicted upon the intended reinforcements that those which arrived would bear small relation to those sent out and would be likely to begin their tasks in the west in a chastened mood. It was, in fact, more than likely that the majority had put back to the shelter of the Norwegian fiords rather than face the long and dangerous passage of the North Sea, Fair Isle or Faroes Channels, and the Atlantic in order to join their comrades in the Biscay ports. On the morning of D-day, moreover, Admiral Ramsay received reports which showed that the U-boats stationed at Brest and in the Biscay ports had not left harbour. Here was encouraging proof that the enemy, knowing invasion to be imminent, was unaware of the date on which it was to be launched.

As soon as the news of the Allied assault in the Bay of the Seine reached the U-boat flotillas, however, they reacted quickly. The U-boats hurried to sea and began to try to close in to the attack on the western flank of the invasion area and its lines of communication with the southern English ports. The Allies, however, were ready for them. It was the time of year when the nights were at their shortest, and therefore when aircraft held the greatest advantage over U-boats trying to make a rapid passage on the surface to the area in which they expected to attack. For this reason, coupled with the very great naval commitments, the outer and main defence against the approach of U-boats from the west was composed of aircraft of Coastal Command of the Royal Air Force. There were, of course, inner defences of anti-submarine vessels and convoy escorts, and these would have had to form the outer as well as the inner defences had the invasion been contemplated in conditions of winter light.

Coastal Command "saturated" the air off the western flank of the invasion and over the approach routes of the U-boats, and the aircraft did magnificent work. During the night of D-day they sighted eleven U-boats and were able to attack six of these; and on the night of D plus 1 they sighted ten U-boats and were able to attack seven of them.

It is worthy of note that no U-boat sightings took place during daylight hours, showing beyond possibility of doubt that our air and sea patrols were so disposed as to preclude the possibility of U-boats proceeding on the surface by day. This itself delayed their passage, for a U-boat's surface speed was roughly four or five times that of its submerged speed, and there were less than six hours of darkness. The results of the air attacks on the U-boats could not be assessed with any accuracy, but even in the well-nigh impossible event of none of them causing even damage, each sighting meant that the U-boat was forced to dive and thus still further to delay its passage. Nor was that all. U-boats of the ordinary type such as the Germans used in the western part of the English Channel immediately after D-day could not hope to operate successfully in the narrow waters of the invasion area unless they arrived there with batteries and compressed air bottles fully charged—and this was impossible in the case of U-boats forced to submerge for long periods during their passage.

It was only after the attempted initial assault of the U-boats on the invasion area and convoy routes had been broken that the Germans tried to use U-boats fitted with the "schnorkel" device in this area. This device consists of a combined air intake and exhaust pipe which is telescopic and which enables the main diesel engines to be run, both for propulsion and for battery charging, while the U-boat is submerged. By enabling the U-boat to make long passages, below the surface and to charge the batteries while submerged, this device very greatly facilitates the operation of U-boats in narrow and coastal waters, particularly where there are many sea and air patrols.

Why the Germans did not use the "schnorkel" in the first U-boats sent out, instead of waiting until the chances of mounting any considerable U-boat offensive against the invasion had almost evaporated, remains a mystery. It almost seems as if the Allies had once again struck before the Germans were quite ready. As it was, they had no success, even with the "schnorkel," against the Assault Areas off Normandy or against the cross-Channel convoy routes which were the vital lifelines of the Allied Armies of Liberation.

The ships of the Allied navies would undoubtedly have broken any attempt at a U-boat offensive just as surely as did the aircraft, but this in no way detracted from their gratitude to the air forces. "Neptune" was a combined operation in the true sense of the term; the navies had plenty to do and they had to guard the eastern flank against all sorts of varied forms of attack. It devolved upon the air forces to guard the western flank against U-boat attack, and this they did with very marked success.

In the Bay of Biscay and the approaches to the English Channel aircraft sighted U-boats on ninety-six occasions between 1 June and 3 July. Of these fifty-nine were attacked. Six U-boats and probably more, were sunk, others

U 185 photographed in August 1943 with the new schnorkel device. The schnorkel is partially raised and is presumably being lowered as the vessel surfaces.

damaged and yet more discouraged. Off Norway, between the beginning of the anti-U-boat offensive in that area on 16 May and 3 July, U-boats were sighted on forty-four occasions; twenty-eight attacks were carried out, sixteen of which were classed as "promising"; and at least thirteen U-boats were probably destroyed.

Although the U-boats were having such a bad time in their attempts to reach the invasion area that their efforts were expensive failures and they proved to be much less of a menace than had been anticipated, the enemy action against the shipping in the Assault Areas and on the convoy routes leading to those areas was always serious. That it was so consistently defeated was due to good planning on the part of the Allies and the determination with which each new attack was met. The enemy mining campaign caused the greatest anxiety and even forced us to modify our swept channels and cleared areas, but the activities of German surface vessels—chiefly E-boats and R-boats— required unrelenting vigilance on the part of our escorts and patrols and led to a number of most determined short-range night actions.

CHAPTER VII

AGAINST THE E-BOATS

Great work of the Light Coastal Forces—The close blockade of Le Havre—
Daring actions under coastal guns—Actions off the Dutch coast—
E-boats fail against a convoy.

It was, of course, expected that the enemy would make great use of his E-boats and other small fast surface forces in his attempts to interfere with the build-up of the strength of the Allied invasion armies. This he did, but he was somewhat slow to react with these craft. With the exception of the one somewhat half-hearted attack on our bombarding forces in the Eastern Assault Area by E-boats from Le Havre, there was no real attempt by German naval forces to interfere with the initial stages of the invasion. For this one can be grateful for the high degree of tactical surprise achieved and also to the neutralising effects of our bombing of enemy ports. Nevertheless, it seemed for a few days as if the Germans were putting their whole faith in their mining campaign. Soon, however, the German surface craft began to operate against the Allied flank, and these led to a number of actions in which the officers and men of our small craft greatly distinguished themselves and asserted even more emphatically than before their moral superiority over the German crews.

Most of those actions were fought at very close range at night between vessels with a relative speed when on opposite courses of as much as 80 knots and more. It was a type of warfare calling for individual initiative and the making of split-second decisions. More often than not the actions had to be fought under the guns of the German shore batteries. Frequently there was confusion, by which our men were quick to profit, which left the bewildered Germans firing spiritedly at one another.

Most of the work of guarding against enemy E-boat attacks, and repelling them with loss when they were attempted, fell upon our Light Coastal Forces—motor torpedo-boats, motor gunboats, motor launches and steam gunboats—together with American PT boats. These small fast craft of the

British and American navies were formed in Light Coastal Forces Mobile Units—the term "mobile unit" meaning, roughly, that they, were based on thin air and had to fend for themselves in nearly all circumstances. They did, however, operate in conjunction with larger vessels, notably frigates. Those little ships achieved mightily, and in order to attain greater efficiency and increase the discomfiture of the enemy they set back the clock of history by a century. The Germans, with a major base at Le Havre and Cherbourg on either flank of the Allied Assault Area and the vital sea communications to the beachhead, were in an ideal position to attack. They could have emerged from their bases, attacked, and regained shelter long before craft operating from the British shore could have intercepted them. There was one answer to this problem. That was to institute a close blockade of Le Havre and Cherbourg.

It had for long been accepted that the coming of the steam engine and the internal combustion engine and the greater range of shore batteries and detecting devices had made the close blockade of an enemy port an impossibility. The strategists and tacticians had maintained that the watch kept by Nelson off Toulon and Cornwallis off Brest would be the last instances in naval history of a close blockade, except possibly by submarines. The little ships of the Light Coastal Forces would have none of this theory. If the only way of making certain of being able to intercept the enemy was to keep a close blockade of his bases, then a close blockade should be instituted and maintained. The German shore batteries would certainly add to the risk, but that would just have to be accepted.

In fact, our losses proved to be much lighter than had been anticipated. Nelson's dictum that the boldest course is often the safest was once again proved true.

The enemy, however, suffered severely. On the eastern flank between D-day and the end of June the German lost five and probably six E or R-boats sunk, and seven E or R-boats damaged, three of them badly, while two torpedo boats were also damaged. The cost to the Allies was two boats damaged, with three killed and ten wounded. On the western flank off Cherbourg no less than thirty actions were fought in these twenty-four nights—seven of them off Cape Barfleur in one night, when the weather was such that it made the craft very difficult to handle. One E or R-boat was certainly sunk, and one destroyer or torpedo-boat was hit by torpedo, while a great many craft were damaged. Severe loss was also inflicted upon German convoys trying to escape to the westward from Cherbourg as the American troops advanced up the Cotentin Peninsula. Farther west, in the neighbourhood of the Channel Islands, one German M-class minesweeper, one armed trawler and two coasters were sunk or severely damaged.

With events moving rapidly in the sea war off Hitler's "Fortress Europe," a German vessel which was damaged was a loss to the enemy during the critical period, and the German surface craft were subjected to so great an attrition that few vessels survived in a seaworthy and operational state.

Far away to the north-eastward other flotillas of British Light Coastal Craft were imposing losses upon the enemy which was seriously affecting the enemy in the invasion area. With nearly all inland transport paralysed by the Allied bombing offensive, the enemy tried to run supplies and reinforcements westward by sea. More often than not these were intercepted by our patrols off the Dutch coast and heavy losses inflicted upon them. The impact of this offensive upon the invasion of Normandy began some time before D-day. During May and June there were thirteen nights of weather so bad that it was impossible for our patrols of small craft to operate off the Dutch coast. During the remaining nights, however, they levied a very heavy toll. Eight armed trawlers, a tug and a gunboat were definitely sunk by torpedoes and another armed trawler and a tank landing craft were possibly sunk. Five more armed trawlers and another tank landing craft were damaged by gunfire.

The night of 9 June proved a profitable one for our little ships in both areas. Off the Dutch coast one of our motor torpedo-boat patrols under the command of Lieutenant-Commander K. Gemmell, DSC, RNVR, found four big German armed trawlers southwest of Ijmuiden. Three of these were sunk by torpedoes and the fourth was badly hit by gunfire and was last seen making for the shore in a seriously damaged condition. Later the same night this British patrol encountered three more German armed trawlers and sank one of these. The night's work cost us one motor torpedo-boat sunk, but there were only two casualties. On the same night in the western flank of the Assault Area a patrol of light coastal forces under the command of Lieutenant J. Collins, RNVR, fought a number of brief actions with German E-boats. These were in the main inconclusive, but damage was certainly inflicted on the enemy, while our forces suffered no damage or casualties.

Next night it was the turn of the steam gunboats on the western flank. It was fifty-two minutes after midnight when a frigate spoke to the gunboats: "There is something to the eastward of you. I don't know what it is. Have a look." The gunboats went off in chase and they sighted something which they had difficulty in identifying. It was not until they had closed the range to a thousand yards that the enemy was illuminated by star shell and seen to be two E-boats in quarter-line so that they presented a single long silhouette. Both sides challenged and opened fire simultaneously. The range was closing rapidly and one of the E-boats was hit and damaged at a range of 100 yards before they turned and managed to escape further punishment. The steam gunboats were not hit.

It had been one of the boats of this flotilla—the *Grey Seal*—which had sighted the first glider-bomb seen in the Assault Area. This was during the night of D plus 1. Of the air raid on the Assault Area on that night the commanding officer of the *Grey Seal* wrote: "As a sight it was quite beautiful, a lovely clear sky lit up by blazing barrage balloons, falling planes, and everywhere criss-cross red with brilliant tracer."

Away to the westward that night was not so brilliantly clear. There was a low-lying fog in the neighbourhood of the Channel Islands. In this fog a group of our motor torpedo-boats located what appeared to be a German convoy, but at once lost it again. Nor was that all. MTB 98 got separated from her consorts and so went on alone. For an hour this MTB stalked and shadowed the German convoy in the fog. Then suddenly she ran into a patch of clear weather and caught a glimpse of the enemy at a range of about 400 yards. The odds against the single MTB were enormous, but she made a snap attack, fired two torpedoes, and disengaged. As she did so she passed within a hundred yards of the nearest German ship and was raked by her gunfire, but she escaped, and as the fog hid her from the enemy her crew heard the explosion of one of their torpedoes. Both the officers of MTB 98 were wounded, the craft was holed and leaking and one engine had been put out of action, yet she was brought safely home.

On 14 June Allied destroyers as well as light coastal forces fought highly successful actions off the western flank. It was soon after midnight when the destroyers HMS *Ashanti* and the Polish *Piorun* sighted seven German M-class minesweepers. The Allied ships were under the command of Commander J. R. Barnes, RN, who at once illuminated the enemy by star shell and joined action at a range of 3,000 yards. The Allied guns began hitting at once. The German minesweepers scattered under the impact of the onslaught and some of them tried to seek shelter under the guns of the Jersey batteries. Nevertheless three of the German vessels were seen to sink and a fourth was so badly knocked about that its survival was most unlikely, while two others were brought to a standstill and left burning furiously. It was a pretty bit of work.

Meanwhile our light coastal forces had found three enemy patrol vessels at sea north-east of Cap de la Hogue, had sunk the leading ship by torpedo and had set the second ablaze by gunfire.

Nor had our patrols been inactive off the eastern flank. Just west of Le Havre a group of R-boats had tried to approach our lines of communication, but had been driven hack, unhappily before they could be brought to decisive action. Torpedo-boats and E-boats had also tried to raid the anchorage and the convoy route, but as soon as they were located and engaged they retired hastily under cover of smoke screens. It was believed that some damage was inflicted on the enemy in at least two of these inconclusive actions.

It was early in the morning of D plus 10 that there was fought in the English Channel an action in defence of a convoy which must surely rank among the great convoy actions of the war. The convoy was composed of landing craft laden with supplies for the build-up of the Allied armies in Normandy, and its escort consisted of one motor launch of the Royal Navy. The ML was under the command of Lieutenant J. C. Lewis, RNVR, and she also had on board Lieutenant B. K. C. Arbuthnot, who was in command of the squadron of landing craft. For an hour and three-quarters the enemy attacked this convoy with ten E-boats but, despite their superior armament, they were fought off time and again by the 3-pounders and machine-guns of the motor launch and the Oerlikons of the landing craft, and all except two of the landing craft arrived safely off the Normandy beaches.

This is how the commanding officer described those crowded hundred and five minutes: "It was about 4 a.m. when we were well out in the Channel that we heard gunfire to the eastward. Five minutes later we spotted two E-boats about 600 yards away. We closed them and opened fire with Oerlikons and machine-guns. The E-boats sheered off at once, giving us a few parting shots as they scuttled away. My experience has been that E-boats are usually shy of returning fire and prefer to make off.

"A minute later we turned our fire against new antagonists. That lot disappeared in a smoke screen, but E-boats seemed to be everywhere. We got close to the convoy to protect it, but we were immediately engaged by another bunch of E-boats. While we were pumping shells at these, yet another E-boat was sighted about 500 yards to port. We turned to engage this one and a very hot duel ensued, during which we received most of our damage. One shell hit our smoke container and we were soon emitting an involuntary smoke screen. At first we thought the ship was on fire. More engagements followed at longer ranges until the Huns retired at dawn. Despite their numerical superiority they weren't prepared to fight it out in daylight. They used flares and star shells to silhouette the convoy, but these proved to be double-edged weapons as they illuminated both friend and foe, and the landing craft fired freely whenever they could see a target. The action took place at such speed that it was difficult to ascertain what damage was inflicted on the E-boats, but we certainly left our mark. The main thing was that we brought the convoy with its reinforcements for the army through intact except for the loss of two landing craft."

CHAPTER VIII

BUILDING THE STRENGTH OF THE ARMIES

Part of the merchant navies—The critical period—Convoys through the Straits of Dover—"Planting" the "Gooseberries" and "Mulberries"— Courseulles and Port-en-Bessin—The great gale.

"The Merchant Navy proved its staunchness and fidelity in whatever circumstances," reported Rear-Admiral Sir Philip Vian, commanding the Eastern Task Force. That was a statement which was gratefully echoed by every commander on the spot, who saw the officers and men of the British Merchant Navy and the American Merchant Fleet doing unaccustomed things under conditions of considerable danger, yet preserving always cool heads and displaying high seamanship and skill as well as great courage. By D plus 2, when General Eisenhower, the Supreme Allied Commander, and Admiral Sir Bertram Ramsay, the Allied Naval Commander-in-Chief, visited the Assault Areas in the cruiser HMS *Apollo*, it could be said with certainty that the initial assault on Hitler's boasted "Atlantic Wall" had been successful. The German defences had been breached, and the follow-up waves of the Allied Armies of Liberation were being put ashore successfully and were pouring into the breaches.

There was reason for great satisfaction and for some optimism—provided the latter was duly tempered by knowledge of the difficulties which lay ahead. The progress of the D-day assaults had varied in the different areas. Perhaps the greatest contrast was to be found between the two American sectors. In the OMAHA sector there had been a bitter and bloody struggle which had prevented the assaulting troops from moving inland until late in the day. In the UTAH sector, however, things had gone well, so well that Rear-Admiral D. P. Moon, USN, commanding in that area, was able to report before noon on D-day: "Initial waves made landings on exact beaches after accurate air and naval bombardment. Fifteen waves landed by 9.45 a.m. Succeeding waves continue to land. Both beaches cleared of obstacles. Roads under construction and vehicles proceeding inland. Little opposition. Coastal batteries under control."

It must not be forgotten, however, that that staccato report was a record of high achievement. Taken as a whole, the first waves of the assault on the Normandy beaches had suffered considerable casualties. Moreover, they were by D plus 1 very tired men. They had had a long and far from smooth and comfortable sea passage, followed by an assault on prepared enemy positions and a day and a night of fighting. Unless the build-up of their strength by the landing of reinforcements and supplies were perfectly carried out there would be danger that these tired men would have to go on fighting without immediate or adequate reinforcement, and possibly under the handicap of shortage of ammunition, fuel for the vehicles, water and rations.

There is always that critical period in an amphibious assault, when the first waves have begun to tire. If the follow-up and the build-up is not quick and sufficient the critical period will be prolonged and become a great danger to the whole enterprise. The military ideal is for the follow-up troops to be in position to attack "through" the assault waves as soon as the latter begin to slow down through fatigue or expenditure of supplies. But like other military ideals in amphibious operations, this is only possible of attainment if the maritime component is perfect in every detail.

The existence of such a critical period was, of course, well known to the German General Staff. It was therefore to be expected that the enemy would launch his strongest attacks on D plus 1 in the hope of meeting only tired troops insufficiently supplied. As it happened, however, the Allied plan had been so successful that the enemy was not ready to counter-attack in any great force at that critical stage—an achievement in which the air bombing of his lines of communication, and particularly of the Seine and Loire bridges, was a potent factor. The latter had virtually transformed North-western France into an island, and had made the German High Command reluctant immediately to rush reinforcements to that "island" because they still could not be certain that we did not intend to land in the Pas de Calais area.

These factors could not, however, be relied upon by the Allied Command, which was very conscious of the great things which remained to be done before the invasion could be accounted successful.

General Eisenhower's and Admiral Ramsay's anxieties were by no means dissipated by the success of the initial assault. It was one thing to land assault troops, particularly when a high degree of tactical surprise had been—almost miraculously—achieved. It was quite another thing to build up the strength, both numerical and material, of the forces landed so that they could fight and defeat the maximum force which the enemy could possibly bring against them. If that were not achieved, if the rate of build-up of the strength of the invading armies were to prove insufficient to their needs in any circumstances which might arise, the invasion must inevitably end in disaster for the Allies—a disaster which must alter the whole future of the world.

Admiral Sir Bertram Ramsay was confident that he had, with the means at his disposal, done all that was humanly possible to ensure that the rate of the build-up would be adequate. He knew, too, that the courage and determination of the tens of thousands of officers and men would not fail. He knew, however, that there were imponderables. The enemy might have at his disposal some strength of which he knew nothing. There was, moreover, the weather. Against the latter, too, all possible precautions had been taken, and even as General Eisenhower and Admiral Ramsay were visiting the Assault Area on D plus 1, the first of the blockships for the "Gooseberry" shelter harbours was arriving and being "planted" in its appointed position. No man, however, can ever say that adequate provisions have been made against the weather, and least of all a seaman of long experience.

During D-day a great deal had depended upon the officers and men of the merchant navies, and particularly upon those who manned the coasters which, having been navigated for long years among the east-coast sandbanks while skilfully avoiding running aground, were driven hard aground on the beaches of Normandy so that they could unload on to dry beach at low tide. In the build-up period even more would depend upon the merchant navies, and ships and men would have to make sure that the armies would not go short, whatever the enemy or the elements might do. The proportion of the whole effort at sea during the build-up period which was made by the merchant navies was, in personnel, roughly one-half of the whole. Thus, on an average day in the first week after D-day, the arrivals of vessels carrying men, equipment and stores for the build-up to the Assault Areas were:

25 "Liberty" ships.
38 Coasters.
9 Troopships.
40 LST's (Landing Ship, Tank).
75 LCT's (Landing Craft, Tank).
20 LCI(L) (Landing Craft, Infantry, Large).

It must be remembered that of the 4,266 Landing Ships and Landing Craft which took part in the assaults on D-day a large number, particularly of the smaller types, had been lost or damaged. Some of these craft casualties had been caused by "marine risk" in the shape of weather, collision, or accidents in beaching or trying to "unbeach"; while others had been the result of enemy shell fire. The great majority, however, were the result of the mined obstacles which the Germans had placed between high and low water marks, and even below the low water mark.

It was only by the application of careful organisation to the detailed plan as laid down in the operation orders for "Neptune" that the gigantic task of the build-up was possible. Everywhere there was team-work, together with a very real desire to simplify tasks wherever possible. The Build-up Control Organisation saw that the loads were ready for the ships at the right place and time. The Turn-Round Control Organisation made certain that no ship or craft would spend more than the minimum of time over the "turn-round" at the end of a voyage. The system of marking ships simplified and expedited the collection and despatch of convoys. The task of the captains of ships and craft where whenever possible made lighter by arranging for them always to load at the same berth. Above all and pervading all was the determination of every officer and man concerned that no individual failure should lead to the troops fighting in Normandy wanting for anything.

It must be remembered that the gigantic task of the build-up was by no means a question only of cross-Channel traffic. The cross-Channel traffic certainly formed the greater part of the build-up during the first stages, but all this had to be dovetailed into other shipping movements, and it was only a short time before a considerable amount of the build-up traffic was coming from the far side of the Atlantic. This certainly came first to British ports and then joined the cross-Channel traffic to Normandy, but the two had to be most meticulously co-ordinated in order to avoid congestion in the British ports which were working far beyond normal capacity in serving the invasion, and to avoid periods of embarrassing plenty alternating with lean periods.

A great deal of the follow-up and build-up traffic, too, had to come from the Thames Estuary. This meant that considerable convoys had to pass through the Straits of Dover, literally under the big guns of the German batteries in the Cap Gris Nez area. Some of the early reinforcements of troops for Normandy, among them the famous 51st Highland Division, had to make this voyage. The necessity for this was beyond question, but it gave Admiral Sir Bertram Ramsay some anxiety. He had ample cause to know the Straits of Dover and the capabilities of the German batteries on the far shore, and these were the first big ship convoys to pass through the Straits since the days before the withdrawal of the Allied armies from Dunkirk. Here was an operation in itself, and it was carried out with great success, the big ship convoys passing through the Straits of Dover unmolested by the enemy and under cover of a diversion and of smoke screens produced by our light coastal forces.

The Allied Naval Commander-in-Chief remarked after the Allied Armies of Liberation had burst out of the Normandy beachhead and were racing after a defeated and disorganised enemy that there was a danger that people would not appreciate the magnitude and difficulty of "Operation Neptune" for the very reason that it had gone "according to plan." It is perhaps fortunate, therefore, that it is possible to record the fact that one ship went astray in that gigantic

SS *Neuralia* was launched in 1912 for the British India Steam Navigation Company. During the War it served as a troopship. It struck an allied mine in Gulf of Taranto, Italy on 1 May 1945—just seven days before VE Day—and sank on the spot.

organisation. This ship was the British India liner *Neuralia*, and the fact that she did not proceed "according to plan" was in no way due to her officers or crew. It was merely the solitary case of a mistake in the organisation.

The *Neuralia* was one of those ships which had come to the south coast from the Thames and had successfully run the gauntlet of the Straits of Dover. She had sailed from the Thames Estuary in the first personnel convoy to leave the Thames for the Isle of Wight area, and she duly anchored at Spithead in accordance with her instructions. The *Neuralia* should have gone over to Normandy in convoy almost at once, and should have arrived in the Assault Area on D plus 2, but it was not until the afternoon of D Plus 5 that she was discovered still anchored at Spithead. It was subsequently discovered that the mistake had arisen through the substitution by the War Office at a late date of the *Neuralia* for another ship, and the notification of this change not having been received by the authorities responsible for making up the outgoing convoys from Spithead.

The *Neuralia* had on board elements of the 7th Armoured Division, and one can imagine and sympathise with their fury at remaining at anchor off the British coast when they should have been in the thick of things in Normandy. It is an astonishing fact, however, that the absence of these important troops was never questioned by the Second Army, which was apparently unaware that they had not arrived in Normandy on the appointed D plus 2. That, perhaps, is an illustration of the speed with which events were moving, particularly in reference to the build-up.

One cannot but marvel at the fact that the case of the *Neuralia* was unique among the many thousands of ships involved in the build-up. If one considers only the ships and major landing craft and excludes hospital ships, tankers, auxiliaries of all types and salvage ships, the total number of arrivals in the Assault Areas between D plus 1 and D plus 24 was 4,257 ships and major landing craft. This total was made up as follows:

570 "Liberty" ships.
180 Troopships.
788 Coasters.
905 LST's (Landing Ship, Tank).
1,442 LCT's (Landing Craft, Tank).
372 LCI(L) (Landing Craft, Infantry, Large).

There were of course, many thousands of minor landing craft, tugs, ferry craft and all sorts of other vessels in addition to the above.

The whole essence of the plan for the build-up had been that it should be as steady as possible and worked on a repetitive schedule in the interests of simplicity. The arrivals of the ships and major landing craft in the Assault Areas day by day are eloquent testimony of how well the plan worked.

The first three days after D-day were abnormal days, for the shipping was recovering from the tremendous effort of D-day and at the same time striving to land the very maximum of reinforcements, equipment and stores on the Normandy coast, irrespective of strain upon men or material. It had never been expected that the build-up organisation would be able to settle down to a regular schedule of deliveries before D plus 4.

Thus the arrivals in the Assault Areas of ships and major landing craft on D plus 1 amounted to 98 vessels, but on the following day the total of arrivals rose to 216. The latter figure was very close to the average daily arrivals of the next week, but D plus 2 was, nevertheless, still an abnormal day because the total figure comprised a very high proportion of LCT's (Landing Craft, Tank), most of which had been pre-loaded, and a very small proportion of LST's (Landing Ship, Tank). The latter were larger and of much greater account in assessing the build-up. On both D plus 1 and D plus 2 the number of LCT's made up over fifty per cent of the total arrivals of ships and major landing craft, while very few LST's arrived on either day. Of the 98 arrivals on D plus 1, only 4 were LST's, while 51 were LCT's. On D plus 2, of the 216 arrivals no less than 110 were LCT's, while only 6 LST's arrived. By D Plus 3 the proportion of the various ships and major craft in the arrivals at the Assault Areas was beginning to approach the desired normal, but the number of LST's, although it rose to 15, was still small by comparison with the other vessels and craft. Yet by the end of D plus 3 no less than 47 convoys had crossed to Normandy.

The arrivals in the Assault Areas on D plus 4 showed that the plan had worked, for they approximated fairly closely to the planned daily normal, not only in the total arrivals, but in the numbers of the various types of ships and craft which made up that total. On D plus 4 the arrivals in the Assault Areas were:

    29 "Liberty" ships.
    44 Coasters.
    31 LST's.
    81 LCT's.
    10 Troopships.
    28 LCI(L).

a total of 223 ships and major landing craft.

Everything seemed to be going exactly in accordance with the invasion plan, and it continued for some time to do so despite the worst that the enemy could do by aircraft attacks and attempted attacks by E-boats, U-boats, and the few other surface forces at his disposal. Moreover, the weather, which had forced a postponement of D-day and continued to be rather uncertain and default from the conception of June weather on that coast, did not for some time play tricks capable of interfering with the steady but enormous flow of the build-up.

And while this was going on the precautions planned against a sudden deterioration in the weather were going ahead as fast as might be. On D plus 1 the majority of the blockships to form the breakwaters of the "Gooseberry" harbours arrived in the Assault Area and were duly sunk in their appointed positions. That was no easy task. Each of the five "Gooseberry" harbours— one off each of the five main assault beaches—had an experienced naval officer in charge who was responsible that the blockships were sunk in the correct positions. This officer was known as the "planter" of the "Gooseberry." He and his men had a very difficult task. The most accurate navigation was demanded of them in the face of strong tides and a wind of no inconsiderable force, for a blockship in the wrong place would not only be waste; it would leave a gap in the projected breakwater through which would surge the seas which it was supposed to impede, and it would almost inevitably result in a major obstruction and navigational danger in an area likely to be so congested with shipping that every square yard of anchorage would be of value.

To add to the difficulties of the "planters," many of the navigational marks ashore were obscured by the "fog of war"—the dust of bursting shells and the smoke of burning buildings as well as the cordite smoke from the naval guns supporting the armies ashore. Marks on the beach, too, were more often than not obscured by other vessels. It was a navigational nightmare, to which was added the distraction of enemy shelling. By D plus 1 many of the German batteries which had been "silenced" during the vital early hours of D-day were "coming to life." Particularly was this true on the flanks of the Assault Area, where the German battery crews were beginning to go back to their weapons and bring them once again into action. Every time they did so they were hotly and effectively engaged by naval gunfire, but they were able to fire several rounds before being again driven from their guns. The Germans, moreover, had by this time brought up mobile guns with which they could shell the flank anchorages—SWORD on the east and UTAH on the west—and these mobile batteries working in the woods were difficult for the bombarding ships to locate and almost impossible for them to knock out. As early as 9.30 a.m. on D-day, Rear-Admiral Vian reported that, although the main German batteries had been silenced, for the time being at least, the beaches and anchorages in the SWORD area were being subjected to an increasing volume of shell fire from mobile guns in the woods south of Franceville (east of the River Orne) which were very difficult to locate and engage.

It is the nature of the Hun when behind a gun to shoot at the target which looks biggest and easiest to hit. That was an enemy trait which was to stand us in very good stead off the entrance to the Scheldt nearly five months later, but that was little consolation on 7 June, when the "blockships" coming in to their sinking positions for the two flank harbours came under a considerable volume of German shell fire, which they could not dodge because it was essential for them to move slowly into their correct positions and maintain these positions while the vessels were settling on to the sea bed.

Despite all the difficulties—and they included one case on the American sector in which one side of the bridge of a blockship was removed by a German shell just after the commanding officer had moved over to the other side of the bridge—the blockships were one and all successfully and correctly placed.

Thus each of the five Assault Areas off the Normandy beaches were speedily provided with a shelter harbour. These, however, could shelter only small craft—the multitudinous ferry craft and light craft of all types which served the beaches and the ships in the anchorages. Shelter against the weather had been provided for the most vulnerable craft, but a great deal more was required before it could be said with truth that everything possible had been done to guard against interruption of the build-up by the weather.

The greater steps to guard against weather interference with the build-up were already in train. The great concrete caissons, the bombardons, the spud pierheads and the pier roadway sections—all of which formed parts of the great prefabricated ports—were already on their way. They had been provisionally assembled and sunk off Dungeness and Selsey Bill, and now they were being raised from those positions and were setting out in tow to their appointed stations off the Normandy beaches.

It was obvious that these artificial "Mulberry" harbours would take longer to assemble off the Normandy coast than the "Gooseberry" harbours. An almost cubic concrete caisson displacing some 6,000 tons is an unwieldy tow even in ideal weather, and its rate of progress cannot be compared with that of a ship under her own power, even if that ship is largely concrete-filled and designated as a blockship. Moreover, the shortage of tugs set a definite limit to the speed of delivery of these great and unwieldy components of a vast project. This was nothing less than the building off the Normandy coast in little more than a week a harbour such as would normally require five or six years of hard and concentrated work to complete.

It is interesting to recall that even in the rush of invasion and the unique task of taking these harbours to France and setting them up off Normandy, tradition was well served. The Naval Officer-in-Charge of the British prefabricated harbour was Captain Christopher Petrie, RN, who had farmed successfully in South Africa for many years, having retired after winning a DSO and bar in the 1914-18 war. Captain Petrie was given as his headquarters ship the old light cruiser *Despatch*, which was lying at the entrance to the scrap-heap, devoid of guns and all stores. By prodigious efforts the ship was "brought forward" and

The breakwater of the concrete caissons of the Mulberry Harbour as they were being sunk into position.

The Mulberry Harbour at Vierville-sur-Mer/St Laurent-sur-Mer for Omaha Beach before the storm. A photograph at the foot of the descent, exit D1; with the Western Pier still under construction, 16 June 1944. The floating docks on their towers from the Lobnitz shipyard on the Clyde, are already in service with the centre pier.

The Mulberry harbour at Arromanches in operation.

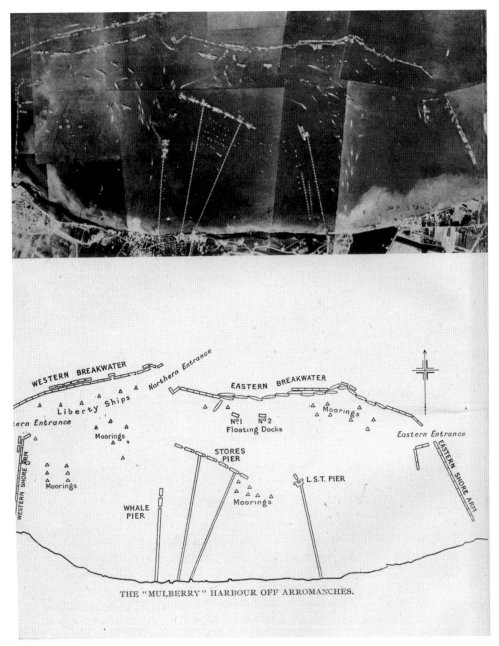

THE "MULBERRY" HARBOUR OFF ARROMANCHES.

A composite aerial photograph and plan of the Mulberry Harbour off Arromanches.

The artificial port of Vierville-sur-Mer/St Laurent-sur-Mer, 'Mulberry A' (Omaha Beach) in operation prior to the destructive storm of 19-21 June 1944

stored, albeit in a manner so unorthodox that it would in normal times have caused great umbrage in high places. Moreover, the ship was armed—with a considerable number of Bofors and other light guns considered primarily as anti-aircraft weapons. These were begged and borrowed, chiefly from the military. Then came the task of manning her, for she required no small complement to man her fine array of guns. Again the army came to the rescue, and the *Despatch* sailed with all her guns manned by soldiers and with a major as the gunnery officer. Tradition had been well served, for the men manning the Despatch's armament belonged to the Queen's Regiment. It had been more than 280 years since the main armament of one of the King's ships had been manned exclusively by soldiers, and then it had been by the "Queen's," who had given their regimental march of "Braganza" to the navy's premier gunnery school at Portsmouth.

By D plus 13 most of the great concrete caissons which were to form the main breakwaters of the artificial harbours were in place off the Normandy coast, and the outer floating breakwaters of "bombardons" had been anchored in position. There were two of the prefabricated "Mulberry" harbours. Both had been built in Great Britain but one was to serve the American sector and one the British sector. The former was placed off St Laurent, in the OMAHA area and the latter off Arromanches in the JUNO area. Although most of the heaviest components of these artificial harbours had been successfully towed to the French coast and placed in position by D plus 13, neither harbour was by any means complete. Pierheads and pier sections were by that time on their way across the Channel. The British "Mulberry" harbour off Arromanches was actually nearer completion than its American counterpart off St Laurent, and the Arromanches harbour was providing considerable shelter, although the discharging of ships still had to be done into lighters, "dumb" barges, DUKW's ferry craft and "Rhino" barges—the latter being little more than large flat-topped caissons with a freeboard when laden of only a foot or so, on to which vehicles were discharged from the ships.

One of the bravest acts of the build-up concerned one of these "Rhinos," which was set on fire while it was lying alongside a ship which had already discharged a number of vehicles on to it. The laden vehicles burnt furiously and there was grave danger that the ship alongside which the "Rhino" was lying would also catch fire, in which case the petrol and loads of the vehicles she carried would very soon have made an end of her. The situation was one of great anxiety when a party of Royal Marines of the ferry service boarded the blazing "Rhino," got the wounded off it, and got it away from the ship's side. For this act of great bravery two of the Royal Marines were awarded the Distinguished Service Medal.

In addition to the shelter harbours, two real French harbours were playing their part in the build-up. Most important of these was Port-en-Bessin, almost on the dividing line between the British and American Assault Areas. This little port had been captured by the Royal Marine Commandos during the night of D plus 1, and by D plus 8 it was handling an average of more than 1,000 tons a day, which must have been far more than had ever been thought of in peace-time. The other captured French port was Courseulles, in the JUNO area to the east of Arromanches. "On paper" Courseulles should have been able to handle more than Port-en-Bessin, but it did not do so, and by D plus 8 it was averaging a bare thousand tons a day. This was an important help to the landing of men, equipment and stores over the beaches, but it had been hoped to achieve more at Courseulles. That we did not do so was due more to the deterioration of the port owing to its neglect than to damage by enemy sabotage or our own bombardments. It would be difficult to over-estimate the importance of these two tiny captured ports. Small as was their contribution to the immense volume of the build-up, it was a contribution which was not dependent upon the vicissitudes of landing over beaches and was therefore one which was doubly welcome as being free from anxiety.

The anxieties regarding the beaches and their exits were many and varied. In the normal course of events one does not think of a beach "wearing out," but that is precisely what they threatened to do and what some of them did. Courseulles was, as has been said, in the JUNO area, and Commodore G. N. Oliver, who commanded in the JUNO area, reported that all the beaches in his sector of the coast began to show serious signs of wear after three days of heavy traffic, and that the deterioration setting in, particularly below the half-tide level, made it essential to work out a system whereby sections of the beaches could be "rested."

Anxieties there were, and of driving relentless hard work, much of it under enemy shell fire, there was certainly no lack, but the build-up was going well. It had fallen slightly behind schedule in the initial stage because of weather and damage to craft, but the leeway had been made up and all was going "according to plan."

In addition to the Supreme Allied Commander and the Allied Naval Commander-in-Chief, other distinguished persons had visited the Assault Areas. On 12 June the destroyer HMS *Kelvin* had brought Mr Winston Churchill, General Smuts; and the Chief of the Imperial General Staff, and Vice-Admiral Nelles of the Royal Canadian Navy visited the area on the same day. Two days later the French-manned "Hunt" class destroyer *La Combattante*—which was afterwards to fall victim to a German mine in the North Sea—took General de Gaulle to the land for whose freedom he had for so long struggled in exile. Then, on 16 June, His Majesty the King, accompanied by the First Sea Lord, the Chief of the Air Staff and the Chief of Combined Operations, visited the Assault Areas in the cruiser HMS *Arethusa*.

Thirteen is held by the superstitious to be an unlucky number. Certainly D plus 13 was the beginning of a three-day period of great misfortune to the build-up of our invasion forces. On that day there arose in the English Channel a gale the like of which had not been known in those waters in June for forty years. For three days it raged with a ferocity so great that a man could hardly stand against the wind; and it blew from the north-east so that the whole of the Normandy beachhead area was lee shore. Along that lee shore as well as out to sea it left such a trail of destruction and chaos that it came near to breaking the hearts of those who had laboured so long and so faithfully to see that nothing should intervene between the armies and their flow of reinforcements and supplies.

Gales, however, cannot break the heart or the determination of the real seaman. Cornwallis, when driven with sprung masts and split sails from his station off Brest during the terrible gales of December, 1803, was always back on his station as soon as the weather showed the least signs of moderating. So it was with the British and American seamen off Normandy. For a short time they were driven from their stations by the great gale, but as soon as it moderated they returned to their greatly increased tasks with fortitude and a determination which soared above all difficulties. Perhaps the greatest trait which British and Americans have in common is that both are at their greatest when they are "up against it." It would be difficult, if not impossible, to point to any fundamental difference between Britain after Dunkirk and the United States after Pearl Harbor. Off Normandy after the great gale that had wrecked hopes and plans as well as vessels and harbours the men of the two nations worked under the spur of the common national characteristic.

The great gale which began to blow in the early hours of 19 June got up very suddenly and increased rapidly to its maximum force. Commodore G. N. Oliver, commanding in the JUNO area, logged the fact that the gale sprang up suddenly at 3.30 a.m. on D plus 13. Throughout that day his headquarters ship HMS *Hilary* rode out the gale, although it took two anchors to hold her. Soon after midday next day (D plus 19), however, even two anchors proved insufficient to hold the ship, which began to drag both anchors.

The American sector "Mulberry" harbour of St Laurent, being incomplete, was vulnerable to the high seas, which could surge over and into the uncovered concrete caissons in a way they were never designed to withstand. The result was that they broke up and great sections of what had been designed as a breakwater sank into the mud of the sea bed. The bombardons of the floating breakwaters broke adrift and drove down upon the wreckage of the artificial harbour, within which the piers were sunk and twisted, and the only pierhead then in position had been utterly smashed by a group of sixteen British LCT's (Landing Craft, Tank) which had sought shelter only to be driven down out of control on to the pierhead. Where there had been a great harbour nearing completion there remained nothing but wreckage dangerous to navigation, with the steel bones jutting menacingly from the concrete. Even the blockships of the "Gooseberry" harbour in the OMAHA area failed to stand up to the gale. They settled in the mud of the sea bed, being worked into it by the sea, so that the waves could break over them at the abnormally high tides built up by the gale in the corner between the Cotentin Peninsula and the Bay of the Seine coast. These made the shelter harbour within them useless and broke up the upperworks of the ships, so that all that remained was a broken and sunken breakwater of concrete-filled hulls which did nothing to break the surface waves. So great was the destruction among the small vessels in the OMAHA area that a survivors' camp containing between 500 and 600 officers and men had to be established on the beach.

The commanding officer of one of the British small craft which sought shelter from the gale in the "Mulberry" harbour off St Laurent described the state of

The destruction at Omaha after the great gale. One theory is that the storm was effectively 'man-made'. From D-Day to the 19th June the sea in a wider area of the Normandy shores was churned and turned up-side-down with vast surface activity, the transportation of vast quantities of materials from thousands of vessel-trips and towing great concrete structures, further exacerbated by countless explosions. From this churning the sea surface got colder. Sun-warmed water was exchanged with deeper and colder water, while the mid June sun supplied a lot of sun ray to the surrounding land masses. That presumably built the ingredients for the making of a devastating storm which started on 19 June 1944 and lasted for three days by which the 'Mulberry A' port at Omaha Beach was so completely wrecked that its further use was abandoned. Luckily the damage at 'Mulberry B' could be repaired fairly soon.

affairs in that harbour in the following words: "The scene inside the Mulberry was one of unutterable chaos. Literally hundreds of landing craft from LCV (Landing Craft, Vehicle) to LST (Landing Ship, Tank) were ashore piled one upon another. The 'whales' (caissons on which the pier roadways floated) had vanished. The bombardons were chasing one another madly round the bay The 'phoenixes' (the big concrete breakwater caissons) had cracked. Even the blockships were breaking up, and what little sea room remained was packed with wreckage, DUKW's and more and more landing craft, coasters and barges, dragging their anchors steadily towards the beach."

The "Mulberry" harbour off Arromanches in the British sector fared much better. Not only was it somewhat nearer completion, at least as far as the breakwaters were concerned, than the St Laurent "Mulberry," but it received a certain amount of shelter from the off-lying Calvados Rocks. Even so, the outer floating breakwater of "bombardons" broke away and its sections became a total loss. Moreover, the completion of the harbour was greatly delayed. When the gale blew up there were at sea on their way to France a great many sections of the piers and pierheads in tow. Every one of the tows which were at sea on D plus 13 were lost. It was, however, fortunate that the breakwaters of the "Mulberry" held, for within their shelter no fewer than 155 ships and craft weathered the gale. The "Gooseberry" shelter harbours in the eastern area also held. Had they not done so the destruction wrought by the gale would have been infinitely worse, for it would have virtually eliminated the ferry service craft, for which there were no replacements available.

As it was, the losses were bad enough. More than 800 craft of all types were stranded. Of the 650 LCT's (Landing Craft, Tank) which had been available for the assault and build-up 320 were put out of action by the gale. On all sides there were calls for salvage and repair. On and off the beaches men worked like demons with tugs, bulldozers and tractors and wire hawsers singing with strain and frequently parting, and flying back with the suddenly released strain to the great peril of all in the vicinity. Had it not been for the tireless efforts of all concerned the gale would have inflicted even greater damage, which would have meant an even greater interruption in the build-up. As it was, the effect of the gale on the build-up extended beyond the period of the gale because of the delay in completion of the Arromanches "Mulberry" harbour and the loss and damage among the ferry craft. Thus the average number of arrivals in the Assault Area of ships and major landing craft was considerably lower during the week after the gale than during the week after D-day.

The great gale had, in fact, accomplished more in three days than the enemy had been able to accomplish in a fortnight, including the Assault period, with all his armies, aircraft, mines, U-boats, E-boats and other surface vessels—and more than he was to be able to accomplish in the future with all his "secret weapons" and other destructive devices.

The figures of craft lost and damaged show conclusively that the gale proved to be the more formidable enemy. During the period of D-day to D plus 6 there were 64 losses due to enemy action and only 34 due to weather, while 106 craft were damaged by enemy action and exactly the same number by stress of weather.

Between D plus 7 and D plus 18, however—which period includes the great gale—118 craft were lost by stress of weather as against 27 by enemy action. And in the same period no less than 297 craft were damaged by the weather, while the enemy damaged only 29 craft.

Over the whole of the first month of the invasion, and including the great risks and inevitable losses due to enemy action during the initial assault phase, the enemy only destroyed or damaged a total of 261 craft as against a total of 606 craft lost or damaged as a result of the weather. The figures for loss and damage by the enemy include, of course, casualties caused by the German underwater obstructions.

By good fortune more ships and major landing craft had arrived in the Assault Areas during the two days before the gale than ever before. This; the providential survival of the Arromanches "Mulberry"; and the little ports of Port-en-Bessin and Courseulles; enabled an, all-important trickle of supply to reach the armies even during the height of the gale. This was as well, for on D plus 14 only 57 ships and major landing craft reached the Assault Areas instead of the usual 220-230; while on D plus 15 not a single ship or major landing craft arrived. Even on D plus 16 there were only 81 arrivals.

One can well imagine the anxiety that was caused to those responsible by the sudden and unexpected freak gale. Never can a wild north-easter have been less welcome.

Several boats ran aground on Omaha Beach after the storm; the gateway and dismantled wreck of a man-made beach in front of 'Mulberry A'.

CHAPTER IX

AFTER THE GALE

Effects of the gale—Salvage and repair—SWORD area abandoned—Gale's effect on German mining campaign—Making good the loss in the build-up.

The great north-easterly gale of D plus 13 to D plus 16 (19-21 June) produced a situation of extreme difficulty in the organisation of the build-up. The whole of the repetitive schedule had been thrown out of gear. For nearly four days the armies ashore had received only the barest trickle of supplies and reinforcements. It was therefore urgently necessary to increase the rate of the build-up in order to make up for the lost days, and in particular to rush to Normandy during the days immediately following the gale the very maximum of reinforcements, supplies and equipment in order to ensure that the military shortages should not become acute and that the enemy should not be able to profit by the situation by launching counter-attacks against tired and ill-supplied troops. It was, in fact, necessary to think in terms of another D-day and its immediately following period.

It was, however, one thing to think in such terms, and quite another to arrange for the maximum to be taken to Normandy in the minimum of time and without considerations of sparing men or material in the process. The gale had done such damage that the material would have to be studied if there were to be no risk of further breakdown owing to shortage of available ships and craft. Numerically, the LCT's (Landing Craft, Tank) had been playing the major part in the build-up, but the gale had put out of action, temporarily at least, just over half the total number of LCT's available. Nor was any useful purpose to be served by rushing larger ships to the Assault Areas when the ferry service, seriously attenuated by loss and damage during the gale, could not compete with the rapid discharge of their cargoes. Such a policy would have led only to a build-up of laden but idle tonnage in the most dangerous area.

The problem which faced the Allied Naval Commander-in-Chief was one which required a nice blend of organisation and improvisation. On the day

Many different kinds of boats beached on the shore. Omaha Beach after the storm of 19-21 June 1944 that destroyed the 'Mulberry A'. The black wavy line shows a redaction by the censors.

before the gale began to blow the British "Mulberry" harbour off Arromanches had handled 1,600 tons of equipment and stores for the army. On 14, 15 and 16 June very few vessels arrived off the Normandy coast, the total arrivals for those three days being 57, nil and 81 respectively. There was, of course, a very large arrival of ships in the Assault Areas on the day after the gale subsided, for ships which had been loaded at British ports but which had not sailed during the bad weather were rushed across the Channel. Thus on that day, 17 June, no less than 281 ships and major landing craft arrived off the Normandy beaches. Arrivals on that scale could not, however, be maintained, and even had that been possible they could not have been unloaded.

The problem on the far shore was complicated by the urgent need to clear the beaches and the waters off them of wrecks and stranded vessels. This was necessary not only in order to clear the beaches and their seaward approaches from obstructions which impeded the unloading of vessels which arrived, but also in order to salvage the craft and get as many of them as might be back into service at the earliest possible moment.

The salvage and repair tasks imposed by the great gale were prodigious. The casualties off the beaches during the assault phase had been far lower than had been anticipated, although a large number of landing craft had been damaged on the beaches or by the enemy's underwater obstacles. The casualties among ships and craft due to the gale, however, were higher than the expected casualties during the assault, and they placed a tremendous strain upon the salvage and repair organisations. By a great and sustained effort, however, these organisations worked wonders. Of rather more than 800 vessels stranded by the gale about 600 landing craft and a few coasters were temporarily repaired and refloated on the next spring tides, while about a hundred more were temporarily repaired and refloated on the following spring tides a fortnight later.

Both the British and United States navies had repair parties ashore in their respective areas; and in the British Assault Area were the two repair ships HMS *Adventure* and HMS *Albatross*. The former had been a cruiser minelayer and the latter a seaplane carrier of the Royal Australian Navy. Both had been specially fitted to work as repair ships during the invasion and they had special repair parties on board in addition to their crews.

These two ships and the repair parties on the beaches proved of the utmost value during the critical stages after the gale. In the British Assault Area alone they repaired 553 ships and vessels. Of these, 90 were HM ships and 80 were naval units of the Light Coastal Forces; 27 were unclassified and 13 were merchant ships. The remaining 315 vessels were landing ships, landing craft and barges.

The *Albatross* alone saved 79 landing craft from probable total loss and restored 132 vessels to fighting service. In order to accomplish this task in the prevailing weather the ship had frequently to go very close inshore in the eastern Assault Area, where she frequently came under heavy shell fire

The remnants of 'Mulberry A' off Omaha Beach after one of the worst June gales in eighty years.

from the German batteries and mobile guns. These scored a few hits on her superstructure, but did no great harm and the *Albatross* continued to give invaluable service off the Normandy coast until she was seriously damaged by an underwater explosion, which necessitated her return to a dockyard port. It is thought that this underwater explosion was due to a hit by one of the very long range circling torpedoes which the Germans sent into the anchorage during July and August.

The repairs carried out to all these craft on the far shore were not, of course, permanent repairs. In the great majority of cases they were temporary repairs only, but they enabled the vessels to continue operating or to make the passage back across the English Channel to a dockyard port where permanent repairs could be carried out. There is no doubt whatever that a large proportion of these vessels would have become total losses had it not been for the work of the naval repair parties and the facilities provided by the repair ships.

Salvage, of course, worked in close conjunction with the repair organisation, particularly in refloating stranded vessels and those which had been temporarily repaired on the beaches. The salvage organisation was also concerned with the dispersal of wrecks which impeded the traffic to and from the beaches and anchorages. When possible such wrecks were moved out of the way in one piece and placed in positions where long-term salvage could be undertaken if desired, but in cases where they could not be moved as a whole they were cut up by divers using underwater oxyacetylene cutters. There were cases in which a decision had to be taken on whether to cut up and dispose of a wreck which, if left, could probably be salvaged in due course. In such cases the necessity of keeping the waters off the beaches clear of wrecks took priority.

When one considers the severity of the gale and the vulnerability, despite the "Gooseberry" shelter harbours and the "Mulberry" harbour off Arromanches, of the great collection of craft off the Normandy beachhead, it seems astonishing that the build-up of the strength of the armies was not even more seriously impeded. Despite the loss and damage to ships and craft and the great artificial harbours, the armies ashore were very soon once more receiving everything that they required, and a progressive increase in their strength.

The gale blew itself out on D plus 16 (22 June), and by 25 June the arrival of ships and major landing craft off the beaches had settled down once more to something approaching what it had been before the gale. In the six days, 25-30 June, the average daily arrivals off Normandy was 171 ships and major landing craft daily, as opposed to an average of 226 arrivals daily during the six days previous to the gale. The lesser number of average daily arrivals after 25 June concerned chiefly LCT's (Landing Craft, Tank). Whereas 462 LCT's had arrived off Normandy between 14 and 18 June, only 291 of these craft arrived off the beaches between 19 and 30 June. This was hardly surprising, since no less than 320 of the total force of 650 LCT's had been put out of action by the gale.

The situation produced by the gale was not the only factor affecting the build-up of the strength of the invasion armies. The enemy's reactions to our invasion was also having its effect. The German minelaying campaign, and the accumulation of mines in the Assault Areas and their approaches due to the period in which the weather made minesweeping impossible, had forced us to accept narrower swept channels in order to be able to devote more mine-sweepers to the clearance of the anchorages and their immediate approaches. Moreover, it was found necessary to abandon the eastern SWORD area, in so far as the unloading of merchant ships was concerned. This decision was not forced upon us by the activities of the German E-boats and other less orthodox weapons loosed against that flank. The naval forces on that flank consistently proved themselves more than a match for the worst the enemy could do at sea. The German shell fire in the SWORD area, however, proved consistently and increasingly troublesome, and it was this which made Admiral Sir Bertram Ramsay decide to abandon that area for the unloading of ships, since to continue to do so invited losses and casualties on a considerable scale.

This German shell fire came mostly from mobile guns which operated in the Franceville area east of the River Orne. Rear-Admiral Vian mentioned in his official report the troublesome nature of these batteries of mobile guns operating in the woods south of Franceville and said that they were most difficult to locate and engage. They were repeatedly engaged by cruisers and destroyers and LCCU's (Landing Craft, Gun) and LCS.s (Landing Craft, Support), but although they seemed on several occasions to have been silenced, they always opened fire again from a different place as soon as our bombardment ceased.

It was just as well that Courseulles and Port-en-Bessin, small ports though they were, were in our hands and being rapidly developed, while great efforts were made, working against time, to replace the "Mulberry" pier and pierhead sections which had been lost when the gale broke while they were being towed across the Channel, and to complete the British "Mulberry" harbour off Arromanches. So well did this work go forward that by D plus 34 (10 July) this artificial harbour was handling an average of 6,000 tons of equipment and stores daily. The great artificial harbour—the only one of the two to survive the gale—proved its worth both during and after the gale. It had originally been planned that a "Mulberry" harbour should survive and work for ninety summer days, but that at Arromanches worked on successfully through the worst of the winter, and when it was closed down as a main supply port the reason was not because it failed to stand up to stress of weather.

The reasons for the eventual closing of the Arromanches "Mulberry" harbour were three. The most important of these was that alternative ports had been captured and cleared in the eastern part of the Channel, in Belgium and in Holland which were much nearer to the fighting line and therefore did not necessitate the long haul up the "Red Ball Route" from Normandy to the front in Holland and on the borders of Germany. The other two reasons were more intimately connected with Arromanches itself. One was the deterioration of the roads in the Arromanches district, which had been literally worn away by the weight of traffic which they had had to bear, and the other was the silting up of the harbour with sand built up into banks in some places and scooped out of other places by the tide. This made parts of the artificial harbour too shallow, while hollows formed in other places on the sea bed into which some of the caissons began to topple and settle.

After it ceased to be used as a main supply port the Arromanches "Mulberry" harbour had one further day of glorious life. That was in the following spring, when it was *en fête* in aid of French prisoners-of-war. It was a fitting end to a project which had demanded the work of many thousands and which had played so tremendous a part in the liberation of France.

The build-up continued steadily after the great interruption caused by the gale. There were, however, other small troubles from time to time. These were mostly caused by the different ideas and requirements of the navy and the army, and all were overcome by
mutual goodwill and appreciation that all were working towards the same goal.

The Naval Commander-in-Chief, for instance, was always concerned that there should be the minimum number of ships lying off the far shore at any given moment, and that all ships arriving there should be completely unloaded at once in order to effect a quick turn round. Their cargoes could be taken to dumps ashore from which the military authorities could draw their requirements as they were needed. Only by working on such a system could full economy in shipping be achieved. The military authorities, however, were prone to take out of the ships on their arrival only the items of cargo which were immediately and urgently required. Thus, they argued, they would save the creation of great dumps ashore, but they did not appreciate at first that they were, in fact, using the ships as dumps and thus impeding their proper use as transport. This army method was given the name of "selective unloading." It was never allowed to assume serious proportions, but it was constantly threatening, and Rear-Admiral Vian, Commanding the Eastern Task Force, had to signal to the Commander in-Chief that "selective unloading is again rearing its ugly head."

CHAPTER X

SEEK AND DESTROY

*Light coastal forces stop Cherbourg evacuation—Dutch coast actions
against German reinforcements—Rendezvous with U-boats and escorts
off Brest—Actions off Le Havre.*

During the period of the great gale of D plus 13 to D plus 16 there was an
inevitable interruption in the series of actions fought by the light coastal forces,
for the weather made it impossible for small surface forces to operate. Even
after the gale had blown itself out some days passed before sea and swell had
gone down sufficiently to allow the light coastal forces to operate successfully.
By that time the American army was advancing up the Cotentin Peninsula
and closing in on Cherbourg from the south. This had a direct effect upon the
actions at sea. The centre of gravity of the coastal force and destroyer activity
shifted to the westward, where it was engaged in preventing the Germans
from escaping by sea from Cherbourg. Thus there set in on the western flank
a period of offensive actions against German escape convoys instead of the
offensive-defensive patrol warfare which had preceded the gale.

The first action against one of these convoys seeking to escape from
Cherbourg took place early on the morning of 23 June, when a patrol of our
light coastal forces under the command of Lieutenant J. R. H. Kirkpatrick,
RNVR, encountered a convoy south of Jersey, sank one of the escorting armed
trawlers and set one of the supply ships on fire in two brisk gun actions.

Early the following morning our light coastal forces had an even more
successful encounter. One of our patrols located a German convoy consisting
of seven small supply ships with the usual escort of armed trawlers. A series
of attacks were made on this convoy as a result of which two of the ships
in convoy were sunk and three more so seriously damaged that they were
considered to be total losses. The remnants of this convoy sought shelter
under the guns of the Alderney batteries. Our forces suffered a few casualties
and some superficial damage.

Three nights later another of our patrol of light coastal forces was in action in the Channel Islands area. This time our patrol, commanded by Lieutenant-Commander T. N. Cartwright, DSC, RNVR, surprised a group of three German armed trawlers and two M-class minesweepers ten miles off the coast of Jersey. Lieutenant-Commander Cartwright at once attacked and considerable damage was seen to be inflicted on the enemy. Then, however, our patrol was illuminated by star shell from the shore batteries and came under such heavy fire from these guns that it was forced to disengage. Shortly afterwards, this force located two M-class minesweepers lying stopped about 5 miles south of St. Helier. Lieutenant-Commander Cartwright approached to within very short range of these vessels and engaged them with gunfire and torpedoes. One torpedo was seen to hit, and the German ship ceased fire as soon as the explosion took place. It was considered that this ship was sunk. Our patrol had two casualties and sustained some slight damage.

Next night the British destroyer *Eskimo* and the Canadian destroyer *Huron* found a group of three German armed trawlers in the same area. Two of the German ships were sunk by gunfire, the third succeeding in making good her escape while her consorts were being sunk.

Meanwhile, the war of attrition against German shipping was being relentlessly waged off the Dutch coast whenever the weather permitted. In the early hours of 27 June an offensive patrol of light coastal forces commanded by Lieutenant-Commander K. Gemmell, DSC, RNVR, intercepted a group of four heavily armed German trawlers. The leading German ship was seen to sink as a result of a torpedo hit, and the second ship blew up. Our craft did not receive a scratch.

Some days earlier Lieutenant-Commander Gemmell had sunk a German gun coaster and heavily damaged an ocean-going tug and an armed trawler in a brisk action off the Texel, also without sustaining casualties or damage to his own force.

Early on 5 July there took place off the Dutch coast a series of actions which inflicted very serious loss on the enemy and demonstrated the value of close co-operation between light coastal forces and aircraft.

The first incident was a running fight between one of our patrols and a convoy of German landing craft escorted by armed trawlers. In this action one of the German armed trawlers was blown up; one landing craft was torpedoed and probably sunk; and another landing craft and an armed trawler were damaged by gunfire. Shortly afterwards our patrol located and attacked a very strongly escorted German convoy, but with inconclusive results. Then the patrol encountered a German patrol, which was presumably acting as a covering force for the convoys. Two of the craft in this German force were set on fire and a M-class minesweeper was damaged by gunfire.

By that time dawn was breaking so our light coastal forces withdrew and Beaufighters of Coastal Command of the Royal Air Force went out. They found one large supply ship on fire, surrounded by nine escort vessels, one of which was also on fire. The Beaufighters attacked with torpedoes, rockets, and cannon fire. The big supply ship was again torpedoed and the blaze on board was increased to such proportions that she must have been a total loss, while eight of the nine escort ships were sunk. This series of actions cost us one motor torpedo boat and one Beaufighter.

In the early hours of 6 July a very different type of action took place off Brest. This was the outcome of a daring plan. U-boats were known to leave Brest in groups escorted by armed trawlers, and a group of Canadian destroyers were sent into Brest roads to meet one of these groups.

The Canadian destroyers were the *Qu'Appelle*, *Skeena*, *Saskatchewan* and *Restigouche* of the Twelfth Escort Group. The Senior officer was Commander A. M. McKillop, DSC, RN in HMCS *Qu'Appelle*.

It was realised that as soon as they were engaged the U-boats would either dive or return to harbour, and that there would be considerable risk of the destroyers being torpedoed by the U-boats. This risk was accepted, however, in the interests of knocking out more of the Germans' dwindling supply of armed trawlers for, if U-boats had to enter and leave harbour without surface ship escorts they could be hunted and destroyed with comparative impunity by our patrols. Moreover, another group of destroyers—the Fourteenth Escort Group—was in the offing about twelve miles to seaward waiting to come in and hunt the U-boats if they tried to continue to seaward submerged.

The Canadian destroyers entered the enemy's water at 25 knots, the speed being carefully worked out and adjusted so that they would be able to approach the expected meeting place with the enemy at 12 knots—at which speed the destroyers would not make high tell-tale bow waves and stern waves.

Let Commander McKillop take up the story in his own words:

"The lighthouse at the southern entrance was working, and it was an eerie feeling taking bearings of a house full of Germans for our safe navigation! Thanks to various navigational aids my position to the nearest twenty yards was never in doubt, and the navigating officer working on the plot was able to keep a careful check an our progress and give me corrections to course and speed in order to keep exactly to my time-table. The other ships knew this time-table, so that if anyone lost touch he would know where we were. It became very dark indeed around midnight, and it looked good.

"As I turned up on to a northerly course well inside the Rade de Brest I got the first report of a group of ships in the Channel. Oh boy, what a thrill! The enemy was at the rendezvous!

"Soon afterwards I saw a light in the entrance to Brest harbour, and it looked like bow and steaming lights. It was on the opposite bow to my target and I decided that it was probably a coastal convoy and so left it alone. As it turned out, I was right.

"As soon as I was well up between the trawlers and their base I went on to 30 knots and passed the enemy's bearing, course and speed to the other ships. When the range was about 3,000 to 4,000 yards the enemy challenged by flashing the letter W. We 'acted wet' and made W's back until the range had been shortened to 2,600 yards. Then I fired my first cluster of rocket flares and the ball opened.

"There were four trawlers in diamond formation with two U-boats in the centre of this diamond-shaped screen. The whole lot, and the land in the vicinity was shown up by our rocket flares.

"We opened fire and at first it was a target shoot, for the enemy seemed to be completely upset by being met on his own doorstep, and from the direction of his tracer he seemed at first to think that he was being attacked by low-flying aircraft. By previous arrangement *Qu'Appelle* went for the leading German ship, and 'A' gun scored a couple of hits before any of his tracer even came in our direction. I saw his 88 mm gun go up in the air and over the side early on.

"Then the enemy realised that we weren't Wellingtons or Mosquitoes and started pointing his guns at us. Very soon tracer was lighting up the bridge and things got pretty lively. I couldn't see what the U-boats did, but it transpired that they turned outwards, and the far one was not seen or heard from again.

"When I guessed that *Restigouche* was clear I turned 180 degrees to port and went back to finish them off. I could see two stopped and burning and I thought at least one had sunk, but it is very hard to tell under these conditions.

"When I was coming back I suddenly found someone shooting very accurately at me from dead ahead—I found out later that it was the port U-boat, which had turned to the southward. I had just told 'A' gun that if they didn't get a hit very soon we would get hit ourselves, when we were. A 40 mm shell passed through the port side of the bridge and burst inside. The Radio-Telephone operator next to me caught most of it—he died four days later—and a look-out and I collected most of the rest. I didn't fall down because I was hanging on to the voice pipe, but I wasn't very comfortable.

"We passed fairly close to the U-boat, and *Skeena* hit him once or twice with Oerlikon, but unfortunately not with 4.7-inch. I turned away to starboard and sent for the First Lieutenant to take over the command. By that time we had 145 holes in the ship, though fortunately very few on the waterline, but the steering was playing up, so, after 'X' gun had registered four hits on the only trawler we could see that wasn't burning, I laid off, telling HMCS *Skeena* to take over the command of the group.

"After that I took less and less interest in the proceedings. The doctor had a busy night for we had several casualties, including an arm off at one of the Oerlikons. Although when I put my hand down to my thigh after being hit my finger went right into the bone, we did not realise that my leg was broken until I got to hospital at Plymouth next morning."

HMS *Thornborough* was a Captain class frigate (K 574) built in the USA where it was launched 13 November 1943. It was returned to the USA in 1947 and scrapped.

The first week in July also saw a sudden great increase in the enemy activity with surface craft off the eastern flank of the Assault Area, but the close blockade of Le Havre maintained by our light coastal forces and the activities of our patrols were too much for them and their sallies led to their repulse, usually with loss and heavy damage.

Actions took place almost every night during this period, but perhaps the nights of 6 and 7 July stand out as full of incident and at the same time typical.

One of the most skilful of our light coastal force commanders was Lieutenant-Commander D. G. Bradford, DSC, RNR. At about 1 a.m. on Friday, 7 July, his patrol intercepted an enemy force off Cap de la Hève. The enemy was greatly superior to our patrol, for it consisted of two M-class minesweepers, one vessel of the corvette type, and seven or eight E-boats or R-boats. Moreover, the enemy was close under the guns of the German shore batteries. Nevertheless, Lieutenant-Commander Bradford attacked and pressed the attack home despite heavy opposition both from the German ships and from the shore batteries. The German corvette-type ship blew up and one of the E or R-boats was seen to sink and another was blazing before the British patrol withdrew, still under heavy fire from coastal batteries. Only one of our craft sustained minor damage and we had one man slightly wounded.

In the early hours of the following morning a light coastal force patrol commanded by Lieutenant J. Collins, RNVR, found a group of E-boats off Cap d'Antifer. There was a brisk engagement in which our boats certainly inflicted damage, and then the E-boats made off towards their base at Le Havre. Before they were able to reach the shelter of that port, however, they were engaged by the "Captain" class frigate *Thornborough* and there is no doubt that some of the E-boats received serious damage before they reached their base.

Shortly after this Lieutenant-Commander Bradford's patrol, which was operating with the "Hunt" class destroyers *Cattistock* and *La Combattante* (of the Fighting French Navy) encountered another group of E-boats. The enemy at once made at high speed for the shelter of Le Havre, but they did not get away. They left one of their number blazing fiercely. Then, as they neared Le Havre, two German 'M'-class minesweepers appeared on the scene. It is probable that these two ships had been ordered out to support the smaller German craft, but mistook the fleeing E-boats for British light coastal craft about to raid Le Havre. Anyway, the German minesweepers hotly engaged the German E-boats, so our forces discreetly withdrew in order to avoid clearing up the misunderstanding and left them to it!

So the war against the German surface units went on night after night, with the Allied forces asserting an ever increasing superiority and inflicting upon the enemy a scale of loss and damage which progressively curtailed his ability to offer any large-scale threat to the build-up of the strength of the invasion armies of the Allies. There is little doubt that the continuous discomfiture of the E-boats and the losses incurred by them led the enemy to divert a great part of his war-effort to the launching of so-called "secret weapons" against the eastern Assault Area.

The first flying bomb had been sighted in the area on 16 June, but these weapons achieved nothing and it was remarkable how many of them were seen flying towards German-occupied territory, having either had gyroscope failures, or possibly due to faulty discharge from hastily improvised ramps.

Eight days later, on 24 June, the first German composite aircraft put in an appearance in the eastern Assault Area. This was a Junkers 88 laden with explosive with a Messerschmitt fighter on top of it. When in position to attack, the fighter could release the explosive-laden bomber and, in theory, direct it on to its target by wireless control. In practice, however, these weapons proved to be failures, and expensive ones, for they were easy to shoot down.

These air weapons were never used on any considerable scale against our invasion forces, and it was not until July, by which time our close blockade of Cherbourg and of Le Havre and our operations off the Dutch coast had seriously depleted the German resources in surface vessels, that the Germans produced their maritime "secret weapons"—the explosive motor boat and the one-man torpedo.

Up to the end of August our light coastal forces had brought the enemy to action on twenty-eight different occasions off the flanks of the Assault Area alone, and on every occasion the loss and damage inflicted upon the Germans was out of all proportion to that suffered by our forces. It was a sustained effort consisting of close blockade and inshore patrolling which called for a very high degree both of skill and of endurance.

This was appreciated at the Admiralty, for the Board of Admiralty made the following signal to all units:

"Their Lordships are particularly impressed with the recent fine work carried out by the Coastal Forces craft off the coasts of France and the Low Countries, and congratulate not only the crews themselves but also those concerned with the direction and administration of the craft. Their efforts have contributed largely to the success of the operations in France."

A *Life* Magazine photograph of tracer fire, early June 1944. The night sky was not a dark and tranquil place in the bay of the Seine off Normandy.

CHAPTER XI

DETAILS THAT COUNT

Keeping the convoy system working—Communications—Meals and mails—
Casualty notification—Further build-up—Operation Pluto.

After the capture of Cherbourg and Le Havre, when there appeared to be little further danger of enemy attack on our cross-Channel shipping route to Normandy, it was strongly urged in many quarters that the convoy system on this route should be abolished and that ships should sail independently as they were loaded. It was argued that this would save voyage-time and therefore shipping, since the speed of a convoy is necessarily that of the slowest vessel in the convoy and the first ship to complete loading or unloading has to wait for the others of the convoy. This argument is perfectly sound, but Admiral Sir Bertram Ramsay stood out against any abandonment of the convoy system on the cross-Channel route.

His reasons were two. In the first place he considered it absolutely essential that the organisation on the far shore should know exactly when ships could be expected and the nature of their cargoes, and that the organisation on the British shore should know when empty ships were leaving Normandy, so that arrangements could be made for their berthing and rapid loading for the next voyage. His second reason, which was a development of the first, was that it was absolutely essential to keep signal traffic down to proportions which could be handled with expedition and without error. As it was, his headquarters signal staff handled more than a million signals in three months, and on some days the signal traffic had reached the 3,000 mark. If independent sailing had taken the place of convoys the signal traffic concerning the sailing and arriving, and loading and unloading of the ships would be multiplied by the average number of ships in convoy—which was sixteen. No communication staff could hope to handle such a volume of signal traffic without danger of delay and mistakes which might well disorganise the whole of the build-up control organisation (BUCO).

Communications had been, from early in the planning stage of "Operation Neptune," a matter which had called for most careful organisation.

Two or three decades earlier a signal officer of the Royal Navy had written:

"Of what avail the loaded tube
The turret or the shell
If flags or W/T default
The Fleet will go to Hell."

(W/T is, of course, the abbreviation for Wireless Telegraphy.) Communications are far more difficult and far more essential in a combined operation in which all three arms of two great nations, together with other Allied forces, are assaulting a fortress continent with nothing less than the future of the world at stake.

The importance of rapid and, above all, reliable communications had been stressed throughout. This was as well, for the signal traffic assumed gigantic proportions. In the GOLD sector alone Commodore Douglas-Pennant's headquarters ship, HMS *Bulolo*, handled 3,219 signals on D-day and 42,298 signals between D-day and D plus 20. Commodore Oliver, who had charge of JUNO area and had HMS *Hilary* as his headquarters ship, had for some time before D-day instituted a special form of training for all those responsible for communications. This was conducted over the internal broadcasting system of the ship and was called "Uncle Taylor's Hour"—"Uncle Taylor" being Lieutenant-Commander Taylor, Commodore Oliver's signal officer. "Uncle Taylor's Hour" was designed to make all concerned "radio-conscious" and inspired with the determination to get signals through with the minimum of delay and the maximum of accuracy. Commodore Oliver paid high tribute in his official report to his signal officer's somewhat unorthodox system of training all those concerned with communications, saying that it had imbued one and all with the spirit that "somehow the message must get through, even if you have to swim with it."

The build-up of the strength of our armies in Normandy was not solely a matter of organisation designed to make the utmost possible use of every craft; of material considerations such as artificial harbours; and of defeating both the enemy and the weather. Admiral Sir Bertram Ramsay had early realised that the essence of the problem lay in hard work in face of difficulties and under conditions of danger and discomfort. For this reason considerable attention had been paid during the planning stage to the provision of such amenities as would be possible to the officers and men working on and off the beaches. The men in the ships would have accommodation and messes and canteens at their disposal if and when they had time to make use of them. Not so the beach parties and the men in the minor landing craft. Self-heating cans of soup and other food would provide a hot meal in emergency, but sufficient supplies of these could not be carried in all the small craft or be landed with the beach parties. It was necessary, however, to produce some means of providing these men with hot meals, for a hot meal is essential to a man who has been wet through for many hours and who has to work on long past the normal exhaustion point and has nothing but a hollow in the sand to sleep in when he can at last snatch a short rest.

Realisation of this truth led to the organisation of what might be termed the "build-up behind the build-up," in so far as it was concerned with building up, both physically and in morale, the men upon whose tireless work the build-up of the strength of the armies so largely depended. To this end there were produced the floating galleys, called LBK's (Landing Barge, Kitchen) which were capable of providing hot meals for upwards of 500 men at short notice. Of all the curious craft which made up the invasion fleet these were among the most odd, and if the Germans ever saw them they may well have wondered whether we had produced some new type of "secret weapon." The LBK was like nothing so much as a large house-boat with the windows boarded up and with its roof a veritable forest of galley funnels. They were clumsy and unsightly, but they proved of incalculable value.

Other amenities were also organised. All depot ships were fitted with canteens, and there were in the British Assault Area two special canteen boats which plied to and fro twenty-four hours a day. It was only in the SWORD area after it had been closed to shipping that the Eastern Flank Support Squadron found itself cut off from this service. Free newspapers were also provided, although it is difficult to see how anybody ever had time to read them. There was also a special organisation for providing new clothing and kits to survivors of sunken craft without the usual delay imposed by "red tape."

The amenities were by no means confined to the British Assault Area. In the American Assault Area special arrangements were made to provide floating mobile "Post Exchanges"—the American equivalent of a canteen known to all American soldiers and sailors as "PX," and where they can get anything from cigarettes and toothpaste to fountain pens and camera films.

There never has been, and probably never will be, an organisation which is perfect. In recent naval history stress has frequently been laid by naval officers upon the importance to morale of ensuring rapid and regular delivery of mails. In "Neptune" every effort had been made during the planning stage to ensure that officers and men engaged in the operation should get their letters from home rapidly and regularly. This was the more important because all concerned knew that London and the southern counties were under constant attack by German "V" weapons. Yet in the reports rendered by commanding officers one finds repeated complaints that the mails were irregular and unduly slow in delivery to the ships and squadrons. To arrange for the delivery of mails to a great floating and constantly moving population under conditions in which the addresses were necessarily kept secret until the last moment and in which the enemy's actions necessarily play a part, is a matter of supreme difficulty. These difficulties should, however, have been overcome to a greater degree than they were.

Another aspect of naval organisation in "Operation Neptune" which was of very great importance to morale was the reporting of casualties and the notification of next-of-kin. This, happily, worked well. A special organisation was set up during the preparatory period to deal with this problem. The big raid on Dieppe two years before had demonstrated that the ordinary method of reporting casualties and notifying their next-of-kin falls far short of requirements in a great amphibious operation in which men are apt to join up with different units at a moment's notice and without the formality of being officially drafted or appointed. If, for instance, a certain LCT is sunk and only three or four of her crew are reported as survivors one cannot, in an operation like "Neptune," conclude that the remainder must be listed as "missing." It is more than likely that some of them have reached the shore, and, finding that an LCA or a beach party are short-handed due to casualties, have joined up with them. To notify the next-of-kin of every man who had in this way temporarily "disappeared" from his proper station or ship that he was listed as "missing" would have led to untold misery and anxiety. In the light of experience gained at Dieppe a special casualty reporting system and centre, with an immense card index organisation, was set up for "Neptune." The extent to which this saved needless anxiety and sorrow may be judged from the fact that of the first 1,500 reports of officers and men being "missing" during "Neptune" rather more than 1,200 were found to be erroneous. In June this special casualty reporting centre was hit and badly damaged by a flying bomb and much of its card index organisation was destroyed. Nevertheless, it continued to function with success until 5 August. By that time the danger of erroneous reports had passed and casualty reporting reverted to the normal Admiralty procedure.

Day after day and week after week the hard slogging work of the build-up went on, and by D plus 28 (4 July) a million men of the Allied Armies of Liberation had been landed in France. With these men had been landed 183,500 vehicles and 650,000 tons of stores, which is roughly equivalent to one vehicle and rather more than three tons of stores for every five men landed. It was a stupendous achievement in the face of great difficulties and a period of bad weather which virtually reduced those twenty-eight days to less than twenty-five. It must be admitted, however, that since the great gale the "build-up" in the British area had been a matter of maintaining rather than reinforcing the troops ashore and trying to make up some of the lost time imposed by the gale. The same applied for a time in the American area, but the capture of Cherbourg on D plus 20 had made an important difference. To begin with, the port could not be used to any great extent, but very soon it was handling a sufficient volume of traffic to enable the strength of the American armies to be considerably augmented. It should be remembered in conjunction with the military history of the invasion that, while an ever-increasing proportion of the American build-up was handled by the great port of Cherbourg and its enormous protected harbour from the last week in June, every man and vehicle and every ton of stores for the British build-up was landed over the beaches, through the Arromanches "Mulberry" harbour and the two little ports of Corseulles and Port-en-Bessin.

While the build-up was going steadily forward during the weeks after D-day, the Royal Navy was standing by to put to practical use yet another great achievement of British ingenuity and engineering. This was the laying of a petrol pipe line across the English Channel to the Normandy coast which would deliver petrol in bulk to the armies without having to employ a large number of tankers which were urgently required for other duties.

The production and laying of these pipe lines—there was more than one—was an organisation in itself, and like everything else, it had a code name. This code name was PLUTO, a name drawn not from the classics or from Walt Disney, but from the initial letters of the phrase "pipe line under the ocean."

The idea, like so many others, had emanated from Admiral Lord Louis Mountbatten when he was Chief of Combined Operations. It was early in April, 1942, after a demonstration of flame throwers, that Mr Geoffrey Lloyd, the Minister in charge of the secret Petroleum Welfare Department, asked Lord Louis Mountbatten whether his Department could do anything further to help the invasion, which was then in the early planning stage. The reply of the Chief of Combined Operations was: "Yes. Can you lay an oil pipe line across the Channel?"

investigation of the problem involved began at once. At first they appeared to be insurmountable and the verdict of the experts was that the project was impossible to carry out.

This was the situation when Mr A. C. Hartley, Chief Engineer of the Anglo-Iranian Oil Company, suggested that it might be possible to make a flexible armoured pipe, rather like a submarine cable without the cores, and to lay this from cable-laying ships. Here was an idea well worth pursuing, and Mr Geoffrey Lloyd at once consulted Dr Wright, Managing Director of Siemens, who agreed to manufacture a trial length of several hundred yards of this flexible pipe. Within a fortnight this trial length had been successfully laid in the Thames from a Post Office Cable-Laying Ship.

The initiation of these trials was reported to the Prime Minister in his capacity as Minister of Defence. Mr Churchill gave orders that the trials and development were to be pressed forward with all speed and also instructed Mr

The Pluto team at Dungeness, 1943.

Geoffrey Lloyd to inform him at once if he should encounter any difficulties which might require Mr Churchill's personal intervention.

This flexible armoured pipe was called HAIS, a portmanteaux word composed of the initial letters of the inventor Mr Hartley, his firm Anglo-Iranian, and the manufacturers, Siemens. It was clear to all concerned that the project of laying such a pipe line across the English Channel in haste and in time of war would be one of great difficulty. Even in the leisurely days of peace it would have been a major engineering feat, but in war the time factor imposed far greater difficulties because of the strong tides and rapidly varying weather conditions in the Channel. It was obvious that the laying of the pipe line, once begun, would have to be carried through to success despite the tides and the weather and in face of any action the enemy might be able to take. There could be no half-way house between success and utter failure. -232

The next step was to carry out large-scale trials by laying a HAIS pipe line across the Bristol Channel, where conditions of weather and tides

HMS *Holdfast* was the first HAIS pipeline-laying ship. She was converted from the Dundee, Perth & London Shipping Company's coastal passenger ship *London*. She was built in 1941 by Hawthorns & Co. Ltd of Leith, Scotland and was of 1,499 gross tonnage. Conversion commenced in the summer of 1942 and was completed later the same year. Other pipeline-laying ships later included *Empire Ridley* renamed HMS *Latimer*, *Empire Baffin* renamed HMS *Sandycroft* and the SS *Algerian* later HMS *Algerian*.

approximated to those between the Isle of Wight and Cherbourg. To this end two 30-mile lengths of 3-inch HAIS pipe were made. At the same time a special laying ship had to be produced, since no existing cable-laying ship was large enough to carry the full length of the very heavy pipe. The Admiralty, therefore, took over the coasting steamer SS *London* and fitted her with special holds and gear for laying the HAIS pipe. In her new role this ship was given the name of HMS *Holdfast*.

In December 1942, HMS *Holdfast* laid a HAIS pipe across the Bristol Channel from Swansea to Ilfracombe, the operation being carried out with the assistance of Combined Operations Headquarters. After many tests and the surmounting of various technical difficulties this pipe delivered petrol in North Devon under high pressure. Petrol consumers in the West Country were unaware that, for more than a year, their supplies had come under the sea from Swansea in a trial PLUTO. The success of this large-scale trial was most encouraging and as a result large supplies of HAIS pipe were ordered. 233*

Meanwhile other engineers had come forward with an alternative proposal. Mr H. A. Hammick, Chief Engineer of the Iraq Petroleum Company, and Mr B. J. Ellis, Chief Oilfields Engineer of the Burmah Oil Company—both of whom were serving with the Petroleum Warfare Department—considered that lengths of 3-inch diameter steel pipe could be welded together and would have sufficient flexibility to be wound on a drum like cotton on a cotton reel, provided the

A drum of Hamel pipe form HMS *Persephone*.

drum was of sufficiently large diameter. Trials proved that 20 feet lengths of 3-inch steel pipe could be welded automatically to any required length and would be sufficiently flexible to be wound on to a drum of 30 feet or greater diameter.

In order to meet this requirement the Admiralty converted a hopper barge and fitted her with a great wheel which rotated in trunnions mounted on her upper deck and on which the steel pipe was to be wound. In this guise she was one of the queerest looking craft afloat and was given the name of HMS *Persephone*.

This form of welded steel pipe was given the name of HAMEL pipe, the word being formed from the first syllable of the names of the engineers who had put forward the idea—Mr Hammick and Mr Ellis.

Trials with HMS *Persephone* showed that the HAMEL pipe could be wound on a big drum or wheel and that it could be laid by being paid out from the drum, which rotated as the ship steamed ahead. The idea was then further developed. Instead of fitting other ships with large drums, model tests in the National Physical Laboratory showed that it would be possible for a tug to tow an enormous bobbin, which would roll round in the water as it was towed and so pay out the pipe along the sea bed. These enormous bobbins were buoyant even with the pipe wound on them because they were hollow. They resembled oil storage tanks or small gasometers lying on their sides in the water and were 90 feet long and more than 50 feet in diameter. The actual drum on which the HAMEL pipe was wound was 60 feet long and 40 feet in diameter. When fully wound with the HAMEL pipe they weighed 1,600 tons—the weight of the average destroyer.

These great floating bobbins were aptly called "CONUNDRUMS," which was soon shortened to "CONUNS," and each of them could carry 70 miles of HAMEL pipe line. While they were being produced, a special factory was set up in which the 20 feet lengths of steel pipe could be welded into 4,000-foot lengths at the rate of ten miles a day. At the same time, arrangements were made for storing 350 miles of this pipe line.

A pump house on the English side for PLUTO.

A camouflaged pump house for PLUTO.

Both HAIS and HAMEL pipes were used for PLUTO, and the laying of the pipe lines under the sea was accepted as a naval responsibility, while the high pressure pumping stations on the English shore, which were cleverly camouflaged in an old fort, an amusement park, and a row of seaside bungalows, were the responsibility of the Petroleum Warfare Department.

To carry out the Navy's part in laying the pipe lines "Force Pluto" was formed under the command of Captain J. F. Hutchings, who had formerly been on the experimental staff of the submarine headquarters at Gosport. This force was composed of ships of all sizes from 10,000 ton ships to barges and motor boats and was manned by merchant navy personnel serving by agreement under the White Ensign. By the time everything was ready for the operation of laying the pipe lines, "Force Pluto" consisted of a hundred

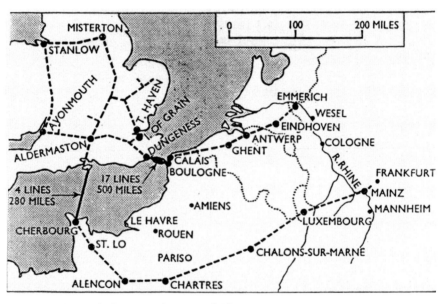

The routes along which PLUTO lines were laid.

officers and about a thousand men. Its main base was at Southampton, with a secondary base at Tilbury. In addition to HMS *Holdfast* two other ships were fitted out with the specially developed cable-laying gear to enable them to lay the HAIS pipe. Two of the ships could each lay 100 miles of HAIS pipe, and the third ship could lay 30 miles. Thames barges were adapted for the handling of the inshore ends of the pipes where the water was too shallow for the ships to operate. "Force Pluto" was also provided with six of the giant "Conuns" for laying the HAMEL pipe. The winding of the pipe on to these "Conuns" was in itself a feat of engineering and seamanship.

The PLUTO Control Room.

A PLUTO line being unreeled across the Channel.

The work of laying the pipe lines across the English Channel from the Isle of Wight area to the Cherbourg neighbourhood was begun some weeks after D-day, as soon as the mines had been swept from the approaches to the tip of the Cotentin Peninsula.

On French soil the pipe lines ran for hundreds of miles, being completed by engineers close behind the advancing armies of liberation. Those pipe lines, once they had been laid across the English Channel, carried all the fuel for the armies and thus contributed very greatly to the build-up, while releasing tanker tonnage for use elsewhere. The pipe lines came as a complete surprise to the enemy, and even the majestic "Conuns" were towed, spinning, across the Channel unscathed and unmolested. The enemy must have seen them during reconnaissances over the Southampton area even if they did not see them at sea, but they were apparently unable to solve these "Conundrums" and assumed that they were some crazy English device of no real importance. They were certainly English; as the Prime Minister said: "'Operation Pluto' is a wholly British achievement and a feat of amphibious engineering skill of which we may well be proud."

Before Pluto, and even for a while during Pluto, fuel was brought in tankers. Here in rural La Cambe, Normandy, American engineers fill hundreds of jerry cans lined up in a pasture. Many GI's have the helmet with white arc of 5th or 6th ESB sector of Omaha. This was 3820th QM Gas Supply Company.

CHAPTER XII

HOLDING THE EASTERN FLANK

The Support Squadron, Eastern Flank—The "trout line"—
German human torpedoes—Booby traps—
Explosive motor boats—Shelling the Germans.

By the third week in June, 1944, the whole of the eastern coast of the Cotentin Peninsula was in American hands and the capture of Cherbourg could be regarded as imminent. There thus remained no threat to the western end of the anchorages off the Normandy beaches, although danger from seaward could not be considered as eliminated so long as U-boats and other vessels could use Brest.

The eastern end of the anchorages off the beaches was, in contrast, still extremely vulnerable. The enemy was still in force in the Franceville-Houlgate area east of the River Orne; the anchorage and "Gooseberry" shelter harbours in the SWORD area was overlooked by the Houlgate and other batteries; and the proximity of Le Havre provided a persistent threat of sea attack. Moreover, intelligence had suggested that the Germans were likely to make use of unorthodox weapons, such as midget submarines and one-man torpedoes. These they could only use against the eastern end of the anchorage.

It was therefore decided to stiffen the defences of the eastern part of the assault area, where such sterling work had already been done by the patrols under Captain A. F. Pugsley, DSO, DSC, RN, and the light coastal forces under Commander Don Bradford, DSO, DSC, RNR. The latter is one of those men to whom war is a magnet. He had already served in South America and with the International Brigade in the Spanish Civil War, yet his hobby is the breeding of thoroughbred arabs.

The new force for the protection of the eastern end of the anchorage was called the "Support Squadron, Eastern Flank." It was formed on 23 June, from the support squadrons of all three of the British Assault Forces. These were no longer required in areas farther to the westward as the army had by that time advanced out of range of their guns.

The SSEF, as it was called for short, was formed under the command of Commander K. A. Sellar, RN. It had the dual role of protecting the eastern flank of the anchorage and of bombarding the German forces east of the Orne. It consisted of seventy-six craft in addition to the Headquarters Ship HMS *Locust*. These craft were mostly LCG's (Landing Craft, Gun), LCF's (Landing Craft, Flak), LCS's (Landing Craft, Support) and motor launches, and they were manned by a total of 240 officers and 3,200 men.

The story of the SSEF is one of great gallantry and of tremendous endurance and keenness over a long period of constant vigilance and activity and of very real hardship. As Commander Sellar said in one of his reports: "The Squadron lived and had its being and operated in a heavily mined area, and were ultimately the only inhabitants of this area, as all the other ships were removed as a result of enemy shelling and mining. Four major attacks were made by night by the enemy, using new weapons. Although losses were suffered, these attacks were decisively beaten."

For the night defence of the exposed eastern flank a line of patrols was established each night. This ran roughly six miles due north from the neighbourhood of Ouistreham and then about two miles in a north-westerly direction to its junction with the area in which Captain Pugsley's patrols operated. This line of patrols, which was established nightly by the SSEF was in reality a double line. The main line consisted of LCG's (Landing Craft, Gun) and LCF's (Landing Craft, Flak) stationed 3 ½ cables (700 yards) apart. As far as possible the LCG's and LCF's alternated in this line. This line was static, in that the craft in it were anchored in their positions. There were certain disadvantages in this practice, but it was necessary because of the ever-present danger from mines and the very limited navigational facilities in these craft. Immediately behind this static line was a mobile patrol of motor launches. One of these motor launches was allocated to every two craft in the static line. In the normal course of events these motor launches lay secured astern of one of the landing craft, but as soon as there was an alarm they cast of and patrolled behind the gaps between the landing craft, ready to give chase to anything that might penetrate the static line.

The whole of this system was called the "Trout Line" and to the westward of it lay the other craft of the SSEF ready to give immediate support if required.

The craft had to move to their positions in the "Trout Line" just before dusk, and if they moved a few minutes too soon they were shelled by the enemy shore batteries, an occurrence which was repeated if they were a few minutes late in leaving their positions at daylight. At night on the "Trout Line" they had to be instantaneously ready for action and exceedingly wide awake. In the forenoons they had to render their reports, replenish with ammunition, and work on the care and maintenance of their craft and armament, added to which there were bombardment commitments to be discharged. The afternoons, therefore, were the only times when the crews of these craft could snatch a few hours' sleep, and that was frequently rudely disturbed by enemy shelling of the anchorage.

This was not a routine which was worked for a few days only, interspersed with periods in British ports. Very few of the craft forming the SSEF returned to England between D-day and the end of August, and some craft did as much as seventy-five consecutive days and nights of this work.

The amenities, moreover, were for the most part conspicuous by their absence in that exposed eastern area. Men lived, or rather existed, for two months and more on "Compo" rations, and none of the craft had trained cooks on board. During the whole period that the SSEF worked in the SWORD area—from 24 July to 11 September—the personnel hardly ever tasted fresh provisions or fresh vegetables. As a result many men came out in boils and suffered from other unpleasant skin eruptions. Mails, too, were irregular and few and far between.

The one occasion when the crews of the craft of the SSEF did get fresh vegetables was when Commander Sellar borrowed a DUKW and went ashore in it. He filled the DUKW up with vegetables which he bought from the local farmers, expending £90 in the process, and then drove it round his command, distributing them to the various craft. To say that the "Vegetable DUKW" was welcome would be a great understatement. Yet when Germany finally collapsed the Admiralty had still not given official approval for the expenditure of that £90.

So strongly did Commander Sellar feel about the lack of fresh provisions that he went so far as to quote in one of his official reports the libellous words of Pepys, when he wrote in 1650:

"Englishmen, and more particularly seamen, love their bellies above everything else, and therefore it must be remembered in the management of the victualling of the Navy, that to make any abatement from them in the quantity or agreeableness of their victuals is to discourage and provoke them in the tenderest part, and will sooner render them disgusted with the King's service than any one other hardship that can be put upon them."

The officers and men of the SSEF, although they were often "provoked," were certainly never discouraged. On the contrary, their spirit and morale as well as their efficiency rose with their increasing moral ascendancy over the enemy and with each action in which the worst the enemy could do with all manner of so-called "secret weapons" and ingenious devices was met and decisively defeated. It was spirit such as this which drew from Rear-Admiral Rivett-Carnac, the Flag Officer commanding the British Assault Area, the remark, after a particularly determined attempt by the enemy to break into the anchorage: "All craft in Trout Line gave their usual display of alertness and excellent seamanship."

There was also high good humour in the SSEF. It had its own newspaper—a 16-page journal issued monthly at a price of threepence, which combined accounts of actions with humour of a high standard. That news-sheet was aptly called *Look Out*. Even one of the LCF's had its own newspaper, a threepenny monthly on ten pages called *Splash*. One marvels that men of whom so much was demanded and who were so short of sleep could bring themselves to produce newspapers in such free time as they had. They lived dangerously *all* the time. On one Sunday Commander Sellar was conducting Divine Service on board one of his craft when there was a sudden whistle and a German shell scored a near miss off the stern—just as Commander Sellar had read the words "fear not, be of good courage." His subsequent remark in his official report was that "A near miss from a shell lent some point to the lesson." At the time, being unaware of the ecclesiastical "drill" for such an occasion, he continued to read, and not one of the men fallen in on the deck moved.

It was on the nights of 5-6 and 7-8 July that the Germans launched their first attacks with human torpedoes. Their attacks came somewhat as a surprise and they succeeded in inflicting fairly heavy casualties. It was estimated that twenty-seven of these weapons were launched on the night of 5-6 July; of these only four were destroyed for certain, and two British minesweepers were sunk.

Two nights later, on that of 7-8 July, came the second attack. It was estimated that thirty-one human torpedoes were launched for this attack, and that twelve of them were certainly destroyed with three "probables" and seven "possibles." Some of these losses were due to Fleet Air Arm Seafires and to Spitfires of the Royal Air Force. Our losses through this agency on that night was one minesweeper sunk, while the old light-cruiser *Dragon* was hit and seriously damaged. This cruiser had been turned over to the Polish Navy, but was serving under her old name. The damage which she sustained was so serious that it was considered not worthwhile to try to get her back to England for repair and she was sunk as an additional blockship in the line which formed the breakwater of No. 5 "Gooseberry" shelter harbour off SWORD beach.

HMS *Orestes* particularly distinguished herself during this attack, destroying no less than four of the human torpedoes. Her log for the latter part of the action reads as follows:

0652—engaged human torpedo. Pilot seen to be hit.
0707—engaged human torpedo. Pilot seen to be killed or severely wounded.
0718—engaged human torpedo. Pilot seen to be killed or severely wounded.
0737—engaged human torpedo. Pilot seen in water and picked up.

Rear-Admiral Rivett-Carnac, commanding the British Assault Area, made the following signal after the action to all ships in the area:

"The valuable work of ships and craft employed in the Defence Lines is reflected in the action taken by HMS *Orestes* and several vessels and craft of the 'Trout Line,' whose vigilance and initiative contributed largely to the frustration of the concerted human torpedo attacks made recently on our anchorage."

Despite the unexpected nature of the attack and the casualties suffered, Commander Sellar was able to say in his report of these attacks that: "The phlegm with which this new weapon was seen, reported, met and dealt with was very noticeable."

On 9 July came the first report of sighting a midget submarine, as opposed to a human torpedo, but these craft never proved a menace off the Normandy beaches.

The so-called "human torpedo" was known by the Germans as the "mother and baby." It consisted of two components. The upper component, which normally travelled awash at a speed of 5-6 knots, was the shell of an old torpedo from which the bulkheads had been removed. In the centre of this upper component was a cockpit with a transparent perspex dome. The pilot of the craft sat in the cockpit, protected by the dome and controlling the entire weapon. In addition to joy-stick-like control, he had an appliance which released the lower component and set it going under its own power. This lower component was, in its essentials, an ordinary torpedo.

The Germans had already produced other special weapons off the British Assault Area. All of these were ingenious and most of them were highly dangerous. The German is an excellent toy-maker, but when he turns this flair to the production of infernal machines he is a menace rather than a joke. All manner of reports of extraordinary-looking objects were reported in the SSEF area at one time or another—so much so that senior officers remote from that troubled sector were apt to consider that the imagination of those manning the "Trout Line" was almost equal to their keenness. Yet most of these apparitions actually existed, and the majority were dangerous, although some were harmless and apparently used as decoys. Among the latter were dummy human torpedo domes with the head and shoulders of a man painted inside. These were apparently dropped to confuse the defence and draw their fire while the real human torpedoes hoped to creep through the patrol lines.

One of the most dangerous of the German devices was a very long range circling torpedo. This weapon was about 8 feet long and rather less than 2 feet in diameter. It had a speed of between 6 and 9 knots and could travel at this speed for up to ten hours. Moreover, its mechanism could be so adjusted that, after it had run straight for the distance required to take it into the anchorage it would start to run in circles as if in search of a victim; and if it "ran down" without hitting a ship it became a very lethal form of mine. These "circling torpedoes" were electric and left virtually no wake so that they were almost impossible to see. It was considered that the damage to the cruiser *Frobisher* and the repair ship *Albatross*, classed as "underwater explosions," as well as the destroyers *Vestal* and *Iddesleigh* were due to these "circling torpedoes."

On the night of 2-3 August the Germans attacked with yet another unorthodox weapon. This was the explosive motor boat. At the time virtually nothing was known of these craft, but gradually a fairly comprehensive idea of their characteristics and capabilities was built up from observation, the interrogation of prisoners, and from the gallantry of a Lieutenant RNVR who boarded one of them and was able to make a brief but invaluable inspection of the craft. These explosive motor boats were, about 16 feet long with a beam of about 6 feet and 2 feet freeboard, and could be driven at between 25 and 30 knots by their two Ford V8 engines. All round the bows there was a spring "bumper" which acted as the "trigger" to detonate an explosive charge of about 250 lbs. carried in the nose of the craft. Some of these explosive motor boats detonated as soon as they touched a ship. Others appeared to have a delay action fuse, for they sank after hitting their target to a depth of 16 or 17 feet and exploded under water. For some time after their appearance it was thought that, although piloted, they were to some extent radio controlled by a "master" boat. This was established as untrue, although there certainly was a "master" boat, which apparently controlled two or three others of a group by a system of simple signalling by red and green lights which could only be seen from astern. These craft were also fitted with an arrangement for their self-destruction in order to prevent them from falling into our hands intact.

The determined and concerted attack delivered by the Germans against the eastern flank of the British Assault Area on the night of 2-3 August did not come as a surprise. Nor, thanks to good intelligence, was the German use of some form of explosive boats altogether unexpected.

As a result of the experience gained in the previous attacks it seemed probable that further attacks were to be expected when conditions of full moon coincided with a west-going tidal stream. On this basis the night of 1 August seemed to be the best for the next series of attacks, but on that night nothing happened. On the next night, however, a lot happened.

At two o'clock on the morning of 3 August the old light cruiser *Durban*, which had been scuttled to form the easternmost of the blockships forming the breakwater of No. 5 "Gooseberry" shelter harbour, was torpedoed. About fifty minutes later the "Hunt" class destroyer *Quorn*, on patrol to the northward, was torpedoed and later sank. Ten minutes later an LCG (Landing Craft, Gun) and a motor launch at the northern end of the "Trout Line" engaged a human torpedo, but without definite results. Nine minutes later, at 3.10 a.m., HMS *Duff* was narrowly missed by a torpedo, and at 3.25 a.m. the minesweeping trawler *Gairsay* was torpedoed and sank.

Things were not going well. All this activity was taking place at the extreme northern limit of the "Trout Line," and was apparently due to human torpedoes. It seemed that these having failed to get through the "Trout Line" on their direct approach to the anchorage on their last attack, were this time trying to skirt the northern end of the "Trout Line" and so work round into the anchorage.

At 3.50 a.m., however, the picture suddenly changed, and it then appeared that the human torpedo attack to the northward was in the nature of a feint designed to cause gaps in the centre of the "Trout Line" or divert the attention of the ships in this line so that the main attack would have a better chance of breaking through into the anchorage.

At 3.50 a.m. an aircraft dropped a red and green flare to the eastward of the "Trout Line." This was obviously a mark and the signal for the main attack to be launched. At 4 a.m. an explosive motor boat was sunk in the Trout Line by an LCG (Landing Craft, Gun). This was the first appearance of one of these weapons. For the next two and a quarter hours successive waves of explosive motor boats attacked and tried to break through the Trout Line. As Commander Sellar said in his report: "A furious battle was waged. When the enemy retired he left 32 explosive motor boats certainly sunk, two probably sunk and one possibly sunk. The Trout Line had lost only one craft—LCG 764, which had sunk one explosive motor boat before being hit by two others. Any explosive motor boats that managed to penetrate the Trout Line were set on and destroyed by the motor launches."

One group of these explosive motor boats tried to work round the northern end of the Trout Line, but they were intercepted by HMS *Gateshead* and ML 185 and four were immediately sunk.

Just after the attack with explosive motor boats developed, some E-boats came into action with our light coastal forces to the eastward. This was apparently a diversion, but it proved an expensive one for the Germans for, without achieving anything, they lost one E-boat sunk and had a second seriously damaged. Our light coastal forces also probably destroyed one explosive motor boat to the eastward of the Trout Line. A group of four other motor torpedo boats—Nos. 252, 253, 257 and 250—which had been sheltering in the "Gooseberry" harbour, were ordered out in support and they did magnificent work in sinking five human torpedoes and taking all five of their pilots prisoner.

The human torpedoes held off during the main attack by explosive motor boats. Then they started attacking, at 6.10 a.m., and kept up their attacks until 7.30 a.m.—an action which cost the Germans twenty-one human torpedoes certainly destroyed, three probably destroyed, and a further eleven "possibles."

The Germans had suffered a most discouraging and costly defeat, which must seriously have shaken their confidence in their new weapons. Commander Sellar reported on this action: "It is considered that the results of what is believed to be the first major attack on an anchorage with these weapons must be somewhat depressing to the enemy and reflects satisfactorily on the vigilance and efficiency of the defenders. It is true, however, that we are becoming used to novel forms and shapes which behave in a whimsical, though dangerous, manner."

The explosive motor boats were promptly christened "Weasels" by those who had destroyed so many of these vicious vermin. An interesting point came to light as a result of the interrogation of prisoners taken from these craft. The men who manned them had apparently been told that their main function was to act as rescue boats for the pilots of the human torpedoes, but that they were to attack any ship if they saw one. Perhaps this was a bit of propaganda designed to induce them to try to get through the Trout Line.

There were three attempts on that night to capture "samples" of the German weapons so that they could be examined in order to determine their weak points and help in the task of producing the best antidote to them. The "Hunt" class destroyer *Blencathra* captured a human torpedo intact, but the self-destruction charge blew it to pieces just as it was being hoisted on board.

The other two attempts at capture were concerned with explosive motor boats, and both were characterised by great gallantry and devotion to duty.

In one case Lieutenant J. P. Fullarton, commanding ML 131, manoeuvred his craft alongside an abandoned explosive motor boat and remained there while a tow was passed, despite the fact that the whirring sound of the self-destruction device could be plainly heard. The explosive motor boat was successfully taken in tow, but unfortunately she blew up about ten minutes later while still in tow.

Lieutenant S. N. Orum, DSC, RNVR, who was afterwards to lose his life in the attack on Walcheren, was the flotilla officer of the 331st LCF (Landing Craft, Flak) Flotilla, but he had embarked for the night in ML 146. Lieutenant Orum saw ML 131 taking the necessary action to tow her abandoned explosive motor boat; then he saw another abandoned explosive motor boat and determined to secure it. It was just dawn when Lieutenant Orum and Sub-Lieutenant I. C. S. Inglis, the First Lieutenant of ML 146, put off from the motor launch in a Carley Raft and paddled to the explosive motor boat. While Sub-Lieutenant Inglis held on to the explosive motor boat and kept the Carley raft in position, Lieutenant Orum made fast a tow to her rudder, deeming it advisable to tow the craft stern first. The two officers regained the motor launch, which began to tow, but the tow parted after ten minutes. Lieutenant Orum and Sub-Lieutenant Inglis set out and passed the tow again. This time Lieutenant Orum shackled a wire strop to a small ringbolt on the after part of the craft. In order to do this he had to board the explosive motor boat, and, in addition to securing the tow he carried out a brief examination of the craft, his account of which was subsequently to prove of great value.

This time, soon after the motor launch had begun to tow, the ringbolt tore out of the explosive motor boat. What was worse, with the ringbolt came a section of her after planking so that the water rushed in and the stern of the explosive motor boat was under water in a minute or two. Seeing this Lieutenant Orum went overboard and attempted to save the craft by passing a tow line through the spring-buffer rail round the explosive motor boat's bows, which, it should be remembered, acted as the "trigger" for the explosive charges in these craft. He was, however, unsuccessful, and the explosive motor boat sank.

On the night of 9-10 August the Germans tried again. It was not so determined or so varied an attack, but it cost the enemy an even higher percentage of loss. It was estimated that the Germans sent just over thirty explosive motor boats on this attack. Of these twenty-nine were certainly sunk, while one "probable" was also claimed, and six prisoners were taken, while there were no casualties to our forces. The Germans showed a very definite reluctance to face the fire of the craft on the Trout Line, and had obviously not recovered from the hammering they had received a week earlier.

On this occasion also the Germans failed to achieve surprise. It was a calm, fine night with a nearly full moon, and in the hours before the attack there had been some sporadic shelling of the No. 5 "Gooseberry" shelter harbour, which had proved to be more of a nuisance than a menace. Shortly after 11.30 p.m. on that night a light was seen to the eastward of the Trout Line, and all craft were promptly warned to be "on their toes."

The attack did not materialise until after 3.30 a.m., but then it led to about an hour and a half of furious activity. As an example of this activity one cannot do better than quote the log of LCF (Landing Craft, Flak) 1, remembering that she was but one of many craft engaged. That log reads:

03.35—Weasel engaged and sunk by starboard after Oerlikon.
03.45—Weasel engaged and sunk by No. 1 4-inch.
04.00—Weasel engaged and sunk by No. 2 4-inch.
04.10—Weasel damaged and stopped. Probably sunk by Oerlikon fire.
04.35—Weasel engaged by Oerlikon assisted by ML 195 and sunk.
05.05-Cease fire.

During the apparent pauses between these quick actions the crew of LCF 1 were far from idle. Not only did the circumstances demand the utmost and continued vigilance, but they were firing star shell all the time, for it was one of the duties of the Landing Craft, Flak, to illuminate the area to the eastward of the Trout Line during an attack in order to show up the explosive motor boats and the domes of the human torpedoes.

The report of Motor Torpedo Boat 714 is even more eloquent of a period crowded with incident. It reads: "The first was sighted to starboard and engaged by gunfire at 03.49 and was seen to blow up. The second was engaged to port and left on fire and well alight. The third was engaged to starboard and was seen to blow up after being on fire for a few seconds. The fourth was closed for some three to four minutes at full speed. This one was set on fire and blew up. The engagements lasted until 04.18. The ranges on firing varied between 50 and 200 yards. No survivors were picked up."

In the whole of this attack only one explosive motor boat penetrated the Trout Line, and this one was promptly chased by a motor launch and suitably dealt with.

As an example of a report by a commander who appreciates that those under his command have established a decisive moral ascendancy over the enemy it would be hard to equal Commander Sellar's report on these actions, the final paragraph of which reads as follows:

"These attacks have been much appreciated by the Trout Line, particularly by the LCF's who nowadays have so little opportunity of showing their skill." (This was because there was at that time a ban on shooting at aircraft.) "It is considered that this attack was detected, met and defeated in a confident and satisfactory manner. Although we were still in a position to field our experienced First Eleven against an indifferent Second Eleven, our bowling was excellent, and for the second time the supports, acting as longstop, had nothing to do."

There was always plenty of humour as well as plenty of work and plenty of danger in the SSEF. After HMS *Locust* had been relieved as headquarters ship on 2 August by HMS *Nith* they could not resist the temptation of replying to signals asking for permission to do this, that or the other by "Yeth" instead of the more conventional "Yes." On one never-to-be-forgotten occasion the squadron received a visit from a gallant ENSA party, complete with girls. Each of them now have a suitably embellished certificate as a holder of the "Order of Neptune, East."

On only one occasion after 9 August did the enemy try to break through into the British Assault Area anchorages with his infernal machines. This was on the night of 18 August. The attack was on only a moderate scale and was somewhat half-hearted, although it caused some amusement because it was directed chiefly against the sunken blockships of the "Gooseberry" shelter harbour. In this attack the poor old French battleship *Courbet* was torpedoed yet again. She was one of the blockships in the breakwater of No. 5 "Gooseberry" harbour. Resting on the bottom she did not draw very much more water than she would have done in full fighting trim, and she used to fly an immense Tricolour and a big Croix de Lorraine flag. The *Courbet* seemed to become something of an obsession with the Germans. She was torpedoed, shelled and bombed, but continued to remain what she was—a very efficient blockship. On 8 July, after the first attack with human torpedoes, the Germans triumphantly broadcast a claim that she had been seriously damaged, and driven ashore, with all her guns silenced! It must he admitted that the German illusion that the *Courbet* was a rich prize was deliberately fostered by the craft of the SSEF, which frequently carried out indirect bombardments of German positions from behind the *Courbet* and under cover of smoke, so that the Germans might well have thought that it was the old French battleship which was causing them so much trouble. Smoke cover was very greatly used in the eastern flank area, because this was so closely overlooked by German batteries east of the River Orne, notably that at Houlgate.

During the abortive attack of 18 August a complete human torpedo unit was captured and brought to the shore. This feat was performed by LCS(L) (Landing Craft, Support, Light) 251, commanded by Sub-Lieutenant Dean, RNVR, in the face of considerable difficulty. The human torpedo was sighted at a quarter to seven in the morning at a range of 400 yards. The LCS at once altered course to close the human torpedo, and opened fire, but the enemy craft took violent avoiding action and was seen to submerge completely for short periods. Sub-Lieutenant Dean therefore gave the order to cease fire, but he continued to close the human torpedo. When the LCS (L) was within 80 yards of the human torpedo fire was opened with machine-guns at the perspex dome. Although some shots ricocheted off this, others pierced it and killed the pilot. Thereupon the human torpedo stopped. The First-Lieutenant and one seaman of LCS(L) 251 went away in the dinghy and went alongside the German contrivance—a ticklish business, for they did not know whether or not it would explode at any moment. However, they succeeded in securing a tow line to the stern of the human torpedo and the LCS(L) began to tow it stern first.

Ten minutes later it was observed that the human torpedo was apparently losing buoyancy and settling deeper in the water, and when LCS(L) 251 stopped her engines the German craft sank, so that it was suspended below the stern of the LCS(L) by the tow line. Fortunately this held. It was brought to the craft's winch and hove up so that the human torpedo broke surface stern first. With great difficulty and care the crew of the LCS(L) succeeded in passing wires round the body of the human torpedo and hove in on these until it rested half out of water, lying horizontally alongside the British craft.

This work had to be tackled very carefully and gingerly, observing that a very dangerous and lethal weapon was being dealt with, and in the circumstances it is hardly surprising that the operation took four hours to complete. Moreover, the whole operation had to be done under cover of a smoke screen laid by another craft, for if the Germans manning the shore batteries had seen what was going on they would certainly have opened fire with every available gun to prevent the capture intact of one of their cherished "secret weapons." Even when the human torpedo was properly slung and secured LCS(L) 251 had to be towed to the anchorage by LCS(L) 260, for it was found that if LCS(L) 251 went ahead on her engines the human torpedo bumped heavily against her side—a singularly unpleasant sensation with a "live" torpedo!

If more attention has been paid in this account to the defensive role of the craft of the SSEF than to their offensive work in bombarding the enemy positions on the flank of the British Assault Area it is because the former were more full of incident of a novel and exciting nature. Nevertheless, the bombardments carried out by the force were of the utmost value to the British troops and particularly to the Royal Marine Commando troops who were holding the Franceville area immediately to the east of the mouth of the River Orne.

Day after day and week after week the craft of the SSEF carried out bombardments. These were of three distinct types. Every day two LCG's (Landing Craft, Gun) carried out harassing fire on the German positions and lines of communication in the Franceville area. There was always opposition to this fire, usually by 88 mm and 105 mm anti-tank guns, although there was a certain amount of heavier shelling from the batteries to the eastward.

Other LCG.s carried out numerous indirect bombardments of enemy positions. These were done in response to a request for fire support from the troops ashore and were controlled by the Forward Observation Officers, Bombardment, attached to the military, who said on several occasions that they were of great value on that exposed eastern flank. Nearly all these indirect bombardments were carried out under cover of smoke screens, and many of them from behind the old French battleship-blockship *Courbet*.

In addition to these types of bombardment, the LCS's (L) (Landing Craft, Support, Light) were almost continuously engaged during daylight hours in "beating up" the coast between Franceville and Cabourg. This was perhaps the most dangerous form of bombarding carried out by the force, for it entailed these little craft working close in off the enemy-occupied coast and virtually under the guns of established coast-defence batteries, and smoke had frequently to be resorted to. At one time or another all the craft engaged on this duty suffered casualties and damage, yet it is on record that the jobs were tackled "with considerable enthusiasm."

Of the effect on the enemy of these bombardments by craft of the Support Squadron, Eastern Flank, there is no doubt. After the Franceville-Houlgate area had finally been occupied by our troops German prisoners testified to its accuracy and to its effect upon the German defensive arrangements. Among other things, they admitted that these bombardments completely denied to them the one main road which formed their main line of communication with the forces holding the Franceville area.

Of the success of the craft of the SSEF against the German infernal machines which tried to break through into the anchorage of the British Assault Area there was forthcoming even more dramatic testimony after the country east of the Orne had been liberated. It was found that the German human torpedoes had been launched from a little village called Villers. A Frenchwoman of that village stated that on one night the Germans had launched and sent out 93 human torpedoes, and that only 18 of this number had come back. The pilots of these 18 were, she said, extremely frightened and needed much brandy to restore them.

In recording this evidence, Commander Sellar commented: "She should know—she was the owner of the 'local.'"

．　．　．　．　．

By September 1944, Havre had fallen, as well as the nearer batteries overlooking SWORD area. No longer was there ever-present danger on that exposed flank from all the enemy could do with orthodox weapons and unorthodox "horrors." The Support Squadron, Eastern Flank was no longer needed in that area, and on 11 September it left the troubled waters in which it had performed so tirelessly and so well since 24 June. It had levied a toll upon the enemy which had proved crippling to his plans with his new weapons, and it had rendered invaluable service to the military forces along the Orne flank. These things it had not done without loss to itself. It had lost four craft. Two LCG's (Landing Craft, Gun) had been mined and sunk. One LCG had been sunk by an explosive motor boat, and one LCF (Landing Craft, Flak) had been torpedoed and sunk. A great many other craft had suffered damage. The cost in personnel had been 8 officers and 57 men killed or missing, and 3 officers and 112 men wounded.

To the Support Squadron, Eastern Flank the Flag Officer commanding the British Assault Area made the following richly deserved farewell signal on 11 September:

"Your work in the British Assault Area in support of the Army and in defending the anchorage has been unfailingly successful. I am very sorry to lose you but the shooting season for you here is now closed. Goodbye and Good Luck."

CHAPTER XIII

BOMBARDMENT AND CAPTURE OF CHERBOURG

"Cruiser Division Seven"—Close range bombardment—Three hours of hot action—importance of Cherbourg—Withdrawal of the Task Forces.

During the third week of June the United States troops were steadily approaching Cherbourg from the southward, and by D plus 18 they were in the outskirts of the town built round the great fortress port which had been the major northern base of the French Navy.

The stage was set for an operation of great importance. The truism that even the first phase of an invasion cannot be considered successful until the invaders have seized a port in which reinforcements and supplies can be landed irrespective of weather conditions had been to some extent modified by the success of the artificial "Mulberry" harbour off Arromanches. The Allies had, however, planned to have two such harbours in operation, but the gale had destroyed the St Laurent "Mulberry" harbour. That made the capture of a big deep-water port the more important. And even if both of the artificial harbours had been completely successful the capture of Cherbourg would have been of great importance, for the "Mulberry" harbours had been designed to last for only ninety summer days.

Even before the war Cherbourg had been a very heavily defended port, and there was no doubt that the Germans had very substantially increased its defences. The port and its defences had been heavily attacked from the air, but it was known that many of the gun positions and strong points were under reinforced concrete of such thickness as to make them immune from air attacks unless each individual position received a direct hit from a penetrating bomb—a most unlikely contingency. Most of the gun casemates, however, had fairly large openings to seaward, for the defences faced the sea and the guns had been mounted in such a way as to give them the maximum arcs of fire. They were, therefore, to some extent vulnerable to low trajectory fire from seaward.

This fact indicated that a naval bombardment from fairly close range would be required to reduce these positions. There was another point which had to be considered. Along the breakwater, which is more than two miles long, there are three forts. These, and the Fort du Homet on the seaward side of the arsenal and naval dockyard, might well have been given guns which would bear upon the sea front and the town. It was quite possible, in fact, that the Germans had moved some of the guns in the forts for this purpose while the Americans were advancing towards Cherbourg from the south. The German coast defences were manned by German naval personnel of a higher quality than the garrison troops, and they were commanded by a young enthusiast who was both a gunnery and a torpedo expert. Rear-Admiral Hennecke was only forty-six years of age and he had been specially selected to command the naval port and defences of Cherbourg.

It was essential that these forts, which might be used against the American troops entering the town and fighting their way through to the harbour, should be silenced, and a naval bombardment promised the best results. If some of the guns in the circular forts on the mole had been moved to the landward side, the empty casemates to seaward would make them the more vulnerable to bombardment from the sea.

It was for these reasons that there was organised a special naval bombarding force for Cherbourg, and this was kept in readiness for several days so that its work should be perfectly co-ordinated with the progress of the troops up the Cotentin Peninsula to Cherbourg.

The Cherbourg bombardment force was Anglo-American and consisted of three American battleships, two American cruisers, and two British cruisers. It was under United States command in the person of Rear-Admiral Morton L. Deyo, USN. The minesweepers allocated to clear the waters ahead of the bombarding force were predominately British, while the destroyers which screened it were American. It was right that the force should be under American command since not only were most of the larger units American, but their bombardment had to be closely co-ordinated with the advancing American army. Any slight delay or confusion in communication might well have led to shells from the American and British warships falling among American troops.

Rear-Admiral Deyo's flagship was the cruiser *Tuscaloosa*. The *Quincy* was the other American cruiser and the British cruisers were the *Glasgow* and *Enterprise*, the latter being commanded by Captain H. Grant, of the Royal Canadian Navy. The American battleships in the squadron were the *Nevada*, *Texas* and *Arkansas*.

The plan was for the *Nevada* to take part in the initial bombardment with the cruisers while the *Texas* and *Arkansas* formed a powerful supporting group slightly to seaward and ready to take part in the bombardment. Rear-

An aerial view of Cherbourg, June 1944.

Admiral Deyo's bombardment squadron was given the title of "Cruiser Division Seven." It was considered that a ninety-minute bombardment by this force should be sufficient to silence the German defences, formidable as these were. They consisted of at least twenty casemated batteries. Of these three were of guns of 280 mm, and at least fifteen housed guns of 150 mm calibre or greater. There were also a large number of smaller batteries.

By D plus 18 (24 June) the situation on the Cotentin Peninsula was developing rapidly. The American troops advancing up the peninsula had compressed the Germans into a narrow strip along its northern coast from Cap de la Hogue to Cape Barfleur. Cherbourg, near the centre of this coast, was by far the strongest German position and, moreover, one which the Allies urgently required for their own use. The time had come for the naval bombardment of Cherbourg and the final assault on the town and port.

Rear-Admiral Deyo's "Cruiser Division Seven" sailed from Portland at dawn on 25 June. It was a beautiful morning as the force was swept across the Channel by the minesweepers. When the ships were still fifteen miles from the coast their crews could see the smoke of fires in Cherbourg, and as they drew nearer they could hear the rumble of gunfire. The battle for the shoreward approaches to Cherbourg was already in progress.

When the bombarding ships were about nine miles from the coast they turned parallel to it. They were steaming in the order *Glasgow*, *Enterprise*, *Nevada*, *Tuscaloosa* and *Quincy*, and were preceded by the minesweepers and flanked by the screening destroyers. The *Texas* and *Arkansas* kept station to seaward.

The ships were well within range of the German heavy batteries, but these showed no sign of fight. The run parallel to the coast was completed without incident and then the minesweepers, followed by the bombarding ships, turned south again to approach even closer to the shore. Still there was no opposition from the enemy defences. Less than five miles from the forts the minesweepers altered course and once again began sweeping parallel to the coast. It was then just before noon.

Then suddenly a German battery opened fire on the minesweepers. At once the bombarding ships replied, and so drew the German fire from the minesweepers and on to themselves.

The action at once became general, with ships and shore batteries engaged in a very fierce and rapid firing duel. The German batteries were shooting very accurately, and the ships were forced to zigzag to avoid the fall of their shells. Up and down off the coast they steamed, almost continuously under helm and yet maintaining great accuracy in the fire they directed at the German forts. The battleship *Nevada*, being slower than the cruisers, and more sluggish in answering her helm, was ill-fitted to take part in this sort of weaving with lighter and faster ships, and about half an hour after opening fire she "cut loose" from the squadron and manoeuvred independently to the northward, still, however, continuing her bombardment.

Despite the almost continuous use of helm, the ships were being repeatedly straddled by German salvoes. In face of so hot and accurate a fire it seemed inevitable that the ships should be hit. Many of them were hit, but not one of them was put out of action or forced to interrupt the bombardment for more than a few minutes.

The first ship to be hit was the American destroyer *O'Brien*. At 12.53 p.m. she was hit by an 8-inch shell. The little ship stood up to it well, however, and was able to continue the action. Twenty-two minutes later both the other American destroyers—the *Barton* and the *Laffey* were hit by heavy shells, but in each case the shell failed to explode. By that time, too, the battleship *Texas* had been hit, but this also was a "dud" shell which smashed against the armour of the ship's conning tower but did not explode.

The planned ninety minutes of bombardment expired at 1.25 p.m., but the German batteries and forts were still very much alive at that time, despite the fact that the aircraft spotting for the ships reported that at least 75 per cent of their fire was effective. RearAdmiral Deyo was determined not to leave the task half completed, although there was considerable risk in extending the bombardment because the military situation on shore was developing so rapidly that it was well-nigh impossible to be certain of exactly where the forward elements of the American troops were at any given moment. He gave the order for the bombardment to be continued.

It was rather more than a quarter of an hour later that the bombarding force suffered the only damage which could be accounted in any way serious. This was to HMS *Glasgow*. The *Glasgow*, which had led the line in the initial stages, had been firing very rapidly and very accurately with her twelve 6-inch guns. It was obvious that the fire of this ship had been causing great annoyance to the Germans, for some of the most belligerent of the enemy's batteries had clearly been concentrating their fire on her and she had several times been straddled and narrowly missed. Then, at 1.42 p.m., she was hit by a salvo. Two shells of this salvo hit and a third was a very near miss. None of these shells was a "dud."

One of the shells which hit exploded in the aircraft hangar just abaft the bridge and started a fire. It was this fire rather than the actual damage caused by the shells which forced the *Glasgow* to interrupt her bombardment and haul away to the northward. In a very few minutes, however, the fire had been got under control and the ship was again in the thick of it, with all her guns in action and wreaking vengeance for the casualties which she had suffered. There were casualties from splinters in ships which were not actually hit, for the Germans were using shells which burst immediately on impact with the water.

After the damage to the *Glasgow* the gunfire of the ships gained a steadily increasing ascendancy over the German forts and shore batteries. Rear-Admiral Deyo kept up the bombardment until it had been in progress for three hours—exactly double the planned time—and although the protected German batteries were never completely silenced, they were all damaged and suffered serious casualties. Moreover, the German guns' crews were kept so busy by the bombarding ships that they were unable to give any attention to what was happening inshore of them, or to the minesweepers which had begun to clear the approaches to the port under cover of the bombardment.

A total of just under 3,000 shells were fired by the ships during the bombardment of Cherbourg. Of these 376 were 14-inch or 12-inch shells from the battleships.

The three hours' bombardment of the forts and heavy gun batteries of Cherbourg from close range in broad daylight was an operation of difficulty

The surrender of Cherbourg, 26 June 1944. German soldiers emerge from underground defensive bunkers with their hands in the air.

and considerable risk. The Anglo-American bombarding squadron, however, manoeuvred so skilfully that no ship was lost and serious damage was avoided. Of the accuracy and effectiveness of the gunfire there is no doubt. Nor is there any doubt that the naval bombardment played a most important part in the reduction of the fortress port of Cherbourg, which fell to the American troops on the following day. The risks taken by Rear-Admiral Deyo's squadron had been amply justified.

American naval personnel played an important part in the actual capture of Cherbourg. These were officers who were working with the army and who entered the town and port from the landward side.

It was, for instance, an American naval officer-Lieutenant John E. Lambie, USNR—who discovered the great underground stronghold which housed the

The surrender of Lt.-General Karl
Wilhelm von Schlieben, Commander
of the Festung Cherbourg, and
Admiral Walter Hennecke.

German military and naval headquarters. He reported his discovery and led
troops to it, which resulted in the final surrender of the German forces in
Cherbourg and the capture of General von Schlieben and Admiral Hennecke.
A brother officer of Lieutenant Lambie—Lieutenant-Commander Leslie E.
Riggins, USNR—was instrumental in discovering in this underground fortress
headquarters certain documents which proved to be of immense value to the
Allies in clearing the port and its approaches.

Thus within three weeks of D-day, and despite the delay caused by the great
gale in the building up of the strength of the Allied armies in Normandy, the
greatest port on the French northern seaboard was in our hands.

Much hard work and great gallantry were required before the port of
Cherbourg was fully available for the requirements of the Allies, but this
could implicitly be relied upon. The important thing was its capture, and this
marked one of the great milestones on the road to ultimate victory.

Admiral Sir Bertram Ramsay, the Allied Naval Commander-in-Chief,
fully appreciated that the capture of Cherbourg was not only of immense
importance, but also that it set a clear limit to the first phase of the invasion.
Hitherto practically every man, vehicle and ton of equipment or supplies had
had to be landed over the beaches or through the artificial "Mulberry" harbour
off Arromanches. Once Cherbourg could be cleared the problem would be
the far simpler one of supply through an established deep-water port. The

Arromanches "Mulberry" and the beaches would still carry an enormous traffic, but they would no longer be the only routes of supply. Moreover, the whole defensive position of the sea lines of communication across the English Channel and the anchorages off the beaches was radically altered by the dislodgment of the enemy from Cherbourg. The enemy had lost a great base of tremendous strategic value on the flank of our main supply line. The threat to the western flank had been enormously reduced. E-boats were no longer seriously to be feared on that flank, although adequate steps would have still to be taken to prevent interference by the U-boats or other craft from Brest. The security of the eastern flank was also affected. There, in Le Havre, the enemy still held a strong strategic position on our flank, but the danger could be reduced because the Allied forces on that flank could be reinforced by forces freed from the western flank.

On all counts the position had been immensely improved. So much so that, as soon as the port of Cherbourg had been surveyed and he had received a report that it would be possible to use a portion of it very soon—a portion

US Army Engineers begin a railway line to the right of the dock of Mielles in the port of Cherbourg.

This series of photographs was taken on 31 July 1944, five weeks after the surrender of the German garrison.

In the early stages of construction a large landing craft shift is utilised. The low number of vessels carrying trains will push the use of LST "specially landscaped Ferry Train", the shallow draft of the LST allows them to land by playing shallow.

The US Army Transportation Corps is responsible for complex operations at Cherbourg Port.

Severe gradient issues need to be overcome to avoid derailment. To successfully unload the train from the LST system a built-mobile ramp is made, the movable ramp slides to arrive at the lower deck of the LST for the final adjustment.

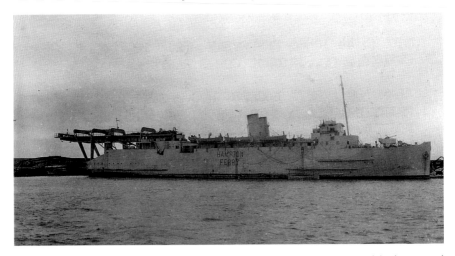

The cross-channel ferry, *Hampton* was re-christened HMS *Hampton* and had a special gantry fitted to her stern which could cope with a load of 84 tons and would first turn a railway engine and then gently drop it on board. The ferry's full load was 16 locomotives and about 20 trucks, with the engines already coaled. To handle the locomotives the ship had a staff of 18 American soldiers who were under the command of Captain Munton. Their first 'delivery' was 30 June 1944, just four days after Cherbourg was captured. Here she is ready on 31 July 1944 to unload her first locomotives for the US Army.

HMS *Twickenham*, sister ship to HMS *Hampton*, stern on, unloads a locomotive onto the rails laid by the Transportation Corps at Cherbourg.

which would increase rapidly as the work of clearance and rehabilitation progressed—Admiral Sir Bertram Ramsay decided that he could make large reductions in the naval forces which he had had under his command since before D-day.

To this end the commanders of the Eastern and Western Task Forces— Rear-Admiral Sir Philip Vian and Rear-Admiral Alan G. Kirk, USN—were withdrawn. Rear-Admiral Kirk, however, remained in general command of all American naval forces. The commanders of the Assault Forces—Rear-Admiral A. G. Talbot and Commodores C. E. Douglas-Pennant and G. N. Oliver in the Eastern area and Rear-Admirals J. L. Hall, USN, and D. P. Moon, USN, in the Western area—were also withdrawn. The places of all these officers were taken by a British flag officer to command the whole of the Eastern area and an American flag officer to command the whole of the Western area. These two officers were Rear-Admiral RivettCarnac in the Eastern area with the title of Flag Officer British Assault Area (FOBAA for short) and Rear-Admiral Wilkes, USN, in the Western area with the title of Flag Officer West. All forces operating in the two assault areas came under the jurisdiction of these two commanders. On the east, forces under the command of FOBAA operated beyond the actual eastern limit of the British Assault Area because this remained the fighting flank where considerable resilience was necessary.

The Task Forces of the Assault Forces were withdrawn and a number of ships thus became available for other duties. In particular, it made possible a greater degree of reinforcement to the Allied fleets in the Far East and the Pacific.

Ships for bombarding duties on the eastern flank and for the bombardment of Brest and the safe conduct of the steady stream of cross-Channel convoys, of course remained available, but they operated under the orders of the Allied Naval Commander-in-Chief only when required. Normally they were administered by the naval authorities at the ports in which they were based. The English Channel ceased to be the responsibility of the Allied Naval Commander-in-Chief, and sections of it once again became the responsibility of the Commanders-in-Chief at Plymouth, Portsmouth and the Nore, and the Vice-Admiral, Dover. The Allied Naval Commander-in-Chief, however, still held the high command of both Assault Areas and the ultimate responsibility for all naval operations connected with the invasion and the maintenance and reinforcement of the Allied Armies of Liberation.

Rear-Admiral Alan G. Kirk, USN, who had commanded the Western Task Force throughout the operations, and who was soon to be promoted to the rank of Vice-Admiral, paid the following tribute in his despatch to the high commanders under whom he had been serving:

"The skilful co-ordination of this vast operation by Supreme Commander General Eisenhower and the high professional skill and sympathetic leadership of Allied Naval Commander Expeditionary Force, Admiral Ramsay, will be remembered by all who served under them in the Western Task Force."

"Operation Neptune" was technically brought to a conclusion by the withdrawal of the Task Force Commanders on 30 June. The consolidation and extension of the successes gained by the operation, however, long continued. These did not end until the Allied armies were fully supplied to a strength which enabled them to launch across the Rhine the great offensive which was to end only with the signing of Germany's unconditional surrender.

The naval responsibility became more and more that of the Royal Navy as the western flank was made more and more safe from enemy interference. For both the American Navy and the Royal Navy there was much hard work to be done in supplying the armies with the sinews of victory, and for the Royal Navy there was still much hard fighting in store in direct continuation of "Operation Neptune."

An LCT (Mark 6), with wounded soldiers being transferred to a large vessel using a conveyor incline. The wounded are covered with a blanket strapped on stretchers. Some of the less badly wounded are reading newspapers.

Part Three

CONSOLIDATION

CHAPTER I

CHERBOURG AND BREST

German strategy of holding and destroying ports—The "Red Ball Route"—Clearing Cherbourg—"Human minesweepers"—Marseilles and Antwerp—Brest

After the break-through of the American Third Army at St Lo and the Battle of the Falaise Gap, enemy resistance in the inland areas of France largely collapsed, and large bodies of German troops were cut off in ports along the Channel coast and in the Brittany Peninsula and the Bay of Biscay.

"The German Command followed a perfectly sound strategic plan. Each port must be destroyed as far as possible and the garrison must resist for as long as possible to enable this destruction to be effected and to deny us the use of the port. On the Allied side, the object was to clear the enemy from the ports before effective demolition could be achieved, and thereafter to repair the port installation as effectively and as expeditiously as possible in order to receive men and equipment.

"The Germans succeeded in achieving their object to a high degree in certain of the Channel ports. Port facilities were demolished, ships were sunk alongside the quays and in the inner harbours, lock gates were destroyed and the entrances to ports were blocked with sunken ships. These ports had also been the target of severe Allied air attacks while in enemy hands. As a result of our own and the enemy's efforts, nearly every port was a scene of utter desolation."

These paragraphs are quoted from a statement made by Admiral Sir Bertram Ramsay, the Allied Naval Commander-in-Chief. They indicate the task which lay before the Allied navies in consolidating the victory over the German armies in the inland portion of France and Belgium, which "Operation Neptune" had made possible.

By the end of September the fighting fronts had moved right across France from Normandy to the German frontier. We had captured the ports of Brest,

Cherbourg, Le Havre, Ostend and Antwerp, but still the vast majority of the supplies and reinforcements for the Allies armies had to come into France by way of Cherbourg and the great prefabricated harbour at Arromanches. Thence they had to be hauled right across France and Belgium. Some of the railways were working, but most of the supplies had to go by road along the famous "Red Ball Route" from Normandy to the German border. That road was so called because it was marked everywhere with a red ball. On it the military traffic stopped neither by day nor night. It was entirely closed to any other traffic and the military traffic knew no speed limit and its drivers no rest. The motto painted on big boards nailed to the trees was "Get on or get off the road." A breakdown meant "ditching" the vehicle to avoid causing any obstruction or delay to others. Drivers used to change over with the vehicle in motion, the relief climbing up behind the driver's shoulders and sliding down into the seat as the driver edged out of it sideways. The thundering tank transporters were fitted with constantly flashing "red ball" lights which gave them absolute priority over everything.

The story of the Red Ball Road is the story of the greatest feat of administration and supply in military history, but behind the Red Ball Road were the ports, which had always been considered the bottleneck in any overseas supply system.

They were not the bottleneck. There was no bottleneck. That this was so was a triumph of the Allied navies and merchant navies, who saw to it that the victory of "Neptune" was consolidated and exploited as the Allies progressed towards the final defeat of Germany.

The seizure of deep-water ports and the ability to make use of them are an absolute pre-requisite of success in invasion. The artificial "Mulberry" harbour at Arromanches had provided us with one such port during the critical weeks of the build-up of the Allied military strength in Normandy. Then, on 27 June, three weeks after D-day, United States troops had captured Cherbourg after bombardment by American and British warships.

Cherbourg was the first French port of any size to fall into Allied hands. Its capture was therefore a matter of the first importance. There was a considerable difference, however, between the port being in Allied hands and the port operating to capacity in the service of the Allied cause.

The Germans, specialists as they had long shown themselves in science and in destruction, had combined the two in an attempt to make the port unusable for the longest possible time. Ships were sunk alongside the jetties and in the entrances to the docks. Cranes had been toppled on top of these, and even railway trucks had been added to the piles of twisted steel which lay mostly below water close up against the jetties so that no ship could come alongside them. Moreover, explosive "booby traps" had been inserted in the tangled wreckage with the object of causing casualties among our salvage experts and discouraging their successors. Add to this the fact that the whole of the great harbour was thickly sown with every conceivable type of mine in all manner of combinations and provided with all sorts of anti-sweeping devices. There were even trip-wires on the sea bed connected with explosive charges to trap and kill divers sent down on the salvage work. It was afterwards discovered that the Germans, with true Teutonic thoroughness, had sent charts of the port and blueprints of its installations to the experts so that a comprehensive plan had been drawn up and followed for the destruction and blocking of the ports. This method had been followed by the Germans in the case of most of the ports to which they clung so stubbornly.

Commodore T. McKenzie, the Principal Salvage Officer on the staff of the Allied Naval Commander-in-Chief, Expeditionary Force, flew to Cherbourg with Commodore W. A. Sullivan, the Chief of the United States Naval Salvage, immediately after the liberation of that port. In Commodore McKenzie's own words: "It was a scene of complete devastation. Quays had been demolished; cranes, elevators, etc., had been blown into the water; dozens of railway wagons had been run into the harbour before the quays were demolished; and sixty-seven ships and craft ranging from 12,000 tons downward to 100 tons had been sunk alongside the demolished quays or near the harbour entrances.

"Six British salvage vessels, twelve lifting 'camels,' and three American salvage vessels were allocated for the work, and as soon as minesweeping permitted they entered the port.

"Inside a few days some berths had been cleared and ships were discharging at the few undamaged quays, while DUKW's and LCT's poured stores and equipment over the beaches. The combined United States and British salvage parties worked at such a speed that inside four months practically every sunken ship had been either re-floated or lifted and dumped in our marine graveyard. In all, 81 wrecks and obstructions were cleared in Cherbourg harbour."

A few years before, even experts would have boggled at the state of Cherbourg, and would have agreed that even its partial rehabilitation must take many months. In the war years, however, the Allies had learnt much of the science of clearing ports and enabling them in a short time to handle a greater quantity of traffic than that for which they had been originally designed.

A notable example was Naples. The Germans had been at great pains to block the port of Naples and destroy not only the port facilities, but the installations which provided the power, light and water for the port. Yet British and American engineers and salvage personnel went to work with such skill, teamwork and friendly rivalry that the shambles which had been Naples harbour soon became a workable port, the capacity of which rose day by day until it was far beyond its original peacetime capacity. The existing jetties were cleared; one hundred and seventy wrecks were lifted and moved; new jetties were built upon the hulls of sunken ships. Thus the wartime Naples which rose from the ruins left by the Germans achieved the amazing feat of handling a greater weight of freight than the port of New York. Not only did Naples supply the Allied armies in Italy, but it was able to handle the additional commitment of being the point of departure for most of the convoys for the invasion of the south of France.

The experience which the Allies had gained at Naples stood them in good stead at Cherbourg. This was concerned not only with the developments of methods but also with the development of port-clearance and salvage "weapons." At Naples the latter had been in short supply and inadequate. At Cherbourg new implements were available, among them a plentiful supply of underwater welding and oxyacetylene cutting plants and fire-fighting appliances.

In the clearance of a damaged and blocked port the navy is responsible for clearing everything up to the point at which the delivery of cargo from a ship normally ends. In other words, the navy is responsible for everything that floats and for moorings and the berths of ships alongside jetties. From that point, it is the responsibility of the military Port Repair Organisation to clear the quayside of obstructions and put the landward facilities and organisation into working order.

The mines which the Germans had strewn on the bottom of Cherbourg harbour were of types which might not reveal their presence until they had been swept over several times. The sweeping of a harbour is at the best of times a tricky job both technically and from the point of seamanship, and Cherbourg had to be swept for magnetic and acoustic operated mines. When the harbour had been swept once the job had to be started all over again, for the sweep passing over a mine would only have given the mine one "click," and some of the German mines had to have eight or ten "clicks" before they exploded.

Only if the harbour had been swept for all types of mines a dozen times or more, and there was certainty that no further mines had been dropped by aircraft, could the harbour therefore be considered as "swept." Even then there would have been an element of uncertainty, for if the Germans could design a mine which required several "clicks" before the one which exploded it, they might well have designed a mechanism which would lie inert for even longer, although it grew more dangerous every time a ship or a sweep passed over it.

To work on the principle of the straightforward sweeping of the harbour would therefore have taken a very considerable time, particularly as enemy aircraft were frequently over the harbour and might be dropping more mines, and time was at a premium for the use of the port was most urgently desired by the Supreme Allied Command.

Fortunately, however, this problem had been anticipated and steps had been taken long before D-day to solve it.

The solution of the problem was the use of "human minesweepers." These "human minesweepers" were underwater bomb disposal experts who could render mines harmless when they were found. When that had been done the safe mines could be raised in order to make assurance doubly sure and to avoid them becoming foul of ships' anchors and cables.

These "human minesweepers" were young men between nineteen and twenty-two years of age who had undergone a difficult and rigorous training for their task. They were all volunteers. They were first trained on dry land on the various types of German mines which they were likely to meet. Then they were trained in the use of shallow-water diving apparatus until they were quite at home under water. The next step was to train them on the mines under water. For this training, of course, the explosive charges had been removed from the mines, but otherwise nothing was made easy for them during their training. It was appreciated that they would have to work on the bottom of harbours where the mud would soon be stirred up so that the mines would be lying in a thick opaque soup. They therefore underwent their final underwater training on the bed of the Lower Thames, where the mud is as thick as it is likely to be anywhere. In these conditions they had to work entirely by the sense of touch, for the visibility was seldom more than a very few feet and often less than a foot. They were taught to move along the bottom like a crab, and to do so very gently, for it was known that the Germans had evolved trip wires and other traps for unwary divers.

These men had to be physically tough as well as possessed of a high degree of fearlessness and coolness. It was found that many of them failed to qualify during their training because they were not sufficiently resistant to the cold. It must be remembered that the low age limits meant that none of them could have had any extensive experience of diving. The vast majority of them had none.

The bottom of Cherbourg harbour was described by an expert on mines, anti-sweeping devices and other devilish contrivances as a "professor's paradise." There is no question that it was a seaman's nightmare.

One good thing could be said about Cherbourg on its capture, the entrances through the breakwaters had not been blocked by wrecks. This was not because the Germans saw no necessity for such a step—they sank ships in the entrances to other harbours—but because they did not have at Cherbourg enough ships of a size suitable for this work.

The fact that the entrances were not blocked by wrecks made the Allies the more wary, for they suspected that the Germans would have laid mines in the hope that an Allied ship or two would do the work for them by being blown up and sunk in the entrances. Thus it was that the initial entry into Cherbourg harbour from the sea was made very gingerly by very small craft, the commanding officers of which had to think in terms of the magnetic field

German mines in a railway wagon at Cherbourg.

of their vessels and the sound of their engines and screws. Thus they almost drifted in, having stopped their engines well outside the gaps between the breakwaters.

For the same reason much of the minesweeping and clearing of the harbour was done from small boats and even from rubber dinghies.

The first vessel to enter Cherbourg harbour was a British naval Motor Launch. This ML was sweeping as she entered the harbour and no sooner was she past the breakwaters than her sweeps became foul of her first "catch." It was obviously something strange and the crew of the ML accordingly hove in their sweep very gently indeed, wondering what sort of "horror" they had got hold of. When the "horror" finally broke surface they saw that they had caught a large section of a crashed German Heinkel bomber!

Other strange things were brought to the surface from the bottom of Cherbourg harbour as well as German infernal machines. One of the "human minesweepers" treasures one half of a hundred franc note which he found in the mud—an indication of how thorough the search had to be.

The clearing of Cherbourg harbour and the rehabilitation of the port was a joint Anglo-American undertaking. It was, of course, in the American area and would be used chiefly for the landing of reinforcements and supplies for the American army, while those for the British army continued to flow into France through the "Mulberry" harbour at Arromanches. Nevertheless, while the Americans did wonders with the jetties and landing stages and the port facilities in general, the clearance of the mines and "horrors" from the bed of the harbour was done by British personnel, working for the most part from the surveying ship HMS *Franklin* under the command of Commander E. J. Irving, RN. Our American Allies realised that we had had longer and more varied experience in dealing with different types of German mines, explosive obstructions, and "booby traps." Moreover, in HMS *Franklin* the Royal Navy had a ship which had been specially fitted and equipped to deal with the problems likely to be encountered. Among other equipment HMS *Franklin* carried a number of small wooden flat-bottomed boats for harbour searching and surveying. These were fitted with small echo-sounding machines which at once recorded the fact if the boat was passing over a pronounced unevenness on the bottom. Such unevennesses were nearly always wrecks, and their position, size and the way in which they lay on the bottom could more often than not be accurately plotted by passing over it several times at different places and in different directions and recording each time the readings of the echo-sounding machine.

Although the searching, surveying and clearance of mines from Cherbourg harbour was done by the British, the American salvage organisation did great work in raising or disposing of wrecks. This organisation was commanded by Commodore W. A. Sullivan, USN, Chief of the United States Naval Salvage. For his work he was afterwards decorated with the CBE by Admiral of the Fleet, Sir Andrew Cunningham. Before, working on the clearance of ports in Northern France Commodore Sullivan had been in charge of raising the French trans-Atlantic liner *Normandie* which became the USS *Lafayette*, in New York Harbour, and had subsequently done much good work in the ports of North Africa and Sicily and at Salerno.

The work of clearing and rehabilitating Cherbourg harbour went forward rapidly despite the destruction and the difficulties left by the enemy. No chances were taken, and yet it was not long before ships could use the sheltered anchorage of the great harbour. The first ships to enter the port with supplies for the armies were four "Liberty" ships. Men watched with bated breath as they entered the harbour, steaming dead slow, but the mine clearance experts were confident. Their confidence was justified. Each one of the ships anchored safely in her appointed berth and was very soon discharging her cargo into DUKW's and lighters and on to the flat "Rhino" ferries.

From that moment the capacity of Cherbourg harbour increased rapidly. By early September it was handling half its full capacity, and not long afterwards as much as 12,000 tons a day were being landed in the port. Cherbourg, like other ports captured by the Allies in both Southern and Northern Europe, was before long handling a far greater quantity of shipping and cargo than it had ever known even in the most prosperous years of peace. DUKW's were for

Docks at Cherbourg after initial clearance.

ever plying to and fro between ships and shore, dashing from one element to another along sloping "hards" specially built for them. Along the water-front were immense stacks of packing cases of military supplies, each of them served by a dozen or more of those fascinating contraptions which are half-trolley and half-lift so that they can carry a load and lift it into its appointed place on top of the dump, practically in one motion. All along these dumps there was always a row of lorries, backed into the dump and being rapidly loaded while their drivers snatched a hurried snack and a smoke before taking the wheel of a loaded vehicle. Day and night the work went on without a break. At first men were inclined to be nervous about lights, but as the Allied Air Forces moved into France, drove back the *Luftwaffe*, and gave Cherbourg a growing assurance of security, arc lights were used with impunity.

And meanwhile the petrol pipe lines of "Operation Pluto" were laid across the Channel, pumping stations were set up, and the pipes ran ever-growing distances across the land of France, their delivery ends keeping always as close as possible to the front line.

The cause of anxiety changed from the ability of the Allies to clear a port and increase its unloading capacity to the upkeep of the roads, and particularly those of the Cotentin Peninsula which had in many places been badly broken up by bombing and by shell fire. Along them gangs of German prisoners were kept at work under guard—working to ensure that the armies pursuing their countrymen did not outrun the supplies which the navies and merchant navies were delivering in such quantities.

After the great break-through of the American army at St Lo part of that army swung westwards into Brittany and finally confined the Germans whom they had driven before them into a narrow perimeter around the great French naval base of Brest.

It was at that time considered that the capture of Brest would be a valuable contribution to the solution of the supply problems of our armies. It was an excellent and large deep-water harbour. It was certainly farther to the westward, but it was found that the railway had for the most part miraculously survived. At that time we required a deep-water port which could take supplies shipped direct from the United States. If ships went direct to Cherbourg from the United States they would have to shape a course up the comparatively narrow waters between Ushant and the Scilly Isles with the U-boat nest at Brest close on the southern flank. There was no denying that the U-boats were still a very real danger, particularly since the "schnorkel" device had just made its appearance. This device enabled the U-boats to remain submerged while ventilating or charging the electric batteries, and even enabled them to proceed on their main diesel engines while submerged. It therefore reduced the reliance which could be placed on patrols, and particularly air patrols, to keep the U-boats away from the convoy route and the focal points of the sea-lanes. Here, then, was another very good reason why the seizure of Brest was very desirable.

A combination of these reasons led to the decision to lay siege to, and finally to assault the fortress of Brest.

Before the final assault on Brest took place, however, other events had taken place which greatly altered the general situation and made it unnecessary to set store upon the possession of Brest as a supply port for the armies. This was as well, for when Brest finally fell to the Allies it was found to be so badly smashed and encumbered with wrecks that it would have needed many months of work to enable it to handle any appreciable quantities of supplies.

These events, which had changed the whole aspect of the supply problem, had happened in both south and north.

In the south "Operation Dragoon" had been carried out with conspicuous success. This was the invasion of Southern France, the naval component of which had been under the command of Rear-Admiral T. H. Troubridge. This invasion had given the Allies possession of the great commercial port of

Assault forces from the US VI Corps file ashore near St Tropez in southern France during Operation Dragoon on 15 August 1944.

Marseilles in an almost undamaged condition. Nor was this all. The American troops landed in the south of France had advanced so rapidly up the valley of the Rhone that they had secured virtually undamaged the magnificent railway running north from Marseilles through Lyons, to Dijon. This was a railway capable of carrying many times the traffic that could have been handled by the Brest railway even at its best and most efficient, while Dijon was comparatively close to the German frontier between Switzerland and Luxemburg, an area in which a considerable proportion of the American armies were assembling. It would be much easier and safer for the direct trans-Atlantic shipping bringing the supplies for the American armies to pass through the Straits of Gibraltar and go to Marseilles, where their cargoes could be rapidly unloaded in an almost undamaged port and whence they could be taken north by rail.

In the north, too, ports had fallen to the Allies. Most important by far of these was Antwerp, and this also had been captured practically undamaged. There is no denying that the dash of the British armoured column to Brussels and down the great double highway past the horror-camp at Breendonck to Antwerp must be accounted a great victory which was to have a far-reaching effect upon the war. It so surprised the enemy by its speed that he had no time to carry out the demolitions in the port as he had planned.

Antwerp was by no means open to traffic. It was obvious that the Germans, realising the danger to which they were exposed by the Allied possession of the great port, would do all in their power to hold their positions along the

Scheldt which denied us the use of the port. Nevertheless, the port was in our hands, and very little had to be done to it to render its facilities fully operative, for they had suffered more from neglect than from the enemy.

Thus the two greatest commercial ports west of the German frontier, and both of them within easy reach of it, had come into the possession of the Allies. Antwerp would be needed, when it had been opened up, chiefly for the supply from the United Kingdom of the British and Canadian armies on the Allied northern flank, but it could if required be used for direct trans-Atlantic traffic which could either pass up the English Channel or north-about round Scotland and down through the North Sea.

The reduction of the fortress of Brest, however, was still important because of its strategic use to the Germans in the U-boat war. The German High Command was well aware that their only salvation now lay in imposing a sufficient delay upon the development of the Allied strategy to allow the "secret weapons" to become fully operative. At the time this German faith in such weapons appeared childish, highly dangerous and unpleasant though those weapons were. The defeat of Germany, however, has brought to light certain facts which give serious food for thought. It is established that the "V-weapons" from which London and Southern England suffered were but samples, and plans were nearing completion in Germany for the daily delivery of a quantity of such missiles as could hardly have failed to paralyse the life of the south-eastern part of England, and might well have done very serious damage elsewhere. At the same time the production was being pushed forward of new forms of maritime weapons which might well have created a serious situation at sea.

In view of the great strength to which the Allied invasion armies had already been brought, and the loss or decimation of valuable German military formations in Western Europe, the main German hope of delaying the Allied progress lay in the U-boats. It is true that the U-boats had suffered a serious defeat two years before, and that since then their own losses had been greater than those which they had been able to inflict upon the shipping of the United Nations. Nevertheless, they had remained a menace, and with the "schnorkel" device—which enabled them to avoid coming to the surface and so to operate in inshore waters instead of being driven even farther away from the focal points of the trade routes as had previously been the case—the menace had greatly increased.

The capture of Brest would rob the U-boats of a base close to the greatest concentration of Allied shipping, and one fitted with virtually indestructible concrete U-boat pens (it is true that one or two Allied bombs had made holes in the roof of these pens but they had obviously expended their energy in so doing, for the glass windows within the pens were not broken.) Brest in Allied hands would not only deprive the U-boats of a great strategic advantage, but

The devastation at Brest.

would also provide our patrols of small craft with a sheltered harbour north-west of the remaining U-boat bases of Lorient, St Nazaire and Bordeaux. It would thus place these patrols in a strategic position to "blanket" those Atlantic ports which remained in German hands.

So the fortress of Brest was attacked with overwhelming weight of air bombing, artillery and men. Even so, it proved to be a very tough nut to crack. The German garrison held on with the grimness of desperation even after they had been forced out of Brest itself and were confined on the Crozon Peninsula on the opposite side of the harbour.

In the assault on Brest the navies played their part, even the battleship HMS *Warspite* coming close inshore to bombard with her 15-inch guns. It seems probable that it was the bombardment from the sea which forced the German garrison to abandon Brest itself and cross the harbour to the Crozon Peninsula.

A U-boat pen at Brest showing the damage done by a 'tallboy' bomb dropped from a Lancaster.

The two great strongholds of the Germans in Brest were the vicinity of the famous École Navale and the tunnelled warehouses off the Quai de la Douane, and both of these were virtually immune to artillery fire from the land to the north of Brest, for they faced south with high ground immediately to the northward of them. In the central quadrangle of the great stone building of the École Navale the Germans had built big concrete "bunkers" with their greater part under ground level, while close to the east of the main building was an even larger bomb-proof "bunker" used as a hospital. The majority of these works, being on the southern slope of the ground, were in "dead ground" to guns firing from the northward. Even more immune to fire from the northward were the U-boat pens, which contained not only shelter for the submarines, but a complete protected dockyard in miniature and comfortable living quarters for the crews of the U-boats and the administrative staff of the flotilla. These pens and their attendant structures of very strong reinforced concrete faced roughly south-south-east and nestled under the cliffs on the top of which stands the École Navale.

On the eastern side of the Penfeld River lies the commercial port with the Quai de la Douane running along its southern side. Immediately to the north of the flat reclaimed surface carrying road and railway rises the cliff upon the

The dry dock at Brest after the siege.

top of which is built the ancient fortress town. Running into this cliff from the port level are a number of tunnels which are both railway sidings and underground warehouses. These the Germans had turned into comfortable living quarters and in them they had stored sufficient food and ammunition to last six months. These tunnels and their entrances, which were closed by great steel doors, were quite immune from any artillery fire from the northward. Bombardment from the sea, however, could be directed at their entrances, which were the only places where they were at all vulnerable.

By the time Brest fell to the Allies there was practically nothing but rubble and gutted buildings in the town and more rubble and twisted steel in the dockyard. The jetties of the commercial port had been destroyed, great craters being blown so that half the crater was under water and the tide was adding daily to the damage. The commercial port and the entrance to the Penfeld River, on which the dockyard lies, were blocked by a tangle of sunken ships, while the latter was also blocked by the wreckage of the high swing bridge.

As a port, it was useless to the Allies, and it was fortunate that the relentless progress of Allied strategy had placed other and more suitable ports in our hands.

No sooner was the last German resistance in Brest crushed than the roads leading away from it were choked with convoys leaving the neighbourhood of the devastated city. The whole army which had reduced Brest was hastening, with all its equipment, to get back into the fight, which had been carried many hundreds of miles farther east.

Much of the equipment of that army went east by road, but its heavy guns and tanks rumbled across the peninsula of Brest to the little port of Brignogan on the north coast, where Tank Landing Craft and Tank Landing Ships were waiting to take them east. The English Channel was providing an invaluable lateral line of communication of which full use was being made.

CHAPTER II

CLEARING THE CHANNEL PORTS

Importance of Le Havre—Successful actions by our patrols stop German attempts to reinforce—German attempts at evacuation have to be abandoned—Fall of Le Havre—
Port clearance organisation—Dieppe—Boulogne—Ostend—Antwerp.

On the eastern flank of the Assault Area the German hold on Le Havre was still the main preoccupation. The capture of Le Havre was very desirable, not so much because it was required as a port for the landing of supplies as because it gave the enemy a strategic advantage on the left flank of the Assault Area and the convoy routes. This the Germans were continually trying to exploit in some new way.

The batteries of Le Havre with their heavy guns were always apt to become a nuisance and demand the use of heavy ships to silence them anew. The E-boats continued to use Le Havre as a main advanced base and were only prevented from causing loss and damage to the Allies by the endurance, vigilance and courage of the men who manned the British motor torpedo boats and motor gunboats and American PT boats which blockaded them and brought them to frequent action. Le Havre, moreover, covered the coastline between the Seine and the Orne, and it was from insignificant points along this coast that the Germans launched their "one-man torpedoes" and explosive motor boats. These were short-range weapons of which the convoy route and the anchorages off the Normandy beaches would be freed from the moment that that coastline was wrested from the enemy, but the capture of Le Havre was a necessary prerequisite to the seizure of the whole of the Seine-Orne coast.

The capture of Le Havre in its turn depended upon other factors. There could be no direct assault on that strongly fortified port. It would have to be taken from the landward side, and this was contingent upon the break-out from the Caen area, the rapid advance to the eastward, and the crossing of the Seine. The latter was complicated by the success with which the Allied air forces had attacked all the bridges in order to isolate north-western France for the initial stages of the invasion.

By the end of the third week in August the Armies had surmounted all these difficulties and were beginning to close in on Le Havre from the east.

At the same time it became clear that there was an abnormal amount of German maritime activity close in to the French shore between Le Havre and St Valéry-en-Caux. It was, of course, to be expected that the Germans would try to evacuate certain instruments and important personnel from Le Havre as soon as they perceived that the capture of their stronghold could not be long delayed. The German naval activity, however, was not by any means all concerned with attempted evacuation from Le Havre. There was also a considerable movement on foot to reinforce the garrison of Le Havre and so prolong its siege.

British naval patrols of light coastal craft supported by "Hunt" class destroyers had long been working off the French coast between Cap de la Hève and the neighbourhood of St Valery-en-Caux. As soon as there was any indication of movement by the enemy the patrols were doubled in strength. Between 22 and 29 August these patrols had a number of encounters with the enemy and inflicted heavy loss and damage upon his vessels.

The first of this series of encounters directly concerned with the situation at Le Havre took place soon after midnight on 23 August, when two German coasters escorted by eight R-boats were encountered west of Fécamp. The action which followed was inconclusive although the destroyer *Talybont* was able to engage for a minute or two at a range of about 4,000 yards. The British motor torpedo-boats tried hard to reach a favourable position from which to attack the German convoy, but they were illuminated by star shell and so heavily engaged by the guns of the shore batteries that they were forced to withdraw.

An hour later this patrol encountered another group of German ships off Cap d'Antifer, but again the motor torpedo-boats were forced out by shell fire from the coastal batteries, and HMS *Talybont* was only able to fire a few shells at a range of about 3 miles. Another of our patrols in approximately the same area had better luck that night. In this case three motor torpedo-boats succeeded in working round inshore of the German convoy and attacked from that direction, hitting a coaster with a torpedo. The destroyer HMS *Melbreak*, which was working with these motor torpedo-boats, engaged the German convoy from seaward at the same time and sank a second coaster by gunfire and also seriously damaged an armed trawler which formed part of the convoy's escort.

That night's work illustrates the great difficulties under which our patrols had to work, since the Germans always kept very close in to the coast and well under the shelter of the coastal batteries. The next night—that of 24-25 August—proved even more eventful. The first clashes with the enemy occurred at about 10.40 p.m., when a patrol of American PT boats (the equivalent to the British motor torpedo-boat) twice engaged a group of enemy ships about six miles north-west of Cap d'Antifer. Both these engagements were very brief and fought at high speed, so that it was hardly surprising that results were not observed and that they were therefore considered to be inconclusive.

After these early clashes nothing happened until about 1 a.m., although our patrols were, of course, searching for the enemy. At about that time, however, a group of our motor torpedo-boats encountered some enemy ships which appeared to consist of a fairly large convoy escorted by armed trawlers and E-boats. The motor torpedo-boats at once attacked, and their attack was followed by a heavy explosion. It was considered that one of the motor torpedo-boats had scored a hit with a torpedo, probably on an armed trawler, and that this vessel had probably been sunk.

Three minutes later the PT boats again made contact with the enemy and they succeeded in inflicting severe damage on an E-boat. Rather less than twenty minutes elapsed after this clash before the destroyers HMS *Talybont* and HMS *Retalick* made contact with the enemy and engaged by gunfire. These destroyers set two of the German vessels on fire, one of which was seen to blow up shortly afterwards, and probably destroyed a third German craft.

Up to this time it had seemed that there was only one German convoy involved in these actions, but it then appeared that the convoy had split into two halves, probably as a result of the last attack by destroyers, and in an attempt to get at least some ships through unharmed.

The next incident of the night was when a group of three British motor torpedo-boats discovered two coasters very close inshore off Cap d'Antifer. They at once moved to the attack, and succeeded in getting within 900 yards of their quarries, but then they were suddenly illuminated by star shells and engaged by the heavy guns of the shore batteries at extremely short range. The motor torpedo-boats were forced to disengage, but while doing so and making an offing they encountered two R-boats, which had presumably been acting as escorts or as a covering force for the coasters. These the motor torpedo-boats promptly attacked by gunfire at a range of 500 yards, leaving one on fire and the other silenced.

Meanwhile a group of two other motor torpedo-boats had been ordered to attack another group of German vessels discovered close inshore off Fécamp. This they tried to do, but found themselves illuminated and heavily shelled by the coastal batteries and were forced to withdraw. A few minutes later this pair of motor torpedo-boats again tried to attack, this time under cover of a diversion caused by the destroyer HMS *Talybont*, but this attack also proved abortive as a result of the interference of the shore batteries.

This group of German vessels, however, were not allowed to escape. Three more motor torpedo boats were ordered to the attack while the Germans were still close off Fécamp. This group succeeded in carrying out their attack on what they were able to identify as a group of five German Tank Landing Craft. One of these was hit by a torpedo and was considered to have been destroyed.

So ended a night in which there had been no less than eight actions between our patrols and the German traffic to and from Le Havre.

On the following night-that of 25-26 August—there was one sustained action and heavy loss was inflicted upon the enemy. It was 1.50 a.m. when a group of three British motor torpedo-boats found a convoy of German coasters escorted by E-boats. These were hugging the French coast even more closely than usual, and were only about 400 yards from shore when the motor torpedo-boats attacked. The motor torpedo-boats were illuminated by star shell and heavily engaged by the shore batteries at this very close range, but they persisted in their attacks and set one coaster on fire and severely damaged one of the escorting E-boats. The motor torpedo-boats then withdrew and allowed the destroyers which were in the offing to "have a go." HMS *Thornborough* most successfully diverted the attention of the gunners in the German shore batteries while the Fighting French Destroyer *La Combattante* closed into a range of 3,000 yards. The French ship then opened a devastating fire, which quickly sank two of the German coasters and one E-boat, while another of the coasters was seen to have been driven ashore to save her from sinking. It had been a highly successful action.

The policy of delivering a rapid succession of attacks by different arms was further exploited on the following night when a convoy of Tank Landing Craft taking supplies and reinforcements to Le Havre was decimated. This convoy consisted of eight LCT's. Despite the very active efforts of the coastal batteries four or five of these LCT's were sunk and another was driven ashore in a badly damaged condition, while the remainder were certainly damaged.

The action was begun by a group of British motor torpedo-boats which succeeded in pressing home their attack despite the interference of the shore batteries and sank two of the LCT's. One of these had clearly been carrying ammunition to the beleaguered garrison at Le Havre, for she blew up with a terrific explosion.

No sooner had the motor torpedo-boats completed their work than the destroyer HMS *Middleton* "took over," attacking by gunfire and scoring many hits on the LCT's. As a result of her fire one LCT was seen to have been driven ashore in a seriously damaged condition. It is safe to say that she would not have been beached in this way had she not been in danger of sinking.

Next it was the turn of a group of American PT boats. These pressed home their attack to a range of under a mile and scored one torpedo hit, sinking yet another of the German craft.

As the PT boats withdrew from their attack, another group of British motor torpedo-boats dashed in. These also attacked with torpedoes and two very large explosions told that they had scored hits and sank two more of the LCT's which had both probably been carrying ammunition.

The Germans had had enough. The losses which they were suffering in their efforts to supply and reinforce the Le Havre garrison were on such a scale that they could no longer continue with their project. So the Le Havre garrison had to be left to its fate without help from outside. After the action on the night of 26-27 August no further attempt was made by the Germans to send ships or craft to Le Havre.

The Germans did not, however, at once abandon their attempt to extricate certain key personnel, instruments and secret material from Le Havre.

It was an evacuation convoy from Le Havre which was intercepted by our patrols shortly before midnight on 27 August. This convoy consisted of two coasters, three armed trawlers and a considerable number of R-boats. They were found close off Cap d'Antifer and the Fighting French destroyer *La Combattante* again distinguished herself. She engaged the enemy by gunfire and illuminated them with star shell as three of our motor torpedo-boats sped in to the attack. Both the coasters were sunk by torpedoes fired by these motor torpedo-boats. The *La Combattante* continued to engage the enemy by gunfire while the motor torpedo-boats disengaged under fire, and she set one armed trawler on fire and damaged another.

After this, even the attempts at evacuation from Le Havre were abandoned by the enemy. As the Commander-in-Chief at Portsmouth stated in his official report to the Board of Admiralty: "This night's operations concluded

Vertical photographic-reconnaissance taken over Le Havre, France after daylight raids by aircraft of Bomber Command on 5, 6 and 8 September 1944. A large area of devastation can be seen in the city centre west of the Bassin de Commerce, over which smoke from burning buildings is drifting. Further attacks on and around Le Havre were carried out on the three following days in an effort to reduce the German garrison still holding out in the city.

the operations off Fécamp and Cap d'Antifer. Our offensive patrols had maintained their stations night after night in this area in face of air attack and shore battery fire for nine weeks."

Although the garrison at Le Havre received no further succour and was in a hopeless situation, it held out until 12 September. When the Allies entered Le Havre they found it in an appalling state. There were no less than 165 wrecks and obstructions in the port, while the approaches to the port and a large part of the lower town had been destroyed as a result of Allied shell fire and heavy bombing attacks. Even as they went down to defeat, the Germans in Le Havre indulged in propaganda of the Goebbels type. They spread the *canard* among the unfortunate inhabitants of Le Havre that the final heavy bombing attack delivered by Bomber Command of the Royal Air Force had been carried out, not in order to achieve any military object, but simply in order to ensure that Le Havre would never again be able to compete with Southampton as a port for the big trans-Atlantic liner traffic.

As has been the case in most of the positions captured from the Germans, there were many "booby traps" in Le Havre. One of these led to an explosion and fatal casualties when someone moved a chair in the main telephone exchange.

Le Havre was for some time useless as a supply port, but it was very soon in use as a base for some of our light coastal craft, and it seemed only right that the flotilla which was first to use Le Havre had been one of the flotillas which had done such magnificent work against the E-boats which had previously been based there.

By the time Le Havre fell to the Allies other ports were beginning to become available as links in the great supply system of the Allied Armies. Up to the fall of Le Havre over 2,200,000 men, nearly 4,000,000 tons of stores and more than 450,000 vehicles had been landed in France, and the great majority of these had been landed over the beaches or through the prefabricated "Mulberry" harbour laid off Arromanches.

Under the direction of the Allied Naval Commander-in-Chief, a special organisation had been set up to ensure that there should be the minimum of delay in bringing a captured port into action in the service of the Allies. This Organisation began considering the problems of the individual ports some time before their capture was expected. As a result, plans were made not only for opening a particular port, but also for clearing the sea routes to that port.

As soon as the most suitable sea route to a port had been decided upon, having regard to known dangers and the probable future course of military operations in the coastal area, arrangements were made for provision of the necessary minesweepers and for the swept channel to be marked by buoys.

Before a port was captured the minesweepers had cleared as much as possible of the channel to that port, and as this preliminary sweeping progressed, the channel was buoyed by Trinity House buoy-laying vessels and surveying vessels.

As soon as the port was captured the sweeping of the channel to the port was completed, and the minesweepers then cleared an anchorage off the port. Thus the minesweepers were always ready to start work in the inshore waters as soon as the capture of a port had led to the silencing of the German batteries. Also in readiness to penetrate the captured port at the earliest possible moment was the advance surveying party, which was usually in a motor launch or a DUKW amphibious lorry fitted with an echo-sounding machine and other specialised apparatus.

The advance surveying party's task was to make a preliminary survey which would allow the surveying ship to enter the port with the main surveying party, whose task it was to survey all wrecks and obstructions and so provide the necessary data for the salvage parties.

In every captured port there was immediately set up a Port Executive Committee, on which all the Services were represented, and which had as its chairman the naval officer in charge of the port. The Port Executive Committee, armed with the knowledge obtained by the surveying parties and the salvage experts, was able to produce a forecast of berths suitable for various types of vessel and an estimated date at which the shipping of certain types could be received in the port. This forecast was passed to the Build-up Control Organisation, whose duty it was to see that the stores the army wanted were loaded into the craft which could be accepted at the port, and that these were in readiness by the date forecast by the Port Executive Committee.

Of the French Channel ports which fell into our hands during the months after the break-out from the Normandy beachhead Dieppe was, apart from Cherbourg, the first to receive convoys of ships carrying supplies and reinforcements for the Army. Dieppe had been severely damaged by the Germans before its capture, and three blockships had been sunk in the harbour, in which there were also eighteen wrecks. Yet before very long Dieppe was handling as much as 7,000 tons of cargo a day, which was many times that which it had averaged in peace-time.

Boulogne was in worse state than Dieppe, and yet Boulogne was of great importance. This was not so much because of the harbour as because, as soon as it was captured, another "Operation Pluto" was carried out. This was the laying of petrol pipe lines across the Channel as had been done from the Isle of Wight to Cherbourg soon after the capture of that port. Boulogne was to become the continental terminal of the cross-Channel petrol pipe system at the eastern end of the English Channel, and this system was far more extensive than that which had been in operation to Cherbourg. There were four "pipe lines under the ocean" to Cherbourg, but to Boulogne there were no less than sixteen.

Allied bombs falling on Dieppe.

At Boulogne the Germans had sunk no fewer than twenty-six blockships across the harbour entrance, and in the harbour itself there were twenty-five wrecks. Yet Boulogne too, was duly cleared by the naval port parties.

The Germans were driven out of Ostend some time before the storming of Walcheren led to the clearing of the Scheldt and the opening of the port of Antwerp, and Ostend therefore assumed for the Allies an importance greater than it would otherwise have done for it was for some time the port nearest to the bitter fighting going on in Holland and along the Belgian-German frontier.

When the naval port party made its preliminary survey of Ostend harbour immediately after its capture they discovered that the Germans had sunk fourteen ships, close together and roughly in three lines, across the harbour entrance. The way in which this problem was dealt with was subsequently described by Commodore T. Mackenzie, Principal Salvage Officer on the staff of the Allied Naval Commander-in-Chief, in the following words:

"The removal of these three lines of wrecks by ordinary salvage practice would have taken three to six months. The use of the port was vital to the Army. I decided therefore to disperse the wrecks by mass demolition. Our wreck disposal vessels were called forward, and a few days after they commenced operations our salvage vessels entered the port astern of the minesweepers and commenced clearing the berths of wrecks. Two days later ships carrying thousands of tons of vital war material for the Army entered the port and commenced discharging. The volume of traffic increased as the channel at the blockships was deepened by our wreck disposal vessels and more berths were cleared by the salvage vessels."

It all sounds astonishingly easy and extraordinarily quick. It certainly was extraordinarily quick, but it was anything but easy or simple. Moreover, it was fraught with considerable risk. Divers and men who are handling explosives and heavy weights and have to deal with intricate problems of buoyancy and ship construction usually have an ingrained aversion to haste, for knowledge and experience has taught them that haste is so often the forerunner of disaster. Yet in the captured ports they were always called upon to work against time, and often fairly close to where mine clearance and disposal experts were working. The latter added to the risks taken by the salvage organisation because there was always the danger of a mine being exploded. Even if it did not detonate other explosives, it would inevitably have a "water-hammer" effect and might well cause a wave capable of upsetting the salvage calculations at a critical moment. Like every other officer and man connected with the "sea affair," however, the salvage crews and the port clearance parties worked with complete singleness of purpose. Their motto might well have been "The Army shall not want."

With every port that had been in German hands clung to by their defenders without any hope of relief, and with each port being blocked and damaged by the enemy before their surrender, it was amazing that Antwerp—by far the greatest port of them all—should have fallen into our hands virtually undamaged. There was some damage in Antwerp. Seven large vessels, including two of 11,000 tons, had been sunk in the port, and there were about twenty smaller wrecks of various types. This damage had not, however, been done by the enemy in order to prevent us from making use of the port. The wrecks and such damage as had been done to the harbour installations, had been caused by Allied bombing raids, and notably the raids of the Royal Air Force in the black days of 1940 when an invasion armada was being collected in Antwerp by the Germans.

Admiral Sir Bertram Ramsay, the Allied Naval Commander-in-Chief, alluded to Antwerp, the third largest port in the world, as a rich prize for the

Allies, but at the same time he struck a note of warning, saying that in the general rejoicing at the fall of Antwerp it was not sufficiently realised that before the facilities of the port could be used the enemy would have to be cleared from both banks of the Scheldt and that thereafter a considerable minesweeping effort would be necessary before the waterway to the port was navigable by Allied shipping.

Nevertheless, possession of the port of Antwerp in good condition was a great and unexpected success. This the Allies owed to the great speed of the advance of the British armoured column and also to some extent to the bravery and resourcefulness of members of the Belgian "underground" movement.

Antwerp was not captured undamaged because the Germans had made no attempt to wreck it, but because the efforts in this direction which were made by the Germans were frustrated and neutralised by members of the Belgian "underground" resistance movement.

Some six miles north of the town of Antwerp, at the extreme north-western end of the great system of wet docks and basins, lie the great locks connecting this tideless system with the tidal Scheldt. This tideless part of the port is quite separate from the miles long ocean quays along the Scheldt where it borders Antwerp town. The Germans had tried to destroy the enormous lock gates controlling the tideless part of the port, and if they had succeeded in doing so they would have closed a large proportion of the three and a half million square yards of dock basins. To destroy the docks the Germans fitted very large demolition charges to the most vulnerable points. Fortunately for the Allies and for the post-war prosperity of the port of Antwerp, the Germans were carefully watched by members of the Belgian "underground" movement while they were engaged on these tasks. As soon as night fell the Belgian patriots emerged from their hiding places and cut the electric leads with which the explosive charges were connected with the distant firing arrangements. Then the Belgians removed the charges and fitted dummy charges in their places, so that the Germans would not think that all their work had been undone. Having fitted the dummy charges in place, the Belgians carefully connected up the wires and, leaving everything apparently just as the Germans had arranged it, disappeared.

CHAPTER III

THE EPIC OF WALCHEREN

Three-fold assault—Bad weather precludes air spotting and support—
Initial bombardment—Great fight of the Support Squadron—Drawing the
enemy's fire—Work of the Commandos—Difficulty in landing supplies.

The capture of the great port of Antwerp in a virtually undamaged condition
was a great success on the road to final victory. It was, however, an incomplete
success, for Antwerp lies more than seventy miles up the Scheldt. So long as
our minesweepers were prevented from clearing the mines from the estuary
and river, so long did Antwerp remain useless to us as a supply port. The
enemy was fully aware that Antwerp, once the approaches were cleared and it
was operating as the main supply port, would be a dagger poised at the heart
of the Reich. They determined, therefore, to deny the use of Antwerp to the
Allies with every means at their disposal.

To this end the Germans clung most tenaciously to both banks of the
Scheldt. They had strong positions on the south bank in the Breskens area. On
the north side of the estuary they were even stronger. The big island of South
Beveland is connected to the mainland only by a causeway which could be
held by few against many. Moreover, west of South Beveland lies the island of
Walcheren, which had been very heavily fortified with nearly thirty batteries
with guns varying in calibre from 9-inch to 3-inch, and many other strong
points.

The importance with which these positions were regarded by the enemy was
shown by a captured German army order which was quoted by Lieutenant-
General G. G. Simonds in his Order of the Day to the First Canadian Army, on
the opening of the Scheldt.

The full text to Lieutenant-General Simond's Order is as follows:

"Headquarters, First Canadian Army.

TO ALL SOLDIERS SERVING IN THE FIRST CANADIAN ARMY

Our victories in the battles for the Scheldt Estuary and the opening of the port of Antwerp mark a decisive step in the final defeat of Germany. There should be no questioning of this fact. It is testified by the following extracts from a captured order issued by the German Army Commander.

'The defence of the approaches to Antwerp represents a task which is decisive for the further conduct of the war. After overrunning the Scheldt fortifications the English would finally be in a position to land great masses of material in a large and completely protected harbour. With this material they might deliver a deathblow at the North German Plateau and at Berlin before the onset of winter. For this reason we must hold the Scheldt fortifications to the end. The German people is watching us. In this hour the fortifications along the Scheldt occupy a role which is decisive for the future of our people.'

The fighting has had to be conducted under the most appalling conditions of ground and weather. Every soldier serving in this army—whether he has fought along the banks of the Scheldt or in driving the enemy from the north-east approaches to Antwerp, and every sailor and every airman who has supported us—can take a just and lasting pride in a great and decisive victory.

In the name of the Army Commander, I thank all commanders and troops for the loyal and able exertions which have contributed to such important successes.

G. G. Simonds, Lieutenant-General,

4.11.44

By the end of October the First Canadian Army had captured Breskens and driven the Germans from the south bank of the Scheldt. On the north side of the estuary they had succeeded, after a grim struggle, in fighting their way over the causeway leading to South Beveland and were gradually clearing the Germans from the whole of that island.

There remained Walcheren, the last bolt which secured the door to Antwerp. Walcheren had been heavily attacked by Bomber Command of the Royal Air Force, and the bombs had breached the great sea dyke about a mile south of Westkapelle, which lies at the western extremity of the island. As a result of this breach in the dyke a great part of the island had been flooded. This, however, did not impair the defences, which were mounted on and in the dykes. At the same time the breach made it possible to contemplate a landing on the island from the sea, which would have been suicidal if the great fortified dyke had had to be frontally assaulted.

Those concerned were under no illusions regarding the strength of the Walcheren defences or the difficulty of carrying out an assault, even upon the breach in the dyke. Yet it was appreciated that this would be the only way in which to capture the island and silence its batteries, so that the minesweepers could set about the task of clearing the Scheldt and opening the port of Antwerp.

A hundred and thirty-five years before, the island of Walcheren had been the scene of a great disaster to British arms, caused by procrastination and disputes between the two commanders. It had been this expedition of 1809 which had inspired the following wellknown quatrain:

> Great Chatham, with his sabre drawn,
> Stood waiting for Sir Richard Strachan;
> Sir Richard, longing to be at 'em,
> Stood waiting for the Earl of Chatham.

The expedition was a complete disaster, thousands of our troops dying of fever before the remnants were at last withdrawn.

In 1944 it was very different. There was complete agreement upon the method of assault and nothing but impatience to see the fortress island reduced and the estuary and river cleared of mines.

The planning of the assault on Walcheren had been begun at the headquarters of the First Canadian Army during the third week of September. Captain A. F. Pugsley had been nominated as the naval force commander, and on 1 October Brigadier B. W. Leicester, Royal Marines, was appointed as the military force commander.

The plan for the assault on the island of Walcheren was for a threefold attack. There was to be a direct attack by the Canadian Army along the causeway linking Walcheren with South Beveland; an assault by Army Commando troops across the Scheldt from Breskens and directed against Flushing; and an assault from seaward in the Westkapelle area by Royal Marine Commandos landed and supported by the Royal Navy. The timing of the Flushing and Westkapelle assaults had, of course, to be closely linked with the progress of the Canadian troops who were clearing South Beveland of the enemy. All these operations were under the general charge of Lieutenant-General G. G. Simonds, Commanding the First Canadian Army.

The force detailed for the assault in the Westkapelle area assembled at Ostend on 27-28 October, Captain Pugsley's headquarters ship being the frigate HMS *Kingsmill*, which had been fitted with more wireless telegraphy installations than had ever before been carried in a ship of this type.

As October drew to an end it became apparent that the Canadian troops in South Beveland would be able to reach the Walcheren causeway by 1 November, and Lieutenant-General Simonds accordingly decided to put in the Breskens-Flushing assault on that day. At the same time it was appreciated

Preparations for the Walcheren expedition at Ostend.

47 RM Commando embark for Walcheren at Ostend on the evening of 31 October 1944. As part of Naval Force T they set sail in the early hours of the next morning.

Above: HMS *Kingsmill*, a photograph while still in port. *Kingsmill* became Captain A. F. Pugsley's command headquarters for the Walcheren expedition.

Left: HMS *Kingsmill* had been fitted with more wireless telegraphy installations than had ever before been carried in a ship of this type.

A view of the gap in the dyke at Westkapelle. The photograph was taken soon after RAF Lancasters had made the breach.

that the weather prospects for the Westkapelle assault were far from good. The urgency of clearing the Scheldt and opening Antwerp, however, was such that it was decided to proceed with the Breskens-Flushing assault and the causeway assault even if the Westkapelle assault proved to be impossible owing to the weather.

Admiral Sir Bertram Ramsay, the Allied Naval Commander-in-Chief, had established temporary advanced naval headquarters in his caravan in the Breskens area, and he and Lieutenant-General Simonds discussed the situation produced by the deteriorating weather.

Since the force which was to carry out the assault in the Westkapelle area had to make the passage from Ostend in assault craft and landing craft, an immediate decision had to be taken to sail or to remain in harbour.

Admiral Sir Bertram Ramsay had had plenty of experience of weather improving suddenly just before a combined operation took place. In the light of this experience, and in view of the immense advantages to be gained by launching all three assaults simultaneously, and the fact that the passage from Ostend would take some time, he ordered the force to sail. At the same time he delegated to Captain Pugsley, the naval force commander, the responsibility for deciding whether or not the assault should go in. This decision Captain Pugsley was to take when he reached a position off Westkapelle and could judge for himself the conditions of sea and surf on the spot.

The passage of the force from Ostend was assisted by motor launches, which marked the channels, and was uneventful.

When the force reached the vicinity of Westkapelle early next morning it was found that the weather conditions were considerably better than had been anticipated, although it was appreciated that air spotting would not be available for the bombarding ships and that the assault would have to go in without air cover. This was because all the airfields in Britain, from which the spotting and supporting aircraft were to have flown, were shrouded in fog. Captain Pugsley and Brigadier Leicester, however, decided to launch the assault, since they considered that the advantages to be gained by timing the Westkapelle assault to fit in with the Breskens-Flushing assault and the causeway attack from South Beveland more than outweighed the disadvantages of having to dispense with spotting aircraft or air support in the early stages.

It is interesting to recall that the sea and surf conditions on the dyke became far worse after 1 November, and had the assault in the Westkapelle area not been carried out it could not have been launched for several more days.

Aerial view of Westkapelle showing the flooding and devastation.

As the force approached Walcheren from the westward it was noticed that the Germans were trying to shroud Westkapelle lighthouse in smoke, apparently in the hope of impeding our navigation and robbing bombarding ships of a convenient point of aim. Their efforts, however, were not very successful.

It had been arranged that H-hour—that is the time at which the landing craft should "touch down" on the tiny beaches on either side of the breach in the dyke—should be 9.45 a.m., but things began to happen long before then.

At 7.15 a.m. the approaching force could see that the battery of 220 mm (8.7-inch) guns at Domburg, north of Westkapelle, was firing. It was apparently firing over the island at Flushing, which indicated that the Breskens-Flushing assault had already gone in and had met with initial success.

Motor Launch No. 902 was the first ship to come under fire at Walcheren. She was acting as a navigational mark when a German battery opened fire on her and she was ordered to withdraw. Ten minutes later the battleship *Warspite* and the monitor *Roberts* opened fire with their 15-inch guns. For some time the big guns of these ships pounded away at the larger German batteries and every now and then a big mushroom-shaped cloud of black smoke showed that a 15-inch shell had struck home hard. Nevertheless, there was no denying that the absence of air spotting very severely reduced the efficiency of the initial bombardment by the heavy ships. The *Warspite* and *Roberts*, however, were able temporarily to silence some of the large German batteries, and notably that known as "W.15." This battery consisted of four 150 mm (5.9-inch) guns and was situated south of Westkapelle and just to the north of the breach in the dyke, so that the assault craft would have had to steer almost straight for it. The big ships fired eight rounds of 15-inch at this battery at 8.30 a.m. and effectively silenced it for half an hour. Moreover, when the Germans got it back into action it was not firing with its former vigour.

The big-gun battery, "W.17," just south of Domburg and consisting of four 220 mm (8.7-inch) guns, was also successfully engaged and silenced by HMS *Warspite*, but it came into action again later. It was, moreover, known early in the day that air spotting would almost certainly be available early in the afternoon and even better results were therefore confidently expected.

At 8.48 a.m. the Support Squadron deployed about five miles off the breach in the dyke. The Support Squadron was commanded by Commander K. A. Sellar and consisted of LCG's (Landing Craft, Gun), LCS's (Landing Craft, Support), LCF's (Landing Craft, Flak) and LCR's (Landing Graft, Rocket).

By 9 a.m. the battle between the German batteries and the craft of the Support Squadron had been joined. It raged unabated for three and a half hours at very close range and was very costly, but it was this squadron which, by its epic fight, made the assault in the Westkapelle area possible and successful. Captain Pugsley, in fact, reported to Admiral Sir Bertram Ramsay

A landing craft nosing into the gap.

m the following words: "This success would NOT have been achieved without the outstanding gallantry and determination displayed by all officers and men of the Support Squadron, under the command of Commander K. A. Sellar, who led the attack and engaged the extremely active enemy batteries."

Elsewhere in his official report Captain Pugsley stated: "From 9 a.m. till 12.30 p.m. the Support Squadron continuously engaged the enemy batteries, firstly in support of the landings and later supporting the Commandos' advance to the southward. Their losses were heavy, but they stuck to their job of engaging the enemy, thereby drawing the enemy's fire and enabling the landings to proceed."

The assault in the Westkapelle area had, in fact, been planned in the light of experience of German tendencies so that the German fire should be drawn by the craft of the Support Squadron away from the assault craft carrying the Commandos.

Experience during and after D-day in Normandy had shown that the Germans, particularly when manning shore batteries, will always fire at the craft which are firing at them. It was this experience which was exploited by the Support Squadron, and there is no doubt that if the Germans had been able to resist the temptation of shooting at the craft of the Support Squadron which were shooting at them and had concentrated the fire of their batteries upon the craft carrying the assault troops, the assault on the Westkapelle sector of Walcheren would have been a costly failure.

Commander Sellar alluded to this in his report on the action. He said: "It was early recognised that we were up against formidable opposition and that losses and damage were to be expected in craft engaging shore batteries at close range. It is considered that this was fully justified because the Commandos got ashore well and lightly. I considered that, so long as the Germans made the mistake of concentrating their fire on the Support Squadron, close action was justified and losses acceptable. In fact, I decided that if there were signs of batteries selecting incoming loaded LCT's (Landing Craft, Tank) as their primary target even closer action would be ordered so as to force the Germans to fire on the Support Squadron."

There can have been few more gallant actions in naval history than the way in which the Support Squadron drew the fire of the formidable German batteries on to itself and so provided the assault forces with a comparative safe conduct to the shore.

The casualties in the Support Squadron during those memorable hours off the west coast of Walcheren amounted to 172 officers and men killed or missing and 125 officers and men wounded—a total of 297. This compared with 5 killed and 28 wounded—a total of 33—in the LCT's (Landing Craft, Tank) and LCI(S)'s (Landing Craft, Infantry, Small) of the assaulting force. By the time the Support Squadron was withdrawn during the afternoon it consisted of only seven craft fit for action, and three of these were vessels fitted only for the laying of smoke screens. Eight craft had been sunk and eight more put out of action, while four had suffered damage which affected their fighting efficiency.

During the whole period in which the vessels of the Support Squadron was in action off Walcheren it lost 20 officers and 152 men killed or missing; 15 officers and 11 men badly wounded, and about 160 officers and men slightly wounded or suffering from shock after the loss of their craft. Of a grand total of 28 craft employed in the Squadron, 9 were sunk, 11 were put out of action, 1 was damaged but still capable of service, and 7 were undamaged and fit for action.

It seems amazing that the casualties in the Support Squadron were not even higher when one considers that the German batteries on Walcheren mounted four 220 mm (8.7-inch) guns, twenty-four 150 mm (5.4-inch) guns, four 120 mm (4.7-inch) guns, twenty 105 mm (4.1-inch) guns, four 94 mm (3.7-inch) guns and four 75 mm (3-inch) guns. These were the guns in the established batteries, and there were also numerous guns, ranging in size up to 105 mm, sited in the various strongpoints.

Disembarking vehicles at Walcheren.

Destruction at Westkapelle.

There were, of course, many instances of outstanding gallantry during this phase of the Walcheren operation, but it must be borne in mind that, where all wrought so magnificently, instances and experiences which may be quoted are typical rather than exceptional.

There was the case of LCG2 (Landing Craft, Gun), commanded by Lieutenant A. Cheney, RNVR This LCG opened fire at a range of 7,400 yards on the battery of four 150 mm guns close to the northern shoulder of the breach in the dyke, and closed that battery to a range between 500 and 700 yards. Then she was hit in the engine-room, which began to flood so fast that the hatches were battened down in order that an airlock over the flooding might support the ship. At the same time she turned away from the dyke but found herself stopped and incapable of moving when only 2,000 yards from the battery. Lieutenant Cheney kept his guns in action until his craft was swung by the tide so that they could no longer be brought to bear on the enemy. Then he hailed another craft to tow him round so that his guns would bear, and opened fire again. About 11.30 a.m. the tide again swung the LCG so that her guns would no longer bear, and at the same time a very big gun began firing at her. Another craft came to her rescue and took LCG2 in tow under very heavy shell fire. She was towed for about half an hour when both vessels struck mines. As she drifted, LCG2 struck another mine and sank by the bows.

The log of LCG10 is laconic in the extreme. It reads as follows:

08.15—Four batteries opened fire on marking ML. (This was ML902.)

08.25—LCG10 opened fire on batteries and drew fire at 08.45.

09.30—Concentrated fire falling all round. LCG10. One cordite locker blown to bits or detonated and three others on fire. Burning cordite everywhere. Hoses got going in a very short time and every sort of extinguisher brought into play. All worked with great courage and calmness. Fire spread to wardroom and accommodation but eventually everything was under control.

10.50—Bombardment resumed with full force, closing range. 543 rounds fired. 46 cartridges and 11 shell destroyed or thrown overboard.

The report of one of the smaller LCG's commanded by Lieutenant A. H. Ballard, RNR, is rather more detailed, but also gives a good idea of what these little craft of the Support Squadron went through. Lieutenant Ballard's report reads:

"At about 09.30 I started to really close the range to about 600 to 800 yards and continued to engage with rapid fire the heavier battery, whilst trying to evade the fire of the 88 mm battery in the sand dunes and engaging them with Oerlikon fire. I had only received three direct hits up to this time. . . . We started to receive further direct hits. One, passing through the bridge, took the compass from under my hands and bursting, knocked me for six, wounding me in the leg and also wounding another officer. I started to get up to give orders through the remains of the voice pipe when the First-Lieutenant arrived on the bridge, I having stationed him forward in case of such an eventuality. Then another shell came and carried away the compass pedestal and voice pipe and knocked me down again. By this time all the officers were wounded and the ship had received numerous direct hits elsewhere. I had, however, passed the order 'Full speed ahead, hard and starboard' to the wheelhouse—it was shouted through the hole in the deck that was all that remained. Then both engines packed up. Their fuel pipes had been severed. We were helpless, with our stern to the shore so that our guns would not bear on the enemy. We had 2 killed and 20 wounded on board and were being heavily pounded by 88 mm's. An LCS(L) (Landing Craft, Support, Light) came alongside and rescued us."

When one thinks of these craft engaging protected batteries of larger guns at ranges of a few hundred yards one cannot but think that Captain Pugsley's remark was an under-statement when he wrote: "The magnificent fight put up by the Support Squadron was indeed inspiring."

Meanwhile the Commando troops were being landed on either side of the breach in the dyke under the covering fire provided by the Support Squadron. Even closer range covering fire for the landings was provided by two medium LCG's. These were Numbers 101 and 102, commanded by Lieutenant G. A. Flamank, RNVR, and Lieutenant D. R. V. Flory, RNVR respectively.

These two craft ran in under very heavy fire from the batteries and beached themselves on either side of the breach in the dyke. From their positions on the edges of the landing "beaches" they were able to give covering fire at point-blank range, and they also drew a great deal of the enemy's fire which would without doubt have otherwise been directed at the personnel craft and the troops as they were disembarking. They were both engaged at very close range by batteries of 5.9-inch and 4.1-inch guns, and both these craft were lost.

"Theirs was a very gallant action," said Commander Sellar in his report, "I cannot speak highly enough of the courage; determination and devotion to duty of these LCG's." No. 102 was soon on fire, but the fire was got under control and the craft remained in action for a time. Then the fire broke out again and she was last seen burning on the beach, broached to. No. 101 remained on the beach and in action against the enemy until shortly after 10 a.m., when she un-beached, but was so badly damaged that she promptly sank. LCI(S) 538 (Landing Craft, Infantry, Small), commanded by Sub-Lieutenant B. S. B. Lingwood, RNVR, un-beached at just about the same time and saw LCG(M) 101 with only her starboard side showing above water. Able-Seaman Green and Able-Seaman Garthwaite of LCI(S) 538 promptly dived overboard to support wounded survivors who were in danger of drowning. As a result,

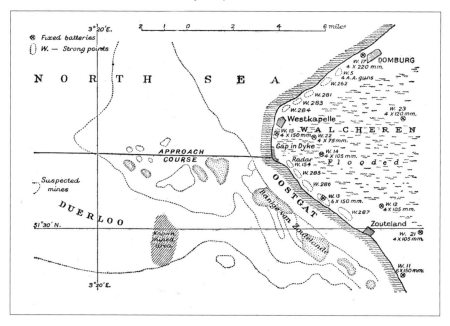

The Walcheren Expedition, November 1944.

A flail tank landing at Walcheren.

six lives, including that of Lieutenant Flamank, the Commanding Officer of LCC(M) 101 were saved. Lieutenant Flamank subsequently reported officially: "I regret to report the loss of my ship off Westkapelle shortly after H-hour on November 1st, 1944, after being in action with a German pillbox at a range of 40 or 50 yards."

The LCG's which were beached on either side of the breach in the dyke were each supported by three LCS(L)'s (Landing Craft, Support, Large) whose duty it was to draw the attention of the enemy as far as possible. All three of the craft which tried to support the LCG(M) on the southern side of the breach were set on fire. It was here that Lieutenant S. N. Orum, RN, RNVR, who led them in and who had so gallantly boarded a German explosive motor boat off the Normandy beaches, lost his life. He led his craft in to "point blank and what proved to be suicidal range of the German strongpoints on the southern shoulder of the breach." It may have been suicidal, but he certainly achieved his object of drawing the enemy's fire away from the landing troops.

It was in one of these LCS(L)'s—No. 260—that a motor mechanic performed an act of great bravery. His craft had been hit by shells and fire broke out in the engine-room and fuel-tank compartment. The fire in the engine-room was got under control with extinguishers, but nobody could get near the hatch of the fuel-tank compartment owing to the heat. Then another craft came alongside and the motor mechanic rigged a hose from it and fought and controlled the fire while sitting in a large shell-hole in the ship's side. This he did without the least thought for his own safety, although about 2,600 gallons of petrol remained in the compartment that was on fire, and there is no doubt that he saved the ship.

The LCF's (Landing Craft, Flak) also did magnificent work, in fact, one of the outstanding features of the assault was the way in which the LCF's engaged the German pillboxes while the landing craft with the Commandos were going in to beach. This they did under heavy shell fire. Lieutenant R. J. Elliott, RNVR, who commanded LCF 32 reported: "Between 10.05 and 11.00 we were under continual accurate shell fire and were hit five times. I reported the damage to the headquarters ship and was told to disengage. The headquarters ship then advised me to increase speed as I was being followed by shells. This advice was rather unnecessary as I was 'emergency full speed ahead' and the bridge had been swamped twice by near misses."

Captain Pugsley, who was anxiously watching from HMS *Kingsmill*, found it difficult to get a clear idea of what was going on during the early stage of the landing, so fierce was the action being fought close to the shore. At 10.15 he signalled to an LCI(S) (Landing Craft, Infantry, Small) which was on her way out from the beaches: "What is happening on beaches?" The LCI(S) replied: "Good beaching. All troops landed."

"This," as Captain Pugsley said in his report, "was most heartening news, since it appeared from my position some 3,000 yards off the beach that the beaching would have been extremely difficult and accompanied by heavy casualties to Commandos and craft."

Captain Pugsley's report, in fact, makes reference to "the apparent impossibility, at the time of ordering the assault groups in, of landing from either LCI(S) or LCT. without severe and possibly crippling casualties" and to "the consequently unexpectedly successful beaching and un-beaching of all the assaulting craft." That is a measure of the success achieved by the gallant Support Squadron.

The first wave of the assault consisted of one Royal Marine Commando landed north of the breach in the dyke, and another landed to the south of it. This initial assault was quickly followed by a second wave, an Allied Commando being landed north of the breach and another Royal Marine Commando south of the breach.

The Marines north of the gap at once found themselves confronted by a German pillbox. This they quickly reduced and pushed northwards, only to be held up by very stiff resistance from the "W.15" battery of four 150 mm guns. By this time, however, a few tanks had been landed and with their help the Marines succeeded in capturing this battery. Once past this battery, they swept on fast along the dyke to the north-eastward. The Germans began to come tumbling out to surrender from the strongpoints and concrete burrows with which the dyke and sand-dunes were honeycombed. In a few hours this Royal Marine Commando reached the neighbourhood of the village of Domburg, but here they encountered stiff resistance from the big battery known as " W.17," consisting of four 220 mm guns. By this time the troops of the Allied Commando had come up with them, and together they fought their way into this powerful battery and killed or captured the whole of its German garrison. Then they halted to consolidate.

The Royal Marine Commando landed on the southern side of the breach in the dyke also progressed rapidly at first. They cleared the radar station and the small battery and strongpoint known as "W.154," and pushed on along the dyke to the south-eastward until they reached the vicinity of the big battery "W.13," with its six 150 mm guns. A quick assault on this battery was attempted, but proved impossible. The leading troop commander in this assault was killed and many of his men became casualties. A second troop at once took over the assault, but it came under such intense mortar fire that most of its men were killed or wounded. This was some of the toughest fighting ever experienced, even by the Royal Marine Commandos. It was hard slogging along the dyke between the sea and the flooded hinterland; through deep sand which clogged rifles and tommy guns and filled eyes, mouth and hair; and in the face of a determined enemy in concrete positions and provided with heavy guns as well as light weapons.

The Royal Marine Commando was held up by the "W.13" battery while fire support was arranged. Some of this came from craft of the Support Squadron which had followed the progress of the Marines along the dyke and were then just to seaward of the big Zouteland sandbank, while some of it came from military field batteries on the southern side of the Scheldt. Moreover, the weather over the British airfields had by that time cleared, and Typhoons of the Royal Air Force were able to make an important contribution by "strafing" the "W.13" battery.

As soon as the support fire ceased a fresh troop of the Royal Marine Commando assaulted the battery under cover of a smoke screen. They succeeded in fighting their way into the centre of the battery and in capturing its control position. The whole of the "W.13" battery was cleared of the enemy during the night and at dawn the Royal Marine Commando pushed on to the village of Zouteland. They had to fight two small battles on the way in order to dislodge the Germans from the sand-dunes dominating the village, but the German Commandant surrendered and resistance virtually ceased in the immediate vicinity of Zouteland.

The two Commandos which had cleared the dyke from the breach to Zouteland rested in that village while a third Commando pushed on farther to the south-east. This Commando pushed on steadily until it reached a very strong German position guarded by an anti-tank ditch and large concrete "dragon's teeth." This was one of the defensive positions covering the " W.11 " battery of six 150 mm guns. Here again, supporting fire was called for and was provided by the field batteries on the south side of the Scheldt, but the weather had closed down again and no air support was available.

With the assistance of the artillery support two troops succeeded in storming across the ditch, but they then came under very heavy mortar fire and suffered severely; both the troop commanders being wounded.

Meanwhile the "W.11" battery itself was being attacked. The leading elements of the Royal Marine Commando almost reached the battery in their initial assault, but in so doing they overran some pockets of German resistance which "came to life" behind them, inflicting casualties and isolating the forward troops. At dusk, however, these German pockets of resistance were dealt with by another troop, and ammunition and supplies were man-handled up to the forward troops close to the battery after dark and just in time to enable them to repulse a sharp German counter-attack during the night.

Early next morning reinforcements were brought up and a determined assault was made on the " W.11 " battery under cover of supporting fire. By noon the Germans had had enough and began to surrender. German officers who were taken prisoner were induced to call upon the Germans in the deep concrete shelters to come up and lay down their arms. When the German Commandant of the battery surrendered he handed over his revolver with the words: "If you think I am a coward, shoot me." It was his way of paying tribute to the irresistible courage and determination of the Royal Marine Commandos.

After clearing the" W.11" battery the Royal Marine Commando advanced fairly rapidly along the dyke until they made contact with the Army Commando which had been landed at Flushing and had been fighting its way north-westwards to meet the Royal Marines.

The junction of these forces completed the clearing of the coast of Walcheren which faced on to the Scheldt Estuary. Much, however, remained to be done in mopping up and consolidating in the north, for it was known that there were a great many German troops on the island of North Beveland which might have put in a strong counter-attack on Walcheren from the north. Such a counter-attack, however, never materialised, and North Beveland was finally cleared of the enemy by the men of the First Canadian Army.

The most critical phase of the Walcheren operations, after the landing and the action of the Support Squadron in the Westkapelle area, was that of landing the supplies for the Commandos. For forty-eight hours after the landings the tiny beaches on either side of the breach in the dyke were under heavy and accurate German shell fire. The Support Squadron had diverted the attention of the batteries with great success during the landing of the assault troops, but it could not continue to do so during the supply phase with the very limited resources which remained available to it.

The force was provided with three LCT's (Landing Craft, Tank) laden with ammunition and stores. This would have been an ample supply for the Commandos if it had been possible to land it at the right time. This, however, was not possible.

The first time attempt was made to beach these LCT's and land their stores one of the three craft struck a mine and sank. The immediately available stores had been reduced by one-third before any supplies at all had been landed. The two remaining LCT's with supplies were sent in at three o'clock on the afternoon of 1 November, but they were ordered back by the Principal Beach Master.

The Principal Beach Master was Commander R. M. Prior, who had walked across France and escaped through Spain after having been left on the beach during the Dieppe raid of August 1942, and who subsequently entered Parliament. Of the work of the Beach Parties Captain Pugsley wrote in his report: "The gallantry and determination shown by the Beach Parties, who worked the beaches under fire for the first forty-eight hours, was in accordance with the highest traditions of the Service."

The decision to order back the LCT's carrying supplies was a most difficult one for Commander Prior to take. He was an experienced officer fully aware of the need to get supplies ashore and up to the Commandos as soon as possible. At the same time, he had seen one of the craft sink and appreciated that the cargoes of the two remaining craft had thereby assumed a greatly added importance. He had been on the beach since the first craft had "touched down" and could assess with accuracy the effect of the German shell fire. This was of such intensity and accuracy that to allow the LCT's to come into the beach would have been virtually to have ensured the loss of the craft and the urgently required supplies which they carried. It was therefore preferable to accept delay in the hope that the German fire would slacken and enable the craft to come in again and beach with the prospect of being able to land their cargoes intact.

Unfortunately, however, the German fire on the beaches did not slacken until the weather had deteriorated to a degree which made beaching Impossible. Several further attempts were made to beach the supply LCT's during the night and the following day, but they met with no success, and it was not until three o'clock on the morning of 4 November that the two LCT's were at last able to beach. Even then, they did so with great difficulty and such an element of danger that both the craft became total losses due to the weather, but providentially not before they had landed their supplies. One of the craft was "broached to" in the breach in the dyke, and the other was driven against a groyne and held there by the seas which battered her to pieces. The wind was lashing up waves eight feet high in the breach. Commander Prior had decided in view of the deteriorating weather and the urgent need of ammunition and supplies for the Commandos that craft carrying supplies would be beached regardless of the virtual certainty of the loss of the craft, provided there was reasonable chance of being able to offload the supplies before the vessels broke up.

The supply situation would have been far more serious had the Commandos not captured quantities of German rations. Even so, the Royal Air Force had to be asked to drop supplies for the Commando troops on the island. This was a matter of great difficulty owing to the widespread flooding of the island, but it was successfully accomplished and greatly eased the situation.

The difficulty of landing supplies, and the delay and difficulty in taking off wounded unhappily increased the sufferings of the latter, but this was inevitable in the circumstances. The assault on the Westkapelle area of Walcheren had been superbly carried out under conditions which demanded the highest form of courage and determination. It was the fortune of war that after a magnificent start, and when the resistance of the enemy had been virtually quelled, the weather made it impossible to give to the troops the supply and succour which every naval officer and man so desperately wished to afford to them.

So Walcheren fell to the United Nations and the gateway to the Scheldt had been forced. In this action the Royal Marines, who had acquitted themselves so well, had been acting strictly in accordance with their traditional role. They had been landed from the sea by the Royal Navy in order to fight for and secure positions which, in our hands, would afford us the use of a great port.

Winter conditions on
Walcheren Expedition.

The fall of Walcheren did not automatically open the port of Antwerp. The river was thickly sown with mines of every known type and with other obstructions. The channel to the port of Antwerp, which had to be cleared of these mines and obstructions, is seventy-three miles long. At Flushing the channel is about a mile wide, and between Flushing and Antwerp it varies in width between 300 yards and 1,400 yards. Here lay a mine-clearance task of great magnitude and complexity, which had to be pushed forward against time—so great was the urgency of opening the port of Antwerp; but the minesweepers proved equal to it as they have to every other call made upon them.

The minesweepers were ready to begin the task at the earliest possible moment. In fact, one group of small minesweepers had actually succeeded in anticipating events by slipping past the Walcheren batteries before daylight while some of these were still in enemy hands. The magnitude of the minesweeping task is illustrated by the fact that nearly 200 minesweepers of different types took part in the clearing of the Scheldt. In the first initial sweep over seventy mines were accounted for.

The job was done. Antwerp was opened to shipping on 28 November 1944, thus setting the seal of a decisive victory upon the successful reduction of Walcheren.

CHAPTER IV

AMPHIBIOUS WARFARE IN HOLLAND

"V" weapons on Antwerp—Von Rundstedt's offensive—Death of Admiral Ramsay—German midget U-boats—Watching, patrolling and raiding—Planting a "Cuckoo" on Overflakkee—Raiding Schouwen—Second battle for Arnhem—The crossing of the Rhine.

It might have been thought, with the opening of so many of the French and Belgian ports, and particularly the clearing of the Scheldt and the opening of Antwerp, that the navy's part in the liberation of Europe and the invasion of Germany would have come to an end, while the part of the merchant navies would he one merely of pouring in supplies and reinforcements.

This was far from being the case, and an official statement issued by Supreme Allied Headquarters on the last day of 1944 sounded a necessary warning. That statement concluded with the words: "The enemy will make every effort he can to interfere with the smooth movement of supplies into Antwerp—the third largest port in the world. So long as Allied armies are fighting on the continent of Europe a great maritime effort will be required and many calls made on the seamen of the United Nations."

The enemy had, in fact, already devoted a very considerable effort to endeavouring to interrupt the flow of supplies through Antwerp by launching against that port large numbers of his so-called "V weapons"—flying bombs and rockets. These did much damage in the town, but they did no appreciable damage to the docks or to the shipping using the docks.

At the turn of the year the German High Command must have realised that the offensive against Antwerp with "V weapons" was a failure. It was for this reason that they embarked upon a far more ambitious plan. This was nothing less than Von Rundstedt's great offensive in the Ardennes. The plan was for the German Ardennes offensive, having broken through the Allied positions where these were weakly held, to swing north-westward across the Maas at Namur or Huy and drive straight for Antwerp. This offensive was to be co-ordinated with a southward attack from the German positions on the islands of Schouwen and Overflakkee and the Dordrecht area. This drive was designed once again to close the Scheldt estuary and then to link up with von Rundstedt's column in Antwerp.

It was a grand and audacious conception. Had it been successful the whole of the British and Canadian armies would have been cut off *without a supply port* in the whole of the area which they occupied. Moreover, Antwerp would have been wrested from the Allies and the threat to the German Westphalian plain removed.

As the world knows, von Rundstedt did succeed in breaking through the Allied positions in the Ardennes, and he caused the Allied Supreme Command no little anxiety for a few days.

It was to a conference at Brussels on the subject of the threat to Antwerp that Admiral Sir Bertram Ramsay, the Allied Naval Commander-in-Chief, was travelling when he was tragically killed in an aircraft accident. Thus the United Nations lost the services of one of the chief architects of victory in Europe. Admiral Ramsay's place as Allied Naval Commander-in-Chief was taken by Admiral Sir Harold Burrough, who had served with General Eisenhower in North Africa.

With the progress, halting, and defeat of von Rundstedt's offensive we are not here concerned, for that was a purely military operation. With the defences of the Scheldt and the sea route to Antwerp we are concerned. These provided a most interesting and unorthodox form of naval and amphibious warfare, in which information of the enemy's movements and intentions was one of the goals and "keeping the enemy guessing" one of the most profitable gambits.

Ever since the landings on the Normandy beaches on D-day, the left flank— which had continued throughout to be the fighting flank at sea—had been held by a motley collection of small craft manned by officers and men who could be surprised by nothing and were always ready for anything. It will be remembered that off the Normandy beaches Captain A. F. Pugsley had been Captain of Patrols and that the Support Squadron, Eastern Flank, which had formed the "Trout line" and repelled the German human torpedoes and explosive motor boats had been commanded by Commander K. A. Sellar, under Captain Pugsley.

It had been these two officers who had so successfully landed the Royal Marine Commandos in the desperate assault on the Westkapelle area of Walcheren. By that time the force had been given the title of "Force T." After the reduction of the fortress island of Walcheren and the clearing of the Scheldt it devolved on "Force T" to guard the northern flank of the Scheldt estuary leading to Antwerp, and in this task they worked in conjunction with the Royal Marine Commandos whom they had got to know so well.

They had a hard task, for the enemy was very active. On the sea route across the North Sea to Antwerp the Germans were doing their utmost with

'Seehund' midget submarines.

more new weapons. These were forms of midget submarine, of which that called the "Seehund" was the most formidable. The "Seehund" was a two-man midget submarine with a radius of action of over 250 miles and carrying two torpedoes. It was by no means a "suicide" weapon, although the German Command obviously considered them to be "expendable." In addition to the "Seehund" and other types of midget submarine the German tried to use explosive motor boats against the short sea route to Antwerp.

There was no doubt that the enemy was operating the explosive motor boats and midget submarines from the large islands which form an archipelago just to the north of the mouth of the Scheldt. These provided an ideal strategic base very close to what was at that period the greatest and most important focal point of maritime trade in the world. The numerous narrow channels between the Islands, and the entrances to the canals made ideal "hide-outs" for these little craft, which could easily be shifted from one such base to another and thus greatly reduce the chance of detection. At sea the patrols and the convoy escorts had to guard against attack by these German weapons, but in the waterways which separated what was then German held territory from that which was in our hands, the patrolling had to be done by the small craft of "Force T." Small support landing craft were used for this patrolling.

It was also necessary for "Force T" and the Royal Marine Commandos with whom they operated to keep a constant watch upon the movements of German troops and formations, for such information might well give warning of some enemy intention. It was, for instance, a raid carried out by "Force T" and the Royal Marine Commandos which told us that the German garrison in Schouwen had suddenly been increased from some 700 men to 6,000—an event which confirmed suspicions that the enemy contemplated an attempt against the islands of North and South Beveland and Walcheren in order to close once again the approach to Antwerp from the sea.

The left flank at that time was a part of the world where men had to keep very wide awake and he very efficient if they wished to live long. Danger and, in winter, extreme discomfort was their portion. They had to operate in gales and pouring rain and sometimes in deep snow. They had to live in scattered villages where their craft could "lie up" in a canal or creek, where there were no amenities and supplies were frequently short. As late as April, for instance, the "Force T" accommodation in Goes on South Beveland had water only every other day and it had to be brought by road.

Nor was "Force T" concerned only with the Dutch islands. The great rivers of the Maas and the Waal on their western reaches across Holland to the sea also had to be watched and patrolled, as had some of the canals in what was for a long time virtually a "no man's land." In retrospect it seems astonishing that this great and dangerous amphibious flank was held so efficiently with so small a force. The truth of the matter is that by sheer audacity "Force T" and the Royal Marine Commandos early established a moral ascendancy over the enemy and this they exploited and continually increased.

In the spring of 1945 the author had the opportunity of spending some little time with "Force T" and taking part in some of the operations and then going with them to the Second Battle for Arnhem. The following accounts were written at the time and may be considered as typical of the activities of "Force T" and the Royal Marine Commandos on this left flank.

The headquarters of "Force T" were then at Bergen-op-Zoom, which was well within sound of the guns which fought a fairly continuous artillery duel between the mainland and the eastern end of Overflakkee. One could not go far from Bergen-op-Zoom without getting into territory where precautions had to be taken against gunfire and even long-range snipers.

It was about midnight on a clear dark night with no wind—the sort of night when sound travels far—when we set off from Bergen-op-Zoom in a jeep. The job was to plant a "Cuckoo" on the island of Overflakkee. The "Cuckoo" technique was one way, not only of gaining information about the enemy, but also of maintaining and increasing our moral ascendancy over the Germans in the islands and keeping them "jittery."

The "Cuckoo," which might consist of a single officer or man or a small party, was landed by night and lay up in the upper part of one of the many flooded buildings among the polders. The "Cuckoo" was then, of course, well within the German nest. Usually he had to swim through the floods in order to reach the building selected as a "hide out" and frequently he remained behind the enemy's positions for as long as three days.

Not only was a close watch kept on the enemy by this means, and sketches made of his strongpoints from the German, and therefore most vulnerable side, but our artillery was frequently "put on" to targets which could not be seen from outside the high dyke surrounding the islands, and of which our gunners would therefore be unaware. This had a pronounced moral effect upon the Germans. Sometimes a digging party working under the shelter of the dyke and out of sight of the British observation posts would suddenly come under shell fire. Sometimes a patrol or fatigue party would be shelled when they considered themselves quite safe. The previous "Cuckoo" which had been landed on Overflakkee had distinguished himself at the expense of a party of German officers. They had emerged from a headquarters and were walking down the road under the shelter of the dyke when shells began to land very close to them. They took to their heels and sprinted for a slit trench, but the shell bursts followed them and probably their last coherent thoughts were wondering how such seemingly miraculous gunnery was achieved. It was all very bad for the German nerves and correspondingly good for our morale. The "Cuckoo" which we had to land, and which consisted of one officer and two men, was, of course, determined to outdo its predecessor.

Half a mile up the road from Bergen-op-Zoom we stopped at a control post and were given the password for the night—it was "Clam." A little farther on we were stopped again—by a sentry who let us pass on giving the word, but told us to proceed without any lights at all. The road was swinging to the northward, that is, towards the German positions on Overflakkee. The enemy was only about two miles away and his look-outs would have seen even side lights. We did not want to arouse his suspicion or draw his fire. Still less did we wish to draw his attention to our activities. The lives of brave men in a very hazardous operation depended upon secrecy and silence.

Before long we were stopped and challenged again. It was the rendezvous. We left the jeep and clambered down the slope from the road. Below us was a lock—one of those which separate the smaller canals from the tidal waters of the channels between the islands. In the lock lay an LCA. (Landing Craft, Assault). In darkness and silence we clambered on board. No man spoke above a whisper, for we were within a few hundred yards of the German positions on the southern dyke of Overflakkee. The lock was flooded slowly and the gates, which had previously been well greased, opened without a creak. The LCA, glided almost soundlessly out into the channel between Overflakkee and the mainland.

The spot chosen for landing the "Cuckoo" was three or four miles up this channel. Going slowly up the channel, the outline of the Overflakkee dyke to port could be plainly seen and it seemed incredible that the LCA. was not seen. It was almost like boating on the Suez Canal with one bank held by a skilled enemy with a plentiful supply of automatic weapons.

The LCA grounded four times in those three miles, but each time only for a very few minutes. That was to be expected, for navigation under those conditions was largely guesswork and luck. None of the channels had been surveyed for five years, and the sandbanks had shifted so that they had little or no relationship to their charted positions. It was for that reason that these operations were always carried out soon after low water, so that there would be a rising tide throughout the operation to float off a craft which grounded, for it would have been certain death to he caught by the dawn while still aground within a hundred yards or so of the German positions.

At last the LCA reached the position where the "Cuckoo" was to be landed. She lay stopped for several minutes while those on hoard stood listening intently and examining the skyline of the dyke through night glasses.

Everything was quiet and there was no sign of movement, so the LCA swung round and glided very slowly towards the Overflakkee dyke until, with a barely perceptible crunch, the bows "touched down" on German-held territory.

In complete silence the commando men who were to guard the LCA from surprise while she lay under the shadow of the dyke clambered up to the top of the dyke and fanned out to port and starboard, There was another silent wait before the signal was made that everything was quiet. Then the three men of the "Cuckoo" went ashore.

For half an hour the LCA lay nosing the bottom of the dyke. Then, from the "Cuckoo's" "walkie-talkie" wireless set came the news that it was established and "happy." The scouts and guards were brought in. Then the LCA went astern, swung round, and headed back to its "hide out" in the lock. The operation of landing the "Cuckoo" had been successfully carried out.

It was three days later that this "Cuckoo" was taken off. An attempt had been made to take them off on the previous night but, although the LCA reached its appointed place, the "Cuckoo" reported that it could not reach the craft as there were Germans between its "hide-out" and the dyke.

That "Cuckoo" had a very successful time. It brought back a detailed sketch of a new strongpoint on which the Germans were working. Moreover, it directed our shell fire on to a German patrol. This it did in such a way that the first shells landed just behind the Germans. No sooner had they begun to run up the road towards the nearest cover than the "Cuckoo" gave a correction to the guns so that the shells began to fall just ahead of them. When the Germans turned about and began running in the opposite direction the process was repeated. As the "Cuckoo" said. "We made 'em sweat before we killed them."

Sitting in an armchair this seems rather cruel, and horrible, and unnecessary, but it was not. Human life was a very cheap commodity in that area, and the more we were able to show the Germans that they were never safe, the safer our own men would be. The incident of that patrol must have been witnessed by many other Germans. The story must have gone round, and the moral effect must have been great.

A few nights later a very different type of operation took place on the island of Schouwen. It was just before the second battle for Arnhem, and it was very necessary to find out what was going on in the islands, and particularly an Schouwen. There had been certain indications of unusual German troop movements, and our air reconnaissance had reported the arrival of some big Dutch barges at Zerikzee, the little port up a canal running north into the island of Schouwen. With the great battle for Arnhem imminent, it was very important to know what these indications meant.

The operation on Schouwen was very carefully planned. For some time the Germans had been showing increasing reluctance to leave the shelter of their strongpoints at night. They had been caught so often when they had sent out patrols which had suddenly become aware that British Commando men had materialised apparently from nowhere and had glided up close behind them, pressed the muzzles of tommy-guns or Sten guns into their ribs and hissed an order to "keep on going"—to a waiting LCA, interrogation and captivity—that they seldom sent out patrols, even when their suspicions had been deliberately aroused. The security of a strongpoint armed with machine-guns and protected by minefields seemed to them infinitely preferable.

Much thought had therefore been devoted to the preparation of a scheme which, it was thought, must force the Germans to send out from one of their strongpoints a patrol to investigate. Moreover, the spot at which the Commando troops were to be landed on the island of Schouwen was carefully selected midway between two known German strongpoints. For this reason, and because of the steps to be taken to lure the enemy into the open, it was a more dangerous operation than an ordinary raid. Moreover, it soon became clear that the Germans were very wide awake and "up to something" unusual.

The operation began when twenty-five men of the Royal Marine Commandos assembled in what had been the bar of a public house on the waterside of Colijnsplaat at dusk. Colijnsplaat is a village on the extreme northern coast of North Bevel and, and opposite to about the centre of the south coast of Schouwen. At that comparatively early hour it was already obvious that the Germans on Schouwen were themselves contemplating some sort of operation that night. First indication of this came just before dusk, when the Germans shelled Colijnsplaat for a short time. This they had not done for some weeks, although it had at one time been a regular occurrence. The shelling did little damage and caused no naval or military casualties, although it killed one girl in her 'teens, blew the leg off another, and inflicted serious head injuries to a small boy. The Royal Marine Commando swore that they would exact vengeance before dawn.

The bar of that little Dutch public house, with its dirty mural paintings, and crowded with men in combat dress and with blacked faces and hands, was thick with smoke and lit only by a hurricane lantern on a central table. It would have made an ideal subject for a Vermeer.

There were snatches of laughter and song. Spirits were undoubtedly high. Then there was a hush as the Commanding Officer came in to give his final "briefing." It was short and very much to the point, and then we filed out and along the dyke to the rendezvous with the LCA which was to take the Commando men over to Schouwen.

The trip across to the selected landing place on Schouwen was fairly long, and it was soon made clear that the Germans really were "up to something." Away to the westward there was great flare activity, which continued through most of the night. This was in addition to the normal German system by which every German post fired a white flare at intervals as a signal that all was quiet. A red flare instead of a white was the alarm signal. These intermittent flares were fired all along the coast of Schouwen, but over at West Schouwen the flare activity was such that there were seldom fewer than fifteen or twenty flares in the air at the same time. What it all meant we had no idea, but hoped to be able to find out.

It was only with difficulty that the selected landing place was found. It was recognisable because the wall along the top of the dyke fell away for a few feet, but it proved difficult to find as, from the direction of our approach, it was in line with the tops of some trees inland on Schouwen. Being midway between two German strongpoints, moreover, there was no margin for error. We crept along dead slow in the still night and keeping about two hundred yards off the dyke—made at intervals to feel very naked by the flares—until the correct spot was identified. Then the LCA turned and glided in towards the dyke.

The LCA "touched down" at the foot of the dyke so gently that it was barely perceptible. Then suddenly we heard a sound and remained absolutely motionless. The sound got louder and was identified as the unmistakable noise of a horse and cart coming along the road which ran about halfway down the landward side of the dyke. It was getting on for midnight. No Dutch farmer would be out with horse and cart in German occupied territory at that time of night, so it must be Germans. The night was so still that a gently rolling stone could have been heard for some distance, so that it was too dangerous to risk trying to disembark the Marines. There was only one thing to do—to keep absolutely still and hope that the Germans would not look over the wall on the top of the dyke. If they did our situation would be exceedingly uncomfortable, for they could not have helped seeing the LCA lying within a few yards of them. The Marines, huddled together in the craft, would have been massacred by automatic weapons—and there was a German strongpoint on each side of where the LCA lay.

The voices of the Germans with the cart could be heard as they passed, but fortunately they were incurious of anything on the seaward side of the dyke and passed harmlessly along the road to the south-eastward.

The moment it was possible, the Marines disembarked and made their way to the top of the dyke. As they reached it they heard the sound of another horse and cart coming along the road. It turned out to be more than one cart. It was a convoy of twenty four-wheeled wagons, heavily laden with equipment and with German soldiers riding on them. The wagons were escorted by other German soldiers on foot and with bicycles. There must have been fully a hundred men, and they passed within half a dozen yards of the Marines lying hidden on the top of the dyke. Had the Marines been in greater force it might have been possible to mop up the entire convoy and its escorts, but it would have been madness to take on odds of more than three to one within a few hundred yards of two enemy strongpoints where there were known to be Spandaus and would probably also be mortars. There was nothing to be done but watch them pass, listen to their conversation, and hope that there would be a straggler or two who could be silently dealt with and taken back to Colijnsplaat for interrogation.

As luck would have it there were no stragglers, so two scouts were sent off to trail the convoy and find out where it was going. After what seemed an interminable wait the scouts came back to say that they had trailed the convoy into the village of Zerikzee, where it had halted near the little harbour where the barges had been reported.

This information was valuable, as far as it went. We had discovered that the Germans were moving troops and equipment out of Schouwen by barge. The barges would have to go "west about" to reach Dortrecht or the Rotterdam area, and this probably explained the flare activity off West Schouwen. Moreover, the shelling of Colijnsplaat may have been intended to discourage our patrols. We did not, however, know the total number of men being moved or their destination, although it looked as if the Germans were either trying to pull out of Schouwen or were sending reinforcements to the area in which we planned to deliver the big attack against Arnhem and the river line. The missing pieces in this jigsaw puzzle might be secured if we could take a prisoner.

After waiting some time to ensure that all was quiet after the passage of the convoy and that no further troops were coming along that road, the plan for tempting a German patrol out of the strongpoints was put into action. This consisted of starting up an outboard motor which sounded like a small motor cycle. Then an explosive charge was to be fired and the outboard motor stopped. This was supposed to represent the motor cycle running into a land mine. Finally, the explosion was to be followed by a voice calling for help in German. It was thought that the Germans would have to send out a patrol to investigate if they thought, as they were intended to, that one of their dispatch riders had fouled a land mine and was injured.

Everything went according to plan, although the noise on that still night seemed deafening after the long silence. Sure enough a red flare went up just to the north-westward. A few minutes later a German patrol of eight men came hurrying along the dyke straight into the ambush which had been prepared for them. There was a flurry of fire. Five of the Germans were killed outright. Two were hit but got away, although it is thought that one was seen falling over the dyke into the floods. The other was also wounded, but was carried quickly down into the LCA to be taken away as a prisoner for interrogation.

The shouting had, of course, well stirred up the Germans. There seemed to be flares everywhere, and there was a certain amount of shooting, but it proved quite ineffective and, with the Marines and the prisoner safely embarked, the LCA went astern out of a position which promised momentarily to become exceedingly uncomfortable. Fortunately there was by this time a slight low-lying mist on the water, which hid the LCA as she made her way to seaward and away from the flares.

As the flares fell farther and farther astern another noise was suddenly heard. The LCA at once stopped and lay motionless. It was the unmistakable slow throb of Dutch barge engines—two of them. Those two barges were going towards West Schouwen, where the flares were still going up. Those in the LCA saw them clearly as they passed within a few hundred yards, but the LCA was not seen by the Germans.

As soon as the barges were clear the LCA made her best speed back to Colijnsplaat to report these curious German moves, and on arrival there the British artillery was "laid on" to hammer Zerikzee, where the wagon convoy had halted and was being loaded into barges. The barges which had been seen on the homeward voyage could not have been these same barges. The time factor made that impossible. It was obvious, therefore, that the German troop movements were more extensive than had at first been thought, and this was confirmed soon after.

With the shells bursting in great profusion over Zerikzee we drove back to Bergen-op-Zoom in the dawn. It was the dawn of the day of the second battle for Arnhem, which proved to be the opening of the final battle for the Three Rivers.

For this battle, in the initial stages of which LCA's of "Force T" were to play a vital part, temporary naval headquarters were set up in the shell-torn village of Huissen, across the river just south of Arnhem. Huissen was closer to the enemy than even the shorter-range light guns which put down so terrific a barrage on Arnhem, and was under enemy machine-gun fire. It was, in fact, a very hot and noisy spot. We drove up to Huissen after the big guns had begun the longer-range bombardment, and found the ruined village illuminated by the flying tracer. To this was soon added the artificial moonlight under which the assault was made and the prolonged flashes as the "mattresses" of rockets landed on the German positions.

The key to Arnhem was the point of land which juts out at the intersection of the Lower Rhine and the River Ijssel. This long narrow point is less than a mile south-east of Arnhem docks and it could only be assaulted by water. The van of the attacking forces, which consisted of an assault company of the Gloucestershire Regiment, were carried in five LCA's under the command of Lieutenant C. W. R. Cross, DSC, RNVR. These had been lying up during the afternoon in the Pannerdensch Canal which connects the River Waal to the Lower Rhine. These craft did the final stage of their voyage under the terrific gun barrage and rocket "mattresses." So effective was this barrage that the LCA's met only slight opposition as they approached the spit and "touched down" on its eastern side from the River Ijssel. As has so often happened, the Germans held their fire until the assault troops were disembarking and then opened a withering fire with Spandaus and other automatic weapons. Fortunately for the LCA's they were by that time shielded from this fire by the bank of the spit.

The assault company of the Gloucestershire Regiment did wonders, but they had a harder task than had been anticipated. The Germans had turned the whole spit into an intricate defence system of great strength, so arranged that the defenders hardly had to show themselves. Moreover, the follow-up waves of troops did not arrive as had been planned. The following waves, which were to be the main body of the Gloucestershires, had been assembled east of the Ijssel River with a large number of "Buffalo" amphibians in which they were to storm across the river and land in the wake of the first wave from the LCA's. To reach the river from the place where they were parked in the shelter of a big dyke, a gap was to have been blown in the dyke. Unfortunately, however, a chance shell had detonated the explosives collected for this purpose, and it was then too late to bring up further supplies. As a result, they had to negotiate the dyke itself as best they could, and for a time only two "Buffaloes" were available in the river instead of the forty which had been expected. Largely as a result of this accident, the spit was not finally cleared of the enemy for some hours, instead of in about half an hour as had been expected.

The second naval part of the operation had therefore to be postponed, since it depended upon the clearing of the spit and the arrival of our troops on its western side, followed by the clearance of mines from a landing place near the dock entrances from the Lower Rhine.

Crossing the Rhine in a Buffalo.

This second naval part of the operation consisted of the landing, on the western side of the spit where it joined the "mainland," of a battalion of the Leicestershire Regiment, which were embarked in landing craft in the Pannerdensch canal for the purpose.

Throughout the day after the night assault, the LCA's which had landed the initial assaulting troops on the eastern side of the spit "lay up" in the Lower Rhine, just round the point of the spit. The shell fire and machine-gun fire all passed harmlessly over them as they lay under the shelter of the bank. Then, as the situation clarified they were placed at the disposal of the military to act as ferries.

Shortly before the attack at Arnhem there had taken place an amphibious operation unique in history, for it demanded the use of naval craft two hundred miles from the sea and in waters to which there was no access by river or canal which was not still dominated by the enemy.

This operation was the crossing of the Rhine, in which craft of the British and American navies played a vital part.

It had for some time been apparent that when the armies forced the Rhine and established bridgeheads on its eastern bank they would need a fast ferry service capable of carrying heavy weights, and would have to rely on the ferry service for all that they would need until bridges, even of a temporary nature, could be thrown across the great river. Exhaustive experiments had been carried out in the United Kingdom on rivers giving similar conditions of banks and current to those of the Rhine. These experiments had been carried out in order to determine which of the available types of craft would be best suited to the task of carrying tanks, bulldozers and mobile guns across the Rhine. Account had to be taken of the fact that the craft selected would have to be taken to the Rhine by road over shell-pitted surfaces and Bailey bridges and through villages and towns.

A 48 Commando Buffalo enters Serooskerke, 8 November 1944. 'A' Troop of 48
Commando was ordered up to Veere to find out what the enemy was doing up there and
to make contact with 52nd Division. The whole of the inland part of the island was under
water so they travelled in four amphibious Buffaloes. Serooskerke was reached without
incident and members of 'A' Troop laughed and celebrated with the villagers on their
liberation.

It was decided as a result of these experiments that LCM's (Landing Craft,
Mechanised) and LCV(P)'s (Landing Craft, Vehicle, Personnel) were the best
craft for the purpose. An idea of the overland transport problem involved can
be gained from the fact that an LCM. weighs 26 tons and, when on its carrier
for overland transport, is 77 feet long, 14 feet wide and 20 feet high.

A considerable amount of training had also to be given to the crews of the
craft chosen for the Rhine crossing, for they were called upon to operate them
in conditions which differed greatly from the beach conditions for which their
former training had fitted them. For the Rhine crossing these craft had to be
launched down muddy banks into a swiftly-flowing river instead of being
lowered from ships' davits. Moreover, when carrying out their Rhine ferry
duties their commanding officers, instead of operating through waves and surf
to beaches constantly changing with the tide, had to manoeuvre their craft to
and from fixed landing places with a strong current running at right angles to
their course.

As the world knows, all difficulties were overcome and the Allied navies
helped the armies across the Rhine as they had placed them successfully on the

Winston Churchill crossing the Rhine River in an amphibious Buffalo vehicle crewed by British soldiers. Germany, 1945.

Normandy beaches. The British craft which took part in the crossing of the Rhine were under the command of

Captain P. G. H. James, RN, and the American craft were under the command of Commander W. J. Whiteside, USNR.

Like all the operations which had carried the Allied Armies from Great Britain to the heart of Germany, the crossing of the Rhine was carried out with an absence of "red-tape" and an unconquerable light-heartedness. Both these factors seem to be demonstrated by a young officer who commanded one of the British craft on the Rhine. This officer was Lieutenant R. O. S. Salmon, RNVR—known as "the Ross Salmon" on account of his initials. He was immensely proud of his command and saw to it that she was always smarter than any other. When attention was drawn by signal to the orders that landing craft were to be painted in light blue and white camouflage, Lieutenant Salmon "scrounged" paint from somewhere and his craft became a very smart olive green with a sheen which told of oil having been put to an improper use. It was Lieutenant Salmon too, who always took his craft across the Rhine, even under fire, wearing a very smart top hat. How that top hat was preserved and kept ironed in the rough and tumble of amphibious warfare was a mystery known only to his crew.

CULMINATION

Scenes at the unconditional surrender of the Germans at Rheims and in Berlin.

By the beginning of May, 1945, Germany was prostrate. The years of blood, toil, sweat and tears were very near their end. The might of Germany, weakened by beating itself against incredible fortitude, had gone down before the "war on two fronts" which had always been so dreaded by the German High Command. From the east the Russians had advanced beyond Berlin. From the west the Allied Armies of Liberation had reached and crossed the last river barrier. The Third Reich was but a narrow corridor between breached walls. The final fruits of "Operation Overlord" and of "Neptune," which made "Overlord" possible—could not long be delayed.

In his capacity of Allied Naval Commander-in-Chief, Admiral Sir Harold Burrough played an important part in the negotiations for the final and unconditional surrender of Germany. It was he who signed on behalf of the Supreme Commander the orders to the German Navy. The following is his description of a sequence of events unique in the history of the world.

By Friday, the 4th of May, it seemed evident that it could only be a matter of days, if not hours, before the German unconditional surrender took place, and that day I therefore left my headquarters at St Germain-en-Laye and proceeded to Supreme Headquarters at Rheims.

Admiral Friedeberg of the German Navy arrived next day, but it soon became apparent that he had not been entrusted with sufficient powers by Admiral Doenitz to negotiate any surrender. Saturday, the 5th of May, was therefore rather a wasted day.

On Sunday, the 6th of May, General Jodl arrived, and at once went into conference with General Bedell Smith, Chief of Staff to General Eisenhower, the Supreme Commander. Negotiations went on all day and well into the night, and

Admiral Sir Harold Martin Burrough, (1889-1977). Burrough joined the Royal Navy in 1903 and during the First World War he was present at the Battle of Jutland in 1916. He was awarded the DSO after a successful raid on the Norwegian islands of Vågsøy and Måløy on 27 December 1941 in which nine enemy ships were sunk by the Navy and Royal Air Force and the garrisons were wiped out by the military forces. In July 1942 he had been given command of the close escort force for Operation Pedestal, and subsequently placed in command of Allied naval forces in the assault on Algiers during Operation Torch. He remained as naval commander occupying post-war Germany.

it appeared that this was going to be another wasted day, so most of us retired to bed before midnight. At 2.10 a.m. I was called and told that the signature would take place as soon as everyone was assembled. By about 2.35 a.m. we were all in the War Room of the Supreme Headquarters.

General Bedell Smith entered the room with General Jodl and Admiral Friedeberg, and the business of signature was accomplished in a very short time. At the conclusion of the signature General Jodl made a short speech, in which he stated that Germany had gained more and lost more than any other country in the war, and said that he hoped for this reason his country would be treated with generosity.

I was particularly impressed with the appearance of Admiral Friedeberg, who appeared to be a very broken man.

A short meeting took place afterwards to report to and to congratulate our Supreme Commander, General Eisenhower. It was difficult to appreciate at the moment the very great historical significance of the event in which we had just taken part.

I returned to my headquarters the following morning, but shortly after my arrival at St Germain-en-Laye on Monday, the 7th of May, I received a message to say that I should be ready to proceed from Rheims to Berlin early on Tuesday, the 8th of May.

I at once returned to Rheims, and at 8.00 a.m. on Tuesday embarked in Air Chief Marshal Tedder's Dakota aircraft. We landed first at an Allied aerodrome in the Allied lines west of the Elbe, where we awaited the arrival of the German delegation, consisting of Marshal Keitel, Admiral Friedeberg and General Stumpf.

The whole party of aircraft took off together a little later, accompanied by an escort of Russian fighters, and we arrived at the Templehof aerodrome at 1.00 p.m.

The Germans were at once taken away to a villa in the outskirts of Berlin. Air Chief Marshal Tedder was greeted with a large guard of honour and band, which he inspected. We then drove off, passing through a part of Berlin on our way to a villa on the outskirts.

On arrival at the villa we were told that Marshal Zhukov would hold a conference at 3.30 p.m. At this conference the formalities for the signature of the German unconditional surrender were discussed. The actual terms of the document of unconditional surrender had not, however, previously been seen by Marshal Zhukov, and he wished to have until 7.30 p.m. to examine them. This, of course, ruled out all our plans for returning to our headquarters on the same day, and it was obvious that we should have to spend the night in Berlin.

Discussions on the terms of the document of unconditional surrender commenced at about 7.30 p.m. and continued until almost midnight. Eventually, however, full agreement was reached on all points, and shortly after midnight we took our places in a very large conference room which had been prepared for the occasion.

As soon as we had assembled, Marshal Keitel, Admiral Friedeberg and General Stumpf entered, with their aides, and were seated at a separate table. Friedeberg looked a very sick man, but Keitel bore himself with all the outward show which one has learned to associate with the Prussian generals.

After a few preliminary questions and answers, Marshal Keitel was called up to sign the document of unconditional surrender, of which there were nine copies in three different languages. He strode up in truly Prussian fashion, removed his right glove and placed his baton and glove on the desk; then adjusted his monocle, seized the pen, and made his signature. Each motion, and his whole bearing, were theatrical in the extreme.

Friedeberg and Stumpf followed, and then returned to their table whilst the witnessing signatures were made.

The ceremony over, we retired to another room for about forty-five minutes, while a host of waiters and waitresses converted the conference room into a banqueting hall. We returned to what had been the conference room at about 1.30 a.m. to sit down to one of those banquets at which the Russians excel on such great occasions.

There was a very good Russian orchestra on a balcony, and each of the many speeches was announced by a flourish, while between speeches a very good selection of music was played.

On 8 May 1945, Doenitz authorised Field Marshal Wilhelm Keitel to sign an unconditional surrender in Berlin. Although Germany had surrendered to the Allies a day earlier, Stalin had insisted on a second surrender ceremony in Berlin.

Most of the toasts were proposed by Marshal Zhukov and replied to by the different distinguished officers associated with the toast.

I was particularly gratified when, at approximately 4.15 a.m., Marshal Zhukov proposed the toast of "The Navies," with which he was kind enough to associate my name.

The banquet broke up at about 5.0 a.m., by which time it was full daylight, and after a short pause we embarked in motor cars and spent an hour and a half driving round and looking at the ruins of what had once been Berlin. It reminded me more than anything of a visit I had made to Pompeii many years before.

We arrived at the Templehof aerodrome at about 7.0 a.m., where Air Chief Marshal Tedder again inspected a large Russian guard of honour and band. Then we embarked in our aircraft and returned to our Headquarters, all suffering in various degrees from fatigue.

THE END